EMERGING AFRICA IN WORLD AFFAIRS

EMERGING AFRICA IN WORLD AFFAIRS

Compiled and Edited by

DAVID K. MARVIN

San Francisco State College

CHANDLER PUBLISHING COMPANY

124 Spear Street, San Francisco, California 94105

The map on page 47 and the chart on page 134
are the work of Zenon Pohorecky.

LIBRARY OF CONGRESS CATALOG CARD NO. 65-12022
PRINTED IN THE UNITED STATES OF AMERICA

Contents

Illustrations

EMERGING AFRICA
IN WORLD AFFAIRS

INTRODUCTION

There is a perhaps apocryphal story of how Mount Kilimanjaro came to be located in Tanganyika rather than in Kenya. Kaiser Wilhelm II, it is said, was in England visiting his grandmother, Queen Victoria, just at the time Great Britain and Germany were trying to work out how, among other things, they would divide up East Africa. Wilhelm was with his grandmother, pouring over a sketch of the proposed boundary between Kenya and German East Africa (Tanganyika). Suddenly, he placed his forefinger on the symbol representing Kilimanjaro and exclaimed, "But, Grandmamma, *I* want the big mountain!" The Kaiser had discovered that the proposed boundary had been drawn *south* of the mountain, thus placing it in Kenya.

The Kaiser got his big mountain; if you trace the border on a map, you will find that it jogs *north* of Mount Kilimanjaro, placing the mountain in Tanganyika.

The tale is symbolic of the colonial era in Africa. The continent became an appendage of Europe, and if the Kilimanjaro story is true, even a kind of plaything of dynasties. Africans in general ceased to have even a minor independent role in international affairs. Their relations with the outside world, and with each other—the languages they now learned, the wars they took part in, the people they fought, even to a considerable extent the new commodities they produced and the markets they sold them in—became functions of the domestic and foreign policies of the various European overlords.

Today most African nations are independent, and the change in status constitutes the underlying reason for this book. Something that happened to Kwame Nkrumah of Ghana symbolizes the change and demonstrates the reason for it. In 1951 Nkrumah was serving a jail sentence for sedition. But the African political party he led won a resounding election victory, whereupon Nkrumah was called from his cell to the colonial governor's office and offered the post of "Leader of

Government Business" in the colonial legislature. Nkrumah thus was transformed in the course of a morning from jailbird to virtual "Prime Minister."

The transformation of Africa has been equally dramatic and sudden. Since World War II, well over two dozen African nations have attained independence, and the process is not yet ended. Like Kwame Nkrumah in 1951, Africans have suddenly achieved a freedom of action sharply contrasting with the previous condition of bondage to the policies and outlooks of Europe. Well may we ask, then, how these new African nations will "shape up." What will be their view of their responsibilities, their interpretation of their interests? What is the prognosis for international relations, both regional and worldwide? Chaos? Disaster? Or can we see the outlines of some less disturbing, or even encouraging, result?

Answers to questions such as these are difficult to come by, and must be of course extremely tentative in nature. Africa is in a state of flux, as Africans attempt to get their bearings in this new situation, to establish institutions fitted to it, and to work out the nature of some satisfactory relationships with each other and the world. The readings included in this book have been selected with an eye to relatively permanent and important elements on the African scene. They focus on trends and tendencies which seem to be emerging, and on the background and apparent causes for them. The book is intended, then, as something more than a report on African current events. It is hoped that the reader will emerge somewhat better informed on typical African attitudes in international affairs, on international issues of a more permanent or perennial nature relating to Africa, and on some possible ways of looking at the new role now being played by Africa in international relations.

The attempt to generalize has, paradoxically, meant a narrowing of focus to that part of Africa south of the Sahara and generally north of the Union of South Africa. Such interesting matters as French-Algerian relations, the future of Saharan oil, or the international ramifications of South African "apartheid" are for example excluded—although the last is so intertwined with sentiments of anticolonialism and the question of race relations as to enter by the back door. The specific and the current issues give way, then, to the general and (if the analysis has been accurate) relatively permanent aspects of Africa's newly established position in international affairs.

I

COLONIAL AFRICA AND AFRICAN AFRICA

During recent centuries that peninsula of Asia known as Europe spawned a series of such revolutionary changes that for several generations the world became little more than a European stamping ground. For present African international relations, the consequences of this explosion of energy have been many and complex.

Perhaps the most important consequences may be summed up under three headings: *First*, the fact of European domination, called imperialism. The elimination of imperialism and the forestalling of any future revival of it are burning issues for Africans. *Second*, race. Widespread contact of peoples of differing color and culture, in a context of domination-submission, has led to an unprecedented "politicization" of race. *Third*, the renascence of Africa. A return to the conditions of "darkest Africa" is impossible, but what may or will be the salient features in the character of the "new Africa"?

Part I is divided into three sections, which deal respectively with these topics: imperialism, the racial issue, and "Africa renascent."

AFRICA PARTITIONED—IMPERIALISM

Imperialism was an experience of transcendent importance for Africa. The European partition of Africa created most of the states and territories of Africa as they appear on the map today. Colonial systems established by the European overlords played a vital role in shaping most African leaders and political institutions. This whole experience in one way or another underlies the attitudes of present-day Africans (and of non-Africans, such as ourselves, as well) toward international events involving African nations.

Selection 1, a textbook description of the European "scramble for Africa," narrates the coming of European domination of the continent. This is followed by several explanations of why Europe happened to expand with such explosive suddenness into Africa in the years after 1885. The explanations offer a choice of two major alternatives—one suggesting that imperialism was largely a political phenomenon, the other that imperialism was the consequence of economic forces and economic rivalries.

The economic explanation lies at the root of some present-day attitudes toward African nations in international relations. Communists subscribe wholeheartedly to it. Many African leaders espouse the idea, proclaiming "neo-colonialism" (by which they mean indirect domination through non-African economic interests) as an ever-present threat to true African independence. The political explanation of imperialism is also, in some guise or other, applied to present-day Africa, often as an adjunct to the economic explanation. These explanations are for this reason alone worthy of study by anyone wishing to gain insight into African international relations.

These explanations also deserve study with reference to current African affairs. How valid for postcolonial Africa is Hall's concept (Selection 2) of the "international frontier"—"an area of low political pressure into which the forces of the strong, well-organized states tend to expand"? Is Lippmann's theory (Selection 3) that imperialism occurs for commercial reasons in areas where political weakness exists applicable to present-day Africa? Can the Communists (and also ourselves) expect that the Leninist theory of imperialism (as set forth by Van Dyke in Selection 4) will hold for the Africa of the future? Can theories such as these be adapted somehow to explain the rather abrupt European abandonment of African possessions in recent years? Answers to these and similar questions are suggested at many points later in the book.

Selection 1

The Partition of Africa*

VICTOR L. and MARGUERITE HALL ALBJERG

Victor L. Albjerg is Professor of History at Purdue University. *From Sedan to Stresa* is one of two among his several books written in collaboration with his wife, Marguerite Hall Albjerg.

AFRICA THE FORGOTTEN CONTINENT

Africa, until the middle of the nineteenth century, was not thought of by the people of Europe as a Continent. To be sure, in the extreme north of the Continent France held Algeria; at the extreme south British and Boers were settled near the Cape; and Portugal, Spain, and Great Britain held a few isolated and neglected trading posts along the coastline, but Africa, as a Continent, was really unknown. . . . During the great explorations of the fifteenth century, Diaz and Vasco da Gama revealed the previously unknown outline of the Continent, but for the white man only the rim of Africa existed, and the rim looked outward. The West Coast of Africa known simply as the West Coast, was occupied by a few trading stations which faced the Atlantic, and from which slave labor was shipped to America. In much the same way, the eastern side of Africa was the western shore of the Indian Ocean. The eastern coast was given over to a few slave stations and became an Arab and Asiatic, more than an African, coast. The southern Cape was long regarded as useful only as a stopping-point on the way to the gems, spices, and riches of the Orient. The interior of Africa remained the mysterious and unknown "Dark Continent" until within the memory of men and women now living. . . .

---

* Reprinted by permission from Albjerg and Albjerg *From Sedan to Stresa*, copyright 1937 by D. Van Nostrand Company, Inc., Princeton, N. J. Chapter XVII, pp. 541, 544–555.

DAVID LIVINGSTON

[David] Livingstone had been sent to Africa in 1840 by the London Missionary Society, and for 30 years he traveled the wilds of central Africa from the Atlantic to the Indian Ocean, discovering the Zambesi River and Lake Nyasa, and publishing many accounts of giraffes and of gorillas and of many strange black races which aroused a lively interest throughout Europe and America.

STANLEY AND LIVINGSTON

In the late 1860's communications from Livingstone ceased to reach England, and a considerable portion of the public became alarmed for his safety. An English expedition was sent in search of Livingstone, but it was forced to return without finding him. At this juncture James Gordon Bennett, publisher of the New York *Herald*, decided that since there was such universal public interest in the fate of Livingstone it would be profitable to equip a searching party. Accordingly, he dispatched to Africa one of the most resourceful, resolute, and eloquent men who has ever graced the newspaper profession. The leader of the *Herald's* expedition, Henry Morton Stanley (1841–1904), not only found Livingstone in 1871 on Lake Tanganyika, but he so dramatized his experiences in a series of lectures, books, and articles that Africa became the chief topic of conversation throughout the civilized world. Stanley's exploits focused the attention of the world on Africa as suddenly and as dramatically as Charles A. Lindbergh's exploits focused the attention of the world on aviation.

ACQUISITION OF THE POWERS

Subsequent explorations by Stanley in the Congo basin revealed the great natural wealth of the region. Repulsed by England, the country of his nativity, in his efforts to secure capital for further exploration, Stanley turned to Leopold II (1865–1909), King of the Belgians, who had previously attempted to secure his services.

LEOPOLD AND THE AFRICAN ASSOCIATION

Leopold, although a sovereign, was primarily a crafty business man, and he had been among the first to recognize the possibilities for immense profit from the newly discovered areas. In 1876 he organized the International African Association—a corporation composed of geographers, explorers, and philanthropists representing many nations, and ostensibly organized to destroy the slave-trade, Christianize and civilize the natives, and explore the interior. . . . He soon managed to squeeze out all the subscribers who were not his satellites, and it was not long before the enterprise passed exclusively into his own hands. Meanwhile, the indefatigable Stanley sailed up the Congo River, and by dint of judicious disposal of trinkets among native chieftains, he secured treaties which gave the President of the International African Association a "protectorate" over the Congo area. By 1882, the skillful and energetic diplomacy of Stanley had secured a colony of 900,000 square miles for Leopold.

THE BERLIN CONFERENCE

Obviously, such significant activities attracted wide attention among the responsible statesmen of Europe. A French explorer, De Brazza, had, during 1877–1878, crossed into the Congo basin, made treaties, obtained concessions, and founded posts. The Portuguese, too, laid claims to the mouth of the river on the basis of early discovery. Great Britain seemed disposed to back the claims of Portugal, but France was adamant, and behind France was Germany. The Congo had attained the dignity of an international question. It appeared that some of the illiterate natives, acting under the influence of gin and intimidation, had been incautious enough to sign treaties with several powers. European statesmen met the dilemma by calling a Conference of the powers to meet in Berlin, in 1884–1885, to discuss the Congo situation and to formulate policies for dealing with the remainder of Africa. The result of the deliberations of the Conference was the Berlin Act, which, in addition to providing that powers making future annexations in Africa must give due notice to other countries, and must make their occupation effective, also provided for: (1) freedom of trade in the Congo basin; (2) free navigation of the rivers; (3) the neutrality and international protection of the Congo basin; and (4) prevention of slave-trading. The Berlin Conference also gave official utterance to the opinion that European activity in Africa should be characterized by uplifting the natives, spreading the Gospel, and advancing science. It was assumed that each of the civilized nations would know best how to achieve these latter points, so no specific recommendations were made concerning them.

CONGO FREE STATE

Shortly after the adjournment of the Berlin Conference King Leopold renamed his possessions in Africa the "Congo Free State," and, after securing the consent of the Belgian parliament, proclaimed the establishment of the new State, and his own advent to the throne. Thus simply did the King of the Belgians present the family of nations with an additional member. The administrative systems of Belgium and the Congo Free State remained entirely separate although a personal union now existed between Belgium and the Free State. In the newly created Congo Free State the King had complete legislative and executive authority, subject to no parliamentary control.

CONGO ATROCITIES

Had Leopold acted in accordance with his many protestations of disinterested humanitarianism, the Congo Free State might have proved a highly interesting experiment in the enlightened administration of an underprivileged people. However, such was not the case. His natural cupidity asserted itself, and Leopold, totally disregarding the welfare of the natives, attempted to squeeze as much wealth for himself as he possibly could from the country. His first act was to reserve the choicest part of the Congo as a monopoly for the State. Private companies were granted monopoly rights in much of the rest of the Congo. In these private concessions natives were driven to work by agents who received a commission on the amount of rubber or ivory, the chief products of the Congo, which were collected. Whippings, brutal punishments, murders, and unspeakable conditions of cruelty and filth prevailed in company labor camps, and almost continuous servitude was the lot of the natives. Conditions on the preserves of the State were, if possible, even worse. No native escaped working for the white man. If all other means failed, he was charged with being delinquent in his taxes, and forced to work them out.

THE BELGIAN CONGO

Eventually revelations of the atrocious conditions prevailing in the Congo reached the ears of an outraged world. Leopold was besieged with requests for reform, and the opposition within the Belgian Parliament demanded that the Congo be converted outright into a Belgian colony. At length, Leopold yielded to the pressure of public opinion, and in November, 1908, the State was transferred to Belgium, and became a Belgian dependency, the Belgian Congo. As a token of gratitude for his numerous sacrifices and generosity, a sum of $10,000,000 was paid over to Leopold. It was not an exhorbitant price for Belgium to pay for an overseas empire with an area almost 80 times her own.

GERMAN ACQUISITIONS

Germany, like Belgium, made her debut as a colonizing nation during the partition of Africa. Even before the Belgian occupation of the Congo, German missionaries had been working among the natives along the southwestern coast of Africa, north of the Orange River. German traders followed, and there came a demand for the protection of these German subjects. The *Kolonialverein*, and other societies which had been organized for the purpose of furthering an aggressive colonial policy, aided by publicists and the nationalist historians, importunately demanded that the government take action. Although Bismarck had been cautious, he had gradually been won over to imperialism, and in 1883, he extended protection to Herr F. A. Lüderitz, a Bremen merchant, who was operating in South West Africa. Lüderitz was promised support on condition that a harbor unclaimed by other nations could be obtained. The Port of Angra Pequena, in the temperate zone and midway between the British-claimed Walfish Bay and Cape Colony, was selected. So successful was Herr Lüderitz that he negotiated in 1884, the purchase of about 3,000 square miles of territory for the modest price of 200 rifles, $500, and an assortment of toys, mostly lead soldiers. British imperialists, who regarded the whole region as theirs, were greatly irritated. However, Lüderitz and his agents assiduously continued their "treaty-making" with the Hottentots until South West Africa contained an area larger than Germany. Since the attention of England was, at the moment, riveted on the Balkan situation and on Egypt, and since France was cordially co-operating with Germany, there was nothing left for the British to do but to show their sportsmanship by cheerfully recognizing Germany's protectorate over South West Africa. Meanwhile, Bismarck had dispatched a noted German explorer, Dr. Gustav Nachtigal, to equatorial Africa in the hope that the natives there might also be made "treaty-conscious." This expedition was also a success, and, with the aid of a warship, Dr. Nachtigal succeeded in outmanoeuvering Mr. Hewett, the British agent. As a result, in July, 1884, the German flag was hoisted in Togoland and in the Cameroons. Two hundred thousand square miles more were thus added to the German Colonial Empire, and the year 1884 may be said to have been a successful one in the eyes of German Imperialists.

EAST AFRICA

Germany next turned its attention to East Africa. Except for a vaguely defined area near the Zambesi, to which Portugal had laid claim since the fifteenth century, the East Coast was fair game for the most energetic bidder. True, the Sultan of Zanzibar held some shadowy claims, but since he was not one of the European Powers he was not to be taken seriously. Accordingly, an expedition led by the youthful Carl Peters set sail for Africa in the autumn of 1884, with all the glamor of adventure that secrecy, an alias, and a disguise could afford. If England was to be outdistanced, he must move quickly. His haste was repaid when, early in 1885, the German flag was raised over a large part of East Africa while slightly befuddled chiefs were affixing their marks on "treaties" which took away their rights. Subsequently, Germany and Great Britain proceeded to define their respective "spheres of influence" in East Africa; Germany took over a colony with an area of more than 300,000 square miles south of the Umba River, and Great Britain a similar amount of land north of the river.

ANGLO-GERMAN AGREEMENT OF 1890

The numerous conflicts between Great Britain and Germany over African territory finally brought about the great Anglo-German treaty of 1890. This agreement settled the main boundaries between Great Britain and Germany in all parts of Africa where the two nations were contiguous. In addition, Germany obtained Heligoland in exchange for recognizing the British Protectorates over Zanzibar and Uganda. To Germany's possessions in South West Africa was added an additional tongue of land which gave Germany access to the Zambesi. Both nations also agreed to recognize the French Protectorate over Madagascar. . . .

FRANCE ENTERS THE GAME

The most active of all colonizing powers in Africa during the last quarter of the nineteenth century were the French. Prior to the nineteenth century France had been interested only intermittently in African affairs, and her few trading stations on the West African coast received little aid from the government. After the Franco-Prussian War, however, the advocates of a "new empire" gained the ascendancy in the government, and under Jules Ferry a vigorous colonial policy was inaugurated. Agents hastened to the West African Coast where they industriously distributed childish presents among the chiefs, plied them with rum, secured signatures to treaties drawn up in the unknown and mellifluous French tongue, and thereby obtained "protectorates" over such strategic posts as St. Louis and Dakar. In Equatorial Africa the Gaboon River area was brought under French "protection," while in 1875, Savorgnan de Brazza had begun the occupation of the right bank of the Congo.

FRANCE AND ALGERIA

. . . At this juncture an inspiration dawned on some unsung hero in the French Colonial Office. It was clear that destiny intended France to unite her small holdings in Equatorial Africa, West Africa, and North Africa into one gigantic bloc of land. Possession of the entire northern half of the Continent loomed as a possibility.

FRANCE EXTENDS HER POSSESSIONS

With true Gallic reverence for logic this grandiose scheme was launched. At the southern entrance of the Red Sea Jibuti was bombarded and a part of Somaliland brought under French control. At the same time French agents on the West Coast made strenuous efforts to secure the areas necessary to give France a united and continuous domain. The remarkable journeys of Colonel Binger (1887–1889, 1891–1893) enabled France to enlarge enormously her protectorate of the Ivory Coast; Dahomey was occupied; Senegal extended into the interior; and the conquest of Timbuctu and the other oases of the Sahara enabled France to unite the French possessions in Algeria with those of West Africa.

FRANCE INTERVENES IN TUNIS

Tunis and Morocco also claimed the attention of French imperialists. Morocco could wait for awhile, but Tunis demanded immediate attention because Italy was vigorously asserting that Tunis should fall to her. Was it not the exact site where Rome had conquered Carthage? Were there not numerous Italian residents in Tunis? And, most obviously and emphatically, was it not just across the straits from Italy's possession, Sicily? These were embarrassing points and France remained passive for a time, but at the Congress of Berlin (1878) she secured the secret assurances of England and Germany that she was welcome to Tunis. In return, the French government had recognized England's acquisition of Cyprus, and had shown less of a spirit of revenge toward Germany. Italy could be dealt with if the need arose. Shortly thereafter, "border incidents" supplied the necessary pretext, and in 1881, French forces occupied the ancient stronghold of Hannibal. The Italians were furious, and for two decades bitter enmity existed between the two Latin nations.

FASHODA CRISIS

The far more serious rivalry between France and Great Britain was, however, rapidly approaching a climax in the Sudan. To complete her ambitious scheme for dominating Africa from the Red Sea to the Atlantic Ocean France still needed to gain control of Eastern Sudan, the Nile valley, and Abyssinia. Unfortunately, England, who had occupied Egypt in 1882, not only showed no disposition to withdraw from Egypt, but was actually preparing to subdue the Sudanese and take possession of the upper Nile Valley. France decided to anticipate England by acting at once. Accordingly, in 1896, an expedition commanded by Captain Marchand departed from the French Congo, and proceeded 3,000 miles through the heart of Africa to the Nile. After two years of terrific hardship Captain Marchand arrived at Fashoda on the Nile, and raised the French flag, in July, 1898. Meanwhile the English had not been idle. A large British army, commanded by General Kitchener, had been slowly moving up the Nile from Egypt. Kitchener not only destroyed the army of the Sudanese as he came, but he built a railroad as well. At Khartum Kitchener learned that a

French expedition was at Fashoda claiming possession of the Nile. Kitchener hastened southward to meet Marchand, who had just been thrown into despair by the news that a large French army from Somaliland, which was to have reinforced him, had been unable to cross Abyssinia. However, Marchand met Kitchener and courageously welcomed him to Fashoda "in the name of France." Kitchener, with a large army at his back, could easily have destroyed Marchand's small force, and a war between England and France would almost certainly have ensued. Both men, however, refrained from overt acts, and agreed to submit the matter to their respective governments. For several months passions ran high in both countries, and it appeared that an Anglo-French war could not be avoided. Eventually a solution, much to the advantage of England, was worked out and accepted by both nations. The Nile valley was to go to England, but France was to get Wadai in the central Sudan.

FRANCE PREPARES TO INTERVENE IN MOROCCO

The amicable adjustment of the Fashoda affair resulted in an *entente* between England and France, and gave the French imperialists courage to renew their agitation for the acquisition of Morocco. This African territory, larger than France, healthful in climate, strategic in position, rich in natural resources, and feebly governed by the Sherifian family was a tempting morsel. Unfortunately, England, Germany, and Spain all had considerable sums invested in the country, and all carried on fairly extensive trade with the Sherifian Empire. But France was determined that Morocco should be hers. Accordingly, the French government made a series of secret agreements which were designed to give her a "free hand" in Morocco. First, Italy was bought off (1900) by a promise of diplomatic support whenever Italy saw fit to seize Tripoli. This recognition of Italian interests in North Africa also served to placate the Italian animosity which had been aroused at the time of the French occupation of Tunis. Next, England's "peculiar interests" in Egypt were recognized (1904) by France in exchange for a promise by England that France would have her cordial support in Morocco. Spain was promised (1904) a slice of the Sherifian Empire after the French had succeeded in making good their position in the major portions of the country. The diplomatic stage having thus been set France prepared to intervene actively in Morocco. The excuses offered to the world were that French investments were imperilled, that the inability of the Sherifian Sultan to end the eternal chaos was a constant threat to the peace of Algeria, and that the life of European residents in Morocco was constantly jeopardized by the incessant civil wars. A formidable bill of indictment—but one which is monotonously familiar in the annals of imperialism. Strangely enough, Germany, which for some unaccountable reason France had failed to buy off, was not properly impressed by the accusations. The Kaiser, who was taking a Mediterranean cruise, suddenly appeared (March, 1905) at Tangier and intimated that he would support the freedom and independence of the Sultan. After a great deal of intense excitement in the Capitals of the world, France finally agreed to arbitrate the Moroccan situation at an international conference to be held at Algeciras, Spain. Delcassé, the French Foreign Minister who had opposed bowing to Germany's demand for a conference, resigned.

ALGECIRAS CONFERENCE

The famous Algeciras Conference of 1906 resulted nevertheless, in a substantial victory for France. While it affirmed the sovereignty of the Sultan, and the commercial equality of all the powers, it gave France and Spain control of the police in Morocco, and virtual control of the financial affairs of the country. It was apparent that France had won a position in Morocco which would before long bring the nation within the French "sphere of influence." Perhaps the most significant part of the conference was that Germany and Austria found themselves alone in facing the other Great Powers.

AGADIR

In 1911 a disturbance in Fez gave France an excuse to occupy the capital city with a large body of troops. Germany promptly dispatched a gunboat, the *Panther*, to the harbor of Agadir to look after "German interests." It became all too clear to France that if she ever expected to occupy Morocco without trouble with Germany, it would be necessary to compensate the German Empire. Accordingly, the two nations came to terms, and Germany accorded France a free hand in Morocco in return for compensation in Equatorial Africa. In 1912 France proclaimed a "protectorate" over Morocco.

GREAT BRITAIN IN SOUTH AFRICA

The French succeeded in gaining control over more square miles of territory in Africa than any of the other European States, but the British Empire came off with the most desirable portions of the Continent. . . . Using the Union [of South Africa] as a base of operations, the British pushed steadily northward until they had secured possession of Bechuanaland, Rhodesia, and Nyasaland. For a time Portugal had attempted to assert claims to all the intervening territory between Portuguese East Africa and Angola, but in the face of a resolute British government the Portuguese relinquished their claims in the Anglo-Portuguese treaty of 1891. England's claim to Rhodesia had been acquired largely from the activities of the South African Company whose occupancy of the area had been successful only after many severe encounters with the Zulus, and with Lobengula, the notable chief of the Matabele tribes. The Nyasaland area came under British influence as a result of the characteristic treaty-making proclivities of Europeans. Before 1889 agents of the African Lakes Company secured the treaties in behalf of British interests, and after that time Sir H. H. Johnston, acting as the direct representative of the government, took over the task of getting those "crosses splodged on treaty-forms" which assured the natives of "protection."

BRITISH IN EAST AND WEST AFRICA

In East Africa, Great Britain established "protectorates" over Uganda (1894) and Kenya (1895) only after disagreements with Germany were adjusted by the Anglo-German Agreement of 1890. It was in Uganda that the long-sought-for source of the Nile was found at Lake Victoria. The protectorate, separated from the Indian Ocean by the breadth of Kenya (500 miles), could scarcely have been effectually occupied and retained but for the construction of the Uganda Railway in 1896. Almost simultaneously with these acquisitions, England was acquiring important areas on the West Coast of Africa. Sierra Leone, founded by philanthropists as a settlement for destitute freedmen (1787), was made a Crown Colony in 1807, and virtually forgotten by the British government until the "scramble for Africa" brought it sharply into focus. Likewise, Gambia, Nigeria, and the Gold Coast, ancient British trading stations in Western Africa, became the centers of an active program of expansion after 1880. In this theater of African enterprise, however, the French gained the advantage, and prevented any of these possessions, with the single exception of Nigeria, from reaching any considerable size. . . .

Selection 2

The International Frontier*

H. Duncan Hall

Australian-born H. Duncan Hall has had a long career as a journalist, British and international (with the League of Nations) civil servant, historian, and writer.

I. THE NATURE OF THE INTERNATIONAL FRONTIER

The international frontier is formed by the zones where great-power interests come together in conflict. It is the main line of structural weakness in the earth's political crust—the main fissure where wars break through. The powers are constantly at work on the frontier trying to patch up the peace by international arrangements of various kinds.

The conception of the international frontier cannot be stated in a sentence. It will emerge from the analysis that follows. But broadly speaking, it is the zone in which the great powers, expanding along their main lines of communication to the limits of their political and economic influence and defense needs, impinge upon each other in conflict or compromise. It is the debatable no man's land into which the interests and policies of more than one great power penetrate, in which they compete for power and influence but in which no one power is supreme. For once a great power becomes supreme in an area,

* Reprinted by permission from *Mandates, Dependencies, and Trusteeship* by H. Duncan Hall (Washington, D.C.: Carnegie Endowment for International Peace, 1948), Chapter I, pp. 3–5, 8–12. (Footnotes that appear in the original source have been omitted.)

even if it is not fully "sovereign" from a legal point of view, that area can hardly be said to fall within the zone of the international frontier. Thus American power and diplomacy as expressed in the Monroe Doctrine (with British support) removed the Latin American continent from the international frontier. So likewise the subcontinent of India, with its congeries of peoples and states, was removed for a century and a half from the international frontier by British power, and given also peace between its races and life for its minorities. Historically the international frontier began to emerge in the sixteenth and seventeenth centuries. It grew with the extension to the New World and South and East Asia of the rivalries of the then major continental powers, Spain and Portugal, Britain, France, and Holland, and the gradual convergence of the contemporary Russian landwise expansion.

The relation between the ordinary national frontier and the international frontier is not easy to define. A national frontier of a great power may coincide in part with a sector of the international frontier. But in general the international frontier is a zone that lies beyond the national frontiers and does not necessarily touch them at any point. When Mr. Stanley Baldwin, before the House of Commons in 1934, spoke of the Rhine as "where our frontier lies today," or when General Carl Spaatz spoke of an American "Arctic frontier," the reference was to the international frontier. . . .

. . . As a volcano is a local vent for widespread pressures in molten depths of the earth's crust, so an outbreak on the international frontier, in some so-called frontier incident, is rarely a local phenomenon but can be traced back to pressures deep down within the states concerned.

A zone of conflict between the great powers forces them to compromise. The international frontier is thus not only an area of international conflict; it has also produced—as will be seen below—nearly all the international territorial regimes in modern history as well as many other international arrangements of various kinds. Such arrangements, which can be classified together as phenomena of the international frontier, have usually had as their objectives the preservation of the general peace, the securing of law and order in otherwise unstable areas, and of proper conditions of life for the local inhabitants, and the facilitating of normal international intercourse in matters of trade, travel, and cultural relations.

Geographical factors such as lines of communication play some part in determining the location and extent of parts of the frontier. It is mostly pure coincidence, though not without symbolical interest, that a fairly typical list of such arrangements can be read off along the line of the Great Rift Valley. The immense unstable line of the Rift Valley runs from Lake Nyasa, past the rock walls of Abyssinia, through the Red Sea, the Gulf of Aqaba, the Dead Sea, and the Jordan Valley. Sunken valleys, deep narrow lakes and seas, mark the Rift. Flanking volcanoes—Ruwenzori and Kilimanjaro—are vents for the eruptions that accompanied the faulting along the Rift. Politically the line of the Rift System, from end to end, from Nyasaland to the Jordan Valley, is a line of typical phenomena of the international frontier: great-power rivalries and conflicting spheres of influence, mitigated by various forms of compromise arrangement. The list, reading from south to north, is as follows: the mandates (now trusteeships) of Ruanda-Urundi and Tanganyika; the Uganda Protectorate; rivalries and spheres of influence over Abyssinia; Eritrea, in turn Turkish, Egyptian, Italian, and now projected international trusteeship; rivalries of Britain and France over Egypt and the valley of the Nile culminating in the Fashoda incident; the condominium of the Sudan; the former condominiums and protectorate over Egypt; the neutralized and demilitarized Suez Canal, with its international regime; the mandates over Trans-Jordan, Palestine, and Syria; the checkered history of Alexandretta, in turn Turkish territory, League mandate, international regime, and again Turkish territory. . . .

2. THE STATE SYSTEM, THE BALANCE OF POWER, AND MANDATES

It is not possible to examine here all the aspects and implications of the international frontier. Its history forms a large part of the history of the relations of the powers. This study will deal with a single aspect. Its theme is the persistent breaking-out along the frontier over the past hundred years, and never more impressively than today, of certain characteristic and closely related phenomena. These include neutralization and demilitarization, condominiums, international mandates and trusteeship, and other forms of international territorial regimes and arrangements. In the past such regimes have not been grouped normally with mandates and trusteeship, which have been regarded almost as an unrelated species.

That international mandates and trusteeship are largely by-products of the working of the state system of the world, of the political relations of the powers, and thus factors in the balance of power, has never been sufficiently recognized. The tendency has been to explain them historically as in the main a product of humanitarianism and of liberal idealism. But these in fact have played a secondary rather than a primary rôle.

Mandates and trusteeship, and the other varieties of the species to which they belong, have flourished in a kind of international no man's land. The characteristic of such no man's land is the absence or breakdown of sovereignty. It is an area of low political pressure into which the forces of the strong, well-organized states tend to expand and where their spheres of influence may overlap and clash. To it belong weak ungrouped and unprotected states, or states which temporarily, through civil war or other factors, have lost their power and cohesion, and thus lie open to pressures and invading forces. But in general it is the area of more or less dependent peoples as distinguished from independent peoples. For the mark of an independent people is that it has a stable internal peace and can offer sufficient opposition to such intrusions to make them difficult if not impossible.

Nearly all mandates and trusteeship areas are to be found in a few great frontier zones of overlapping interests or spheres of influence of the powers now fused together into the international frontier. But they may also arise at points of direct frontier contact between the great powers, as in the Saar Basin. In such cases resort may be had to some compromise form of international regime such as that set up for the Saar Territory, or the Free Territory of Trieste under the Italian Peace Treaty of February 10, 1947.

There are no mandates, no trusteeships, no dependent peoples within the well-ordered peace area of a strong, advanced national state, such as metropolitan France or Great Britain. But within the metropolitan area of a number of the states members of the United Nations, including more than one of the five great powers permanent members of the Security Council, there are internal dependent areas and depressed peoples. Though these peoples are depressed, in need of tutelage and assistance and of effective guarantees of their human rights, they are not made the subject of annual reports and petitions to any international body. Their populations are without any special international safeguards (though they do come within the general field of "human rights" of the Charter). No example of international trusteeship, and few if any of the other phenomena of the international frontier, are to be found in the Western Hemisphere, in which there is a single great power—the United States of America. The international frontier threatened to run through the Americas; the series of episodes whereby it was eliminated from the Western Hemisphere forms the central thread of the history of American diplomacy. . . .

. . . even a great state which has fallen into a condition of prolonged internal weakness and civil war, and so become incapable of excluding, controlling, or protecting the foreign trader or traveler, may be subjected to a species of limited international tutelage. Thus, China in the nineteenth century became a semicolonial area open to intrusions from her land and sea borders, and was subjected to the "unequal treaties." These limited her tariff autonomy, made her customs revenue security for foreign loans, imposed a one-way open door, and gave foreign states jurisdiction over their own subjects in Chinese territory, with the right to establish extraterritorial zones in Chinese ports. China had temporarily lost her full sovereignty and was partly merged in the international frontier. Only in recent times have the Western powers enabled her to close at least her sea borders by giving up their special privileges.

Phenomena such as those mentioned in the last two paragraphs are not commonly associated with international mandates and trusteeship; but they are due to the same political causes as mandates and trusteeship and have elements in common with them. They all involve some kind of tutelage; they are all the result of the intrusion of outside forces, whether those of a single state or of several states, or of an international body. Greece in 1947 afforded an example of tutelage, a special form of protectorate with trusteeship features, falling short of full international trusteeship. The United States intervened at the request of the Greek Government to give aid and protection, training and supervision, thus supplementing the aid given hitherto by Great Britain. The action was taken in conformity with the Charter. It was formally notified to the United Nations, to which some kind of accounting was to be made. The possibility was held open that the United Nations itself might take over ultimately the responsibility if it desired and were able to do so. And a United Nations frontier commission was appointed as an insurance against violations of the Greek frontier. This was tutelage with some international elements but not full international trusteeship in the technical sense of the Charter.

Thus the varieties of the species shade off into one another. Spheres of interest and national trusteeship shade off into protectorates; or into various forms of condominiums. These shade off into other forms of international regimes, like Danzig or Tangier; and these in turn shade off into mandates and the several kinds of United Nations trusteeships. For the United Nations Charter itself recognized at least four distinct varieties of trusteeship: the strategic-area type; trusteeships exercised by one state; or by several states; or by "the Organization itself." . . .

Nothing, it will be noted, has been said so far of the African mandates south of the Sahara. The reason is that historically international mandates and trusteeship did not originate mainly in Africa. Their significance cannot be understood if they are studied mainly in relationship to Africa. The theory and ethics of national trusteeship developed first in relation to the vast dependency of India. International mandates of a primitive kind developed first in relation to the Mediterranean-North African-Middle East frontier zone, especially in the eastern Mediterranean and the Turkish Empire from Egypt to the Balkans. Mandates in tropical Africa were a secondary phenomenon. The idea that both historically and as a contemporary phenomenon mandates and trusteeship involve primarily Africa south of the Sahara and the Pacific Islands is a misreading of the facts. Yet the idea has gained considerable currency. Thus in a recent publication of high authority, the history of mandates becomes almost wholly an African affair; it is told in terms of the humanitarian movement, the abolition of slavery, the development of national trusteeship, colonial self-government, equality of commercial access, the Berlin-African Conference of 1884–85, and, finally, the setting-up of the League African mandates in 1919.

All this is no doubt important but it is less than half the story. By leaving out all reference to the political background of the mandate and trusteeship systems it obscures the relationship of mandates to other varieties of the species. It fails to explain why the League mandate system was applied only to ex-enemy territory and nowhere else. It minimizes the great importance historically of the Near East mandates. It gives the wholly misleading impression that historically the "A" mandates, set up in the areas liberated by the collapse of the Turkish Empire, were special cases, outliers as it were of the central range in Africa; whereas they are in fact the main range itself, and the African mandates are the lesser ridges branching off from it. They were a further stage of the partition of Africa under a more elaborate formula. The partition of Africa, the greatest example of peaceful adjustment in the history of the international frontier, combined national trusteeship with international obligations under the Congo Basin treaties. The mandates added the principle of international accountancy. The partition was accomplished by the Concert of Europe without war, though not without friction between the powers. It was friction between France and Germany that permitted King Leopold of Belgium to slip in between them and to secure from the powers at the Berlin African Conference of 1885 the mandate to govern the area now known as the Belgian Congo. . . .

Selection 3

Arenas of Friction*

WALTER LIPPMANN

For the past half-century Mr. Lippmann has played a prominent part in American life, as an editor, author of numerous books, and commentator, particularly in the area of foreign affairs.

There are in the world to-day not more than eight Powers which really count—Great Britain, France, Russia, Italy, Germany, Austria-Hungary, Japan, and the United States. When I say "count," I mean that the effective force of the world is in their hands, and that the decision of world affairs is for them. The other nations lie in the orbit of the Great Powers. They follow but do not lead. . . .

There is an incessant competition between governments to attach

* From *The Stakes of Diplomacy* by Walter Lippmann (New York: Henry Holt and Company, 1915), pp. 82–83, 87, 93–95, 98. Reprinted with the permission of The Macmillan Company.

these smaller states to themselves. At no point can one say that specific trade opportunities are the prize. The real prize for the diplomats is an increase of power, a greater emphasis to their word. Their nations rally behind them—the interested business men see it as dollar diplomacy, the mass of the people, hardly aware of the concrete issues, see it as a gigantic competition involving their own sense of importance. The diplomatic struggle is played in Morocco, at Constantinople, in Pekin, wherever there are stakes for which to play. At home there is joy in victory, anger at defeat. Armament is added as an "insurance" for diplomacy, and of course military preparation always calls forth military preparation. Every international incident is seen then, not on its "merits," but in its relation to the whole vast complicated game, forever teetering on the edge of war. . . .

This whole business of jockeying for position is at first glance so incredibly silly that many liberals regard diplomacy as a cross between sinister conspiracy and a meaningless etiquette. It would be all of that if the stakes of diplomacy were not real. Those stakes have to be understood, for without such an understanding diplomacy is incomprehensible and any scheme of world peace an idle fancy.

The chief, the overwhelming problem of diplomacy seems to be the weak state—the Balkans, the African sultanates, Turkey, China, and Latin America, with the possible exception of the Argentine, Chile, and Brazil. These states are "weak" because they are industrially backward and at present politically incompetent. They are rich in resources and cheap labor, poor in capital, poor in political experience, poor in the power of defense. The government of these states is the supreme problem of diplomacy. . . .

It is essential to remember that what turns a territory into a diplomatic "problem" is the combination of natural resources, cheap labor, markets, defenselessness, corrupt and inefficient government. The desert of Sahara is no "problem," except where there are oases and trade routes. Switzerland is no "problem," for Switzerland is a highly organized modern state. . . .

The weak states, in other words, are those which lack the political development that modern commerce requires. To take an extreme case which brings out the real nature of the "problem," suppose that the United States was organized politically as England was in the time of William the Conqueror. Would it not be impossible to do business in the United States? There would be an everlasting clash between an impossible legal system and a growing commercial development. And the internal affairs of the United States would constitute a diplomatic "problem."

This, it seems to me, is the reason behind the outburst of modern imperialism among the Great Powers. It is not enough to say that they are "expanding" or "seeking markets" or "grabbing resources." They are doing all these things, of course. But if the world into which they are expanding were not politically archaic, the growth of foreign trade would not be accompanied by political imperialism. Germany has "expanded" wonderfully in the British Empire, in Russia, in the United States, but no German is silly enough to insist on planting his flag wherever he sells his dyestuffs or stoves. It is only when his expansion is into weak states—into China, Morocco, Turkey, or elsewhere that foreign trade is imperialistic. This imperialism is actuated by many motives—by a feeling that political control insures special privileges, by a desire to play a large part in the world, by national vanity, by a passion for "ownership," but none of these motives would come into play if countries like China or Turkey were not politically backward. . . .

The whole situation might be summed up by saying that the commercial development of the world will not wait until each territory has created for itself a stable and fairly modern political system. By some means or other the weak states have to be brought within the framework of commercial administration. Their independence and integrity, so-called, are dependent upon their creating conditions under which world-wide business can be conducted. The pressure to organize the globe is enormous. . . .

Selection 4

Imperialism as a Stage of History*

Vernon Van Dyke

Vernon Van Dyke is Professor of Political Science at the University of Iowa.

Of the Marxists, and of those who regard imperialism as an inevitable stage in the development of capitalism, Lenin, the Russian Bolshevik leader, has been most influential. . . . [Lenin] based his theory on the "general and fundamental law" that under capitalism both the means of production and the money available for investment are concentrated in fewer and fewer hands. In other words, capitalist economies come to be dominated by monopolies or trusts, supplemented internationally by cartels. At some point in this process capitalism is transformed into imperialism. According to Lenin's "briefest possible definition," imperialism is "the monopoly stage of capitalism."

Capitalism in its monopolist or imperialist stage, according to Lenin, is necessarily expansionist. It is expansionist in part because the monopolists come to control "surplus" capital. They will not use the surplus for the purpose of raising the standard of living of the masses, for this would mean a decline in profits. They cannot keep on investing within a strictly national economy, because as capitalism matures the rate of profit on investments within the country tends to decline. So they invest abroad, in less advanced countries, where the rate of profit promises to be higher. Having invested, they want their investment to be secure. "The necessity of exporting capital gives an impetus to the conquest of colonies, for in the colonial market it is easier to eliminate competition, to make sure of orders, to strengthen the necessary 'con-

---

* From *International Politics* by Vernon Van Dyke (New York: Appleton-Century-Crofts, 1957), pp. 105–106.

nection,' etc., by monopolist methods (and sometimes it is the only way)."

Monopoly capitalism is also expansionist, Lenin held, because of the need for foreign raw materials and because of the competition among capitalists of various countries for control over them. "Colonial possession alone gives complete guarantee of success to the monopolies against all the risks of the struggle with competitors. . . . The more capitalism is developed, the more the need for raw materials is felt, the more bitter competition becomes, and the more feverishly the hunt for raw materials proceeds throughout the whole world, the more desperate becomes the struggle for the acquisition of colonies."

As the reference to the acquisition of colonies suggests, Lenin was not speaking solely of economic expansion. Under his analysis, monopoly capitalists dominated not only the economic but also the political life of imperialist countries. In general, he regarded all governments simply as instruments of a ruling class. Whether governments were monarchical or republican, dictatorial or democratic—in fact, regardless of their form—they would be class instruments in societies divided into classes. Under monopoly capitalism, they would be tools of the monopolists. Thus, if the monopolists wanted to render their foreign investments secure, and if they wanted to gain control over the sources of needed raw materials, they would simply use government to serve this end. Whether the nation as a whole gained or lost through imperialist expansion was an irrelevant question; it was only the interests of the monopolists which counted. Thus through their economic power and through their use of the state the monopoly capitalists engaged in struggles for territorial expansion. The fundamental forces at work were economic, but Lenin admitted the existence of a "non-economic superstructure" which stimulated the striving for colonial conquest. What he meant was that the monopoly capitalists developed ideologies and principles which justified and reinforced their pursuit of economic interests.

In Lenin's description, the process of imperialism went on until the whole world had been divided up among the imperialist powers, but even then it did not stop. Enduring stability was out of the question. Lenin held that capitalism develops unevenly in different countries. Power relationships among countries therefore change, and as they change there are demands for a redivision of the world. Imperialist countries which in the days of their strength seized foreign territories are thus compelled to disgorge their gains when other imperialist countries become more powerful.

Lenin simply assumed that wars arise naturally out of the imperialist struggle. He thought it "naive" to talk about peace under imperialism. There would be wars among the imperialist states themselves over the division and redivision of the world, and wars between imperialist states and the colonial areas. . . .

THE RACIAL ISSUE

If the experience of imperialism looms large for Africans (sometimes a little larger than life, perhaps), it does so partially because domination came at the hands of people of another race. Race and "the race question" constitute a significant part of the history or background and the present reality of African international relations.

We cannot here do more with this large and important concept of race than to define terms and, with three selections, to impart some notion of past and current racial attitudes relating to Africa.

A noted anthropologist, the late Ruth Benedict, noted that: " . . . racist dogmas as they are stated today are modern. But they express an old human obsession and only the 'reasons why' have altered. . . . "*

What are some of the typical racist dogmas applied to the African scene?

A generation or two ago it was widely accepted that race and human social development were closely connected. Primitive peoples, according to theory, were inferior by reason of inherited racial characteristics, and thus presumably would continue indefinitely in this status. Racial mixture was to be avoided as damaging to

* Ruth Benedict, *Race: Science and Politics* (New York: Viking Press, 1945), rev. ed., p. 221.

the capacities of the "superior," better adapted races. We can note some echoes of this theory in discussions of our own racial troubles, particularly in the South.

Such ideas were current in the early days of colonialism in Africa. But Selection 5, written by a European resident ("settler") of a white-dominated area of Africa, is a more typical expression of modern racist belief. One might call it the "only 50 years out of the trees" theory. (Belgians in the Congo are supposed to have made it explicit—a favorite epithet applied to Africans is said to have been "monkey.") This conception of racial differences drops the frank assertion of hereditary, biological inferiority. There is left a paternalistic concern for the African, oddly intermingled with arrogant contempt for his backward condition.

The author of Selection 6 is concerned with the kernel of truth in the "settler" point of view. As he shows, science has been unable to demonstrate probable connection between biologic differences and variations in achievement. But differences there are, as the "settler" points out, and Mr. Mason is concerned to establish that these "reasons why" should not justify the dogmatic racial attitudes assumed by the "settlers."

Black racism exists also. A Negro journalist who traveled in Africa recently returned to report that "racism in reverse" was rising on the continent. It is only fair to note, however, that African leaders are obviously very aware of the danger that resentment of European imperialism offers a handy "reason why" for black racism. Selection 7, from the debates in the Tanganyika National Assembly on extending citizenship to non-Africans, indicates clearly the differing African attitudes with respect to racially connected issues.

Selection 5

Eden and the Volcano*

Letter from a White Settler

We have, I am happy to say been remote from any of the disturbances so far . . . but there is no doubt that we are living on the edge of a volcano. The cause of it all? Well, I think that it is quite natural for the ignorant to want to bite the hand that feeds him. That, and infection from surrounding black states plus too much interference with bias from Britain. I can assure that the average [man] is quite liberal-minded, wants to see the African advance but not as quickly as others would have it happen. Nobody who does not live in the country can realise the problems—the [illiteracy], lack of the remotest sense of responsibility and complete absence of appreciation for what European good will and money has and is doing for the African. The greater number of them are little removed from savages and the few who have had advanced education are only out for power for themselves. As an example, the disgraceful and impossible behaviour of Dr. Banda in England at present. After all we didn't become civilised in 70 years and how on earth can anybody expect the African to be a responsible citizen in that time. BUT, in the meantime we have the Reds waiting like hyenas and the problem now is how to carry on our plans to educate and uplift our African population on a steady and progressive basis. Left to ourselves I am absolutely convinced that we could have done it but what we do now with interference all round, I don't know. I do know this, however, that this will not be a second Belgian Congo with the Europeans taking to their heels and running without a shot fired. This country and it is a good country has been built with the blood and sweat and tears of the European. His roots and heart are here and he will not sit down and give it up to a mob of thugs

* Excerpt from a letter to Mr. William A. Boekel of San Francisco. Reprinted by special permission of Mr. Boekel.

and ignorant people, mad with the lust for power for the individual, if he can do anything about it. I can't understand why the world has not learned a lesson from the Belgian Congo for if it wasn't so desperately serious, the situation there would be a first class comic opera. Surely that has proven that a people not trained steadily for responsible government, taking the reins into their own hands, can only lead to tragedy and bloodshed. We know that the African must advance to our standards, but what we don't want is for him to revert to what he was before we came, to lead the miserable existence that he did perpetually waging war on his next door neighbour and to plunge the country in which we have a stake into ruin just because others thousands and thousands of miles away will persist in looking on him as a poor down trodden person who must at any cost have everything handed to him on a plate. We feel that he must earn some of it at any rate as we have had to do. In the meantime, . . . relations between us could not be more pleasant and cooperative. We do our very best for them and though that doesn't even vaguely enter their heads, their tummies are full, they have good housing and a beautiful hospital exclusively for them and a good school. They are happy and content and know that their sons will have every chance of advancement. Oh, how I wish we could keep it that way but, as I say, we can't delude ourselves that we are anywhere but on the edge of a volcano.

Selection 6

The Sciences, Race, and History*

PHILIP MASON

Philip Mason, a British writer and a former administrator in India, is at present Director of The Institute of Race Relations in London.

THE ANSWER OF BIOLOGY

. . . The answer of biology . . . must be that biology is unable to detect any hereditary difference between races which would seem likely to involve any necessary superiority of mind or character on one side. But that is not to say that some superiority is not there. The answer which physical science gives to this problem is limited; only if it is positive can it help the inquiry. If the answer is negative, it means no more than that we must shift our ground. There is a difference in achievement between the races which must be faced and taken into account. Not only that, but stabilizing devices are supported with passion and conviction; it would be to fly in the face of evidence to ignore that fact. It would be no use telling, let us say a South African miner or a Rhodesian farmer, that science states positively that there is no difference which has significance in the field of human development between himself and his Native employee. His reply is likely to be: "Then the more fool science; there plainly is a difference. What is the reason?" . . .

THE ANSWER OF STATISTICAL PSYCHOLOGY

There is in fact a fundamental limitation in the extent to which the methods of physical science can be applied to the realm of the human mind. . . .

* From *An Essay on Racial Tension* by Philip Mason (London: The Royal Institute of International Affairs, 1954), pp. 52–57, 59–61, 64. Reprinted by permission of the publisher and the author.

. . . this is not to decry the value of the inductive physical sciences but only to say that they cannot tell the whole truth about human beings. In this particular field all they can hope to say is one or the other of two things. Either they may say that there is a difference between races, whether a bodily or a mental difference, so great that it hampers one race permanently in the field of human performance, or they may say that they cannot find a difference of that nature which can be measured in their quantitative terms. They cannot say that there is no difference. And in any case such an answer would be far from satisfactory to observers who perceive an actual difference in achievement today.

With this warning in mind it is possible to pass on to the second approach which may be made to the question we have asked, the approach of statistical psychology. By this I mean the compilation of statistics about intelligence and character, an attempt to apply the methods of physical science to the measurement of the human intelligence. The most obvious example is the intelligence test, and here it is worth considering what it is that you are looking for in an intelligence test. . . .

Today most intelligence testers are aware of the limitations of their method. In Klineberg's words: "The history of mental testing of ethnic or racial groups may almost be described as a progressive disillusionment with tests as measures of native ability and a gradually increasing realization of the many complex environmental factors which enter into the result. . . . "

. . . It is in the United States that most of this work has been done; if the difficulties of excluding environment have been great here, they are infinitely greater in Africa where backgrounds are so much wider apart. Biesheuvel in his monograph on *African Intelligence* concluded that it was virtually impossible to compare in numerical terms African and European intelligence in South Africa. It is a judgment which would apply with even greater force in Central or East Africa, where the impact of industrialism has been less.

Statistical psychology then returns the same report as biology. When allowance has been made for environment, no differences can be detected which are not greater within the races than between them and therefore no argument is provided which might justify domination. There is, however, room for more work in this field; it should be possible both to improve the tests and to cut out the environmental differences further. . . .

HISTORY, CLIMATE, DIET

The methods of physical science have then returned negative results. But this is not enough; we are faced by life and human beings, not by tables of statistics. It is no use showing tables of statistics to a man who has all his life been dealing with African miners and field hands. He will ask why Africans have made so insignificant a mark upon the world. He will ask why they have added no great buildings to humanity's achievement, why they never learnt to write or to plough, why in fact when Africans have been left to manage their own affairs, as in Liberia and Abyssinia, they have not been notably successful. He will point to the fate of the settlements of the Bastards in Griqualand and to other missionary settlements in South Africa which have fallen back—the springs silted up, the fields eroded, the houses unrepaired—as soon as missionary influence was removed. He will ask how it is that while he can teach Africans a skill, his employees never make any suggestion for improving the way the work is done. He will in short apply a pragmatic test. . . .

Why then has Africa south of the Sahara produced no civilization? There are people who will tell you that it has, and it is true that we now know of more highly developed cultures in Africa's past than we once did. But if world history is considered with a sense of proportion, the question can surely stand unaltered. . . .

. . . history cannot be said to return an entirely conclusive reply to this question. Much closer investigation of the subject is required. It is however worth remembering that it is approximately 350,000 years since man in a form biologically modern appeared on the earth's surface and that the history of which we have knowledge covers at the most 5,000 years. It is not therefore surprising to find that over so long a period some people have obtained a start over others. There was contact between the Mycenaean Bronze Age civilization and the people who built Stonehenge; a thousand years later Mycenae had developed into Athens but fifteen hundred years later the inhabitants of Britain were painting themselves blue and burning people alive in wicker cages. The most intolerant judgment passed on the African today might well have been passed on the German in the time of

Tacitus and it would have been easy to conclude in the tenth century that European civilization was receding into barbarism, while Indian civilization at the same date compared poorly with that of the Guptas or the Mauryas six hundred and fourteen hundred years earlier. Go back only two hundred and fifty years and compare the poorer parts of London in the reign of Queen Anne with Moroka or Newclare or Sophiatown on the fringes of Johannesburg today, and it is impossible to conclude that the African slum-dwellers as compared with the English are more dirty, drunken, criminal, or callous of human life and suffering. Or, to come closer home, quote the Premier of Southern Rhodesia, who finds his African tribesmen today very like the people of the East End of London whom he used to doctor when first he was qualified. "We are a people," said an African character in a recent short story, "still in God's dressing-room, still waiting to come on the stage."

Selection 7

White Citizens in Black Africa?*

TANGANYIKA ASSEMBLY DEBATES

MR. MWAKANGALE: Mr. Speaker, Sir, whatever we say in this House is what the ordinary African thinks. Again whatever we say here does not mean at all that we have got hatred against people of other races. I wish this hon. House to be able to understand that whatever I say does not at all mean that I hate non-Africans.

. . . Mr. Speaker, Sir, we all believe and accept the doctrine of human rights. When I say we, I mean we Africans. I don't think people of other races really mean it. It is through the undisputed leadership of Mr. Nyerere and his followers that we have racial harmony in Tanganyika. Believe me Mr. Speaker, Sir, I think 75 per cent of the non-Africans in Tanganyika still regard an African in

* From *Tanganyika Assembly Debates* (Hansard). Tanganyika National Assembly, Official Report, 36th Session (5th meeting), 10–20 October 1961, columns 329–330, 333–339.

Tanganyika as an inferior human being. Why is it so, Sir? It is because the white population has been dominating us both economically and politically, and their neighbours the Asians too have been economically dominating us, we Africans. This domination will not end just because we are politically mature. The main foundation of political freedom is the economic soundness of a country. At this point, Sir, I can guess that we are economically 50 years behind non-Africans who live here and who choose to remain in Tanganyika.

The African cannot be blamed for this. It is the retiring administering power which is to be blamed for creating this wide gap. Both the white people and the Asians have been exploiting the African for the last seven decades. The wealth they have exploited and obtained was not being evenly distributed between the exploiters and the exploited. This is the main cause of the gap.

Mr. Speaker, Sir, can we fill this gap by miracles? Do you think that an ordinary African forming the vast majority of the population will agree at this stage to have equal rights with the Europeans and the Asians? My answer is no, Sir. The non-Africans are economically sound and have the means to obtain money on loan because they have the security, while an African, due to land ownership titles and land tenure does not possess this advantage. Thus if we say, "All right, we are equal, all citizens of Tanganyika," the non-Africans will settle on the land. I know they will increase the economy of the country, but they will want to own the land, and for many years to come we will only be labourers on their farms. The question of the Civil Service and the present doctrine of Africanisation will lose its meaning, although in ten years to come we hope the output of qualified Africans will probably justify the Africanisation of say 60 per cent of the Civil Service. Now will the Government in power then say, "Now, non-African citizens in Tanganyika, leave the Service in favour of African citizens?" Will this not mean discrimination? Now Sir, if we return to what the hon. Mr. Joseph Nyerere said yesterday with regard to the relationship between the white, yellow, brown and the American negroes in the United States of America, of course I think the hon. Member is aware of what has been happening, or is still happening, in the southern states of the United States of America. Now, Mr. Speaker Sir, in that so-called civilized country, in that so-called democratic country, how many years has it taken to correct the situation? Furthermore, Sir, the United States of America cannot be compared with Tanganyika. Those who form the Government in the States were colonizers and the American negroes, though they were brought to America as slaves, I feel, Sir, that was an indirect way of colonization. The inhabitants of that country were Red Indians, just as we are in Tanganyika. Do you hear of the Red Indians playing a full part in the government now? Do you? The answer is no.

LADY CHESHAM: Mr. Speaker, Sir, on a point of information. Yes, Sir. A leading General, and one of our Chief Justices, are Red Indians.*

MR. MWAKANGALE: Mr. Speaker, Sir, is it fair for only one or two Senior officials to take part in the Government of their country?

The same thing, Sir, might happen here in the future. Although we cannot see it, those people can see it. They have already seen what is going to come. But some of we poor Africans cannot see what can happen here in Tanganyika in the future.

Now, Sir, another point. Again I repeat, the non-Africans are economically sound, and if we allow them now to become citizens and when they get well established on our land, it is quite possible—I cannot prove it now, but it is quite possible—that when elections will take place on different government institutions in future they could easily buy our votes, the poor Africans' votes—it is quite easy to do that.

Now, Mr. Speaker, Sir, some people will think that we are objecting to some proposals contained in the Government Paper just because we are planning to create another South Africa, apartheid policy in Tanganyika. I say no, Sir. The situation here is quite different. In South Africa it is the foreigners, the imperialists, who are claiming superiority against the indigenous Africans there. What the Africans want in South Africa, Sir, is democracy. What form of democracy? That the Africans should govern that country, giving allowance to foreigners to enjoy certain rights—not all rights as bwanas—until such time when they will realize that Africans are also human beings, just as much human beings as the whites are. . . .

THE PRIME MINISTER: Mr. Speaker, Sir, I do not intend to answer for my hon. Colleague, the Minister for Home Affairs, certain matters of detail which have been raised on the Government White Paper on Citizenship. But I would like only to tackle the matter of principle

* Editor's Note: Lady Chesham is of American birth.

which has been raised by a substantial number of potential Verwoerds.

Now, Sir, what are we trying to do? We are establishing a citizenship of Tanganyika. What is going to be the basis of this citizenship of Tanganyika? We, the Government, elected by the people of Tanganyika say loyalty to the country is going to be the basis of determining the citizenship of our country. In order to be certain as far as humanly possible to be certain that citizens of Tanganyika are going to be loyal to Tanganyika and Tanganyika only we have said, although other countries do accept it, we have said we are not going to accept dual citizenship in Tanganyika.

A fairly large number of speakers have stood up here. They claim they speak for the majority of the people of Tanganyika and I am going to take them very seriously, because I believe they did intend to be taken very seriously. They stood, Sir, and said they speak for the vast majority of the people of Tanganyika, and they are asking us, Sir, to base citizenship not on loyalty to our country, but on colour.

Now, Sir, this is a big difference of principle. And there cannot be a bigger difference between the speakers and this Government here. And, Sir, I intend to take them very seriously. They have challenged us on democracy, we are a democratic Government. They have said they speak for the vast majority of the people of this country. We claim we do, and now Sir, I am going to make a very serious statement, because I don't want people coming in this House, getting drunk with the atmosphere of the House and talk rubbish in this House, hoping some people will clap for them and get away with it. I am going to deal with it very seriously.

We are committed to democracy here, and the organization that we represent is committed to democracy. They claim they are speaking for the majority of the people of this country, I say on this Paper, though we are going to treat it as a matter of principle, we are going to be even more democratic than other democratic countries. We are going to make it a free vote, completely free, no whip, nothing. But we are going to treat it as a matter of principle. Let the representatives here of the people of Tanganyika reject this Motion and we shall resign immediately, and I mean it. (Applause.) I mean it, because we are not here on the basis of fooling our people. We are here to tell our people what we believe.

Sir, a great American once said, "As a nation we began by declaring that all men are created equal. We are now practically reading it all men are created equal except negroes. When the know-nothings get control it will read all men are created equal except the negroes and foreigners and catholics. When it comes to that," Abraham Lincoln said, "I shall prefer emigrating to some country where they make no pretence of loving liberty, where despotism can be taken pure, without the base alloy of hypocrisy."

Sir, our own know-nothings, if they got control, would say, I am sure, that all men are created equal, except white people, Indians, Arabs and Chinamen, who happen to live in Tanganyika. But they will not stop there, Sir. They will continue; for principles have a way of revenging themselves. If you break a principle, it will find a method of breaking you. And if a people try to break a major principle, those principles will find a way of breaking that people.

If we begin now in Tanganyika saying that all people in Tanganyika are equal except the Indians, and the Arabs and the Europeans, and the Chinamen, who happen to live in Tanganyika, we shall have broken a principle. It won't let us stop there. If we in Tanganyika are going to divorce citizenship from loyalty and marry it to colour, we won't stop there, Sir. We will go on breaking that principle, and I have heard people here already doing it. I have heard several times, and I was noting it, the phrase "indigenous African." They are beginning to draw a distinction between Africans too. This is the beginning of breaking that major principle, and going downhill until you break up the country, until that country is left without an ethic at all.

Sir, if we begin, if we were to accept what our friends would claim they are speaking for the vast majority of the people of Tanganyika, if we were to accept what they are saying, Sir, a day will come when we will say all people were created equal except the Masai, except the Wagogo, except the Waha, except the polygamists, except the Muslims, etc. We will continue breaking these principles. For what is colour. If we are going to base citizenship on colour, we will commit a crime. I cannot change my colour. Ideology, one can understand, because I could change my ideology, it is something I accepted on conviction. Religion, Sir, I can change my religion. If somebody convinces me I am wrong as a Catholic, I change my religion. I decided to become a Catholic, I can still change it. I still don't like people being persecuted or discriminated against because of their ideology or because of their religion, but at least there, Sir, there is something. Discrimination against human beings because of their colour, is exactly what we have been fighting against. This is what we have formed T.A.N.U. for—(applause)—and so soon, Sir, so soon, before even 9th of December some of my friends have forgotten it. Now they are preaching discrimination, colour discrimination as a religion to us. And they stand like Hitlers and begin to glorify the race. We glorify human beings, Sir, not colour. You know what happens when people begin to get drunk with power and glorify their race, the Hitlers, that is what they do. You know where they lead the human race, the Verwoerds of South Africa, that is what they do. You know where they are leading the human race. These people are telling us to discriminate because of the "special circumstance of Tanganyika." This is exactly what Verwoerd says. "The circumstances of South Africa are different." This is the argument used by the racialists.

My friend there talks as if it is perfectly alright to discriminate against the white, against the Indian, against the Arab, against the Chinaman. It is only wrong when you discriminate against a black man.

Sir, what is the crime in the world today? It is the oppression of man, by man. It is the treatment by those in power, of those who have no power, as if they are goats and not human beings; that is the crime of this world, that is what we have been fighting against. People come here and stand as if they are the only people who know that here in Tanganyika we have racial difficulties. I do not have to be told that the African of this country is poor. But when I am told that the way to raise the standard of living of the African peoples of this country is to base our citizenship on colour, I cannot believe, Sir, that the people who utter this rubbish have ever given very much thought to the problem at all. I have said, Sir, because of the situation we have inherited in this country, where economic classes are also identical with race, that we live on dynamite, that it might explode any day, unless we do something about it. But positively, not negatively. Sir, I said I was not going to try and answer matters of detail raised on the White Paper. But I am going to repeat, and repeat very firmly, that this Government has rejected, and rejected completely, any ideas that citizenship, with the duties and the rights of citizenship of this country, are going to be based on anything except loyalty to this country. (Applause.) We Sir, the Government, are committed to that principle, . . .

Mr. Wambura: Mr. Speaker, Sir, although the Prime Minister has just warned us that some of us, after having got drunk return to this House and claim to represent the view of the vast majority of the people. I am one of those, Sir—a few who got drunk, Members—who should not stand here and speak. At the same time, Sir, I would also like to speak as a Hitler, who has been referred to in that sense by the Prime Minister. Mr. Speaker, Sir, it must be known that we are also Members representing the people, just as well as the Members of the Cabinet do. Now when certain matters are brought before this House, we have an equal right to discuss it without any fear, well, I am not going to have any fear, I am going to speak with my power and ability. Now then, it appears that the Prime Minister thinks that the people outside this House do not support the proposals made by the hon. Members, Mr. Tumbo, Mr. Msindai, Mr. Mtaki, and Mr. Mwakangale. I want to repeat that the vast majority of the people support it wholeheartedly. This is what the people believe, and if the Prime Minister thinks that we are just pretending I can only ask the Government to put a referendum on these proposals, and see what will be the outcome. Now, Sir, I do not think there have been any Members in this House, or that there are any who think in terms of colour bar or who believe in racialism. We do not want any racialism. What the Members are saying is that there should not be an automatic offer of citizenship to non-Africans. (Applause.) . . .

Mr. Wambura: . . . If for instance, God sends a message to Tanganyika today, he perhaps drops in at this House, God says, "Within six months to come, Tanganyika will be set on fire." Everybody now Sir, will look for his own place. Tell me, by March next year, how many non-Africans will be in this country? None. They will have gone, they will have gone to their original places. . . .

(*At this stage the Deputy Speaker took the Chair*)

Mr. Tumbo: I would repeat what I said earlier, last night, that Africa is our home. If, as the hon. Member, Mr. Wambura said, there was someone to burn us, the Europeans would go to Europe in their situation.

Mr. Wambura: Now, Mr. Deputy Speaker, Sir, Government

knows that this is wrong. But as usual they are just trying to pursue with their White Paper. They shout and keep on shouting; the Cabinet goes on laughing, and when the time comes, they say "Aye" and the Paper is approved. I would say this time it is not going to be so easy to say "Aye." I do not like to bet because I know the Members will go against it.

The Minister yesterday amended clause A of subsection 2 of section 4 to read as follows: "If there are minors, within one year of reaching the age of 21 years." Well, this is all right. This has now been amended, but what I wanted to say, what about those citizens who are adults by the date of Independence? What citizenship are they to be given, because the Minister did not mention it here, and I would suggest, Sir, that they should not be given more than six months to decide whether they want to be citizens of Tanganyika or whether they will return to their homes.

The second point, Sir, is that which has been raised by Mr. Msindai and that is that only Africans will become automatically citizens of Tanganyika on Independence Day. All non-Africans will be subject to application or to registration and by saying so, we do not mean to say we are discriminating. We don't discriminate. We are not causing discrimination. Why should the Government decide for these people? Why don't the Government let them decide for themselves? How does the Government know that these people will agree or not? Why should the Government give them an automatic offer for citizenship?

I regard this, as an example. When I was young, in our family we used to share a bed—about four of us. Our grandmother used to cover us with one blanket. I got used to my grandmother's blanket. But then I went to visit my uncle and I was also covered with another blanket with the children of my uncle, I did not like that blanket, so instead of sleeping in the middle, I had to move and sleep at the very end of the bed so that when I did not want to be covered with that blanket, I could just leave it to cover the other children. And I chose to sleep without it because I hated the blanket for one reason or another which I know myself.

This is what Government is doing. It is going to cover Africans as well as non-Africans with the same blanket which some Asians and Europeans might not like. Supposing these people whose parents were born in Tanganyika are not interested in becoming Tanganyika citizens. We are offering them citizenship and they will reject it because they are not interested in living in Tanganyika. We never know. There are some people who have been here for centuries and yet they still might not like to become citizens of Tanganyika. Some of them have already made up their minds to live in their own countries. Why should we offer them this automatic citizenship? Why don't we put registration and see how many people are interested in the citizenship of Tanganyika. It is not a very big job. I would not associate myself with the views of Mr. Mwakangale that we give them five years. We don't need five years. We should give them two years from independence in which to register, and by the end of 1963 we would then know how many citizens of Tanganyika we have. Then if anybody becomes a citizen of Tanganyika, they will be treated equally with the African, and I hope he will also believe himself to be an African. We are not discriminating. All we are saying is that the application and the method used to offer citizenship to non-Africans is wrong.

Now, Sir, we have another Commonwealth clause. The Government has felt that the Commonwealth citizens should enjoy better privileges than even Africans from other parts of Africa whose countries are not in the Commonwealth. Well, Sir, this again is wrong and I think the time has come when the constitution of this Commonwealth has also got to be redrafted. What is the use of giving a man from a Commonwealth country a privilege simply because he comes from the Commonwealth. During the death of Mr. Dag Hammarskjoeld recently in the Congo, some newspapers of Ghana stated that the British Government was involved in his death. When Britain heard this, they sent their Minister for Commonwealth Relations to see Dr. Nkrumah and discuss that. The reason was that Ghana was a Member of the Commonwealth. Now, are we really accepting this Commonwealth as a means of shutting our mouths so that we may not speak freely according to our opinions? This was an affair in which the British were involved. Why should not they say freely that Britain was involved? How many times has the British Government supported Portugal? How many times has the British Delegation to the United Nations voted against the African resolutions?

The Minister for Home Affairs: I regret I have to get up again and correct the hon. Member. Perhaps he might have read newspapers which I did not read but an official communiqué from Ghana stated quite clearly that when the statements appeared in the Ghana Press, Dr. Nkrumah and his Government dissociated themselves from those statements.

MR. WAMBURA (*continuing*): Mr. Deputy Speaker, Sir, Dr. Nkrumah might have dissociated himself but this does not alter the principle of the Commonwealth. Suppose he had associated himself—what would have happened? Are we going to dissociate ourselves from things which we think are right?

Another point, Sir, is this Republic of Ireland. I don't know what relationship we have with the Republic of Ireland, but the Republic of Ireland is recognized in Tanganyika. Should we not use this opportunity of fitting in the Congo? It is a shame for an independent Tanganyika bringing in citizenship rights and mentioning the Republic of Ireland but failing to mention the Congo and other African countries which are not in the Commonwealth. This is a shame! I think, Sir, the Government ought to take this opportunity of implementing, adding some African countries which are not in the Commonwealth, so that when the Africans of those countries visit Tanganyika, they also enjoy the same privileges as those enjoyed by members of the Commonwealth.

The Africans of other countries who are in Tanganyika, I think, should also be given a special provision, not those five years just like other people, . . . I know there are many non-Africans in this country who are very happy to be Tanganyikans. They like the word "Tanganyika." Tanganyika citizenship? "Yes, this is very sweet. I am going to become a Tanganyikan." But they would not like to be known as Africans. They don't like the word Africans for reasons known to themselves. Africans? No! "Are you a Tanganyikan?" "Yes." "Are you an African?" "No, I am not."

Now, I know in U.S.A. and Canada you have French Canadians and French Americans. This is nonsense. We are not going to adopt Asian Africans, European Africans or whatever it is. We want these people right from the time of obtaining their citizenship of Tanganyika to know that they are going to be Africans and not Tanganyikans. It is wrong and it is just this consideration—if these people agree to be Africans, I am sure we will have no quarrel with them. But I know many of them will not like it. Europeans do not like it. I think a few Asians would be willing to be Africans. Europeans—No! No! "Me—

an African?" Because an African means a black skin. Now, the word African has nothing to do with skin as far as I know, because we have Moroccans and Tunisians who are Africans. They are not black. Those who attended the Assembly Youth Conference at Msimbazi last time saw there quite a number of them who are white people, participating and they are all known as Africans. Now this we like. But when people who have been here don't like to be known as Africans—this I think is wrong. These people must get used to the word Africans. We are going to forget the word "Tanganyika" just now because we are now talking of the African unity and it is only as Africans we can be known. I wonder how one can accept it to be Tanganyikan and at the same time reject African, because Tanganyika is a daughter of Africa. Now, if you say Hadija is the daughter of Salum and Salum is the son of Mohamed and you say, "Hadija are you a daughter of Salum?" "Yes." "Are you a grand-daughter of Mohamed?" "No." "Are you a Mohammedan?" "No." "Are you a Salummedan?" "Yes." I think the time has come now when people should understand this word African. It is when they have identified themselves to be Africans that the question of segregation will not arise again. . . .

AFRICA RENASCENT

The map on page 47 demonstrates in graphic form African progress toward independence—from only four states as late as 1955 to over thirty in 1962. But while precise, the map is neither a very complete nor even an accurate guide for the student of present-day African international relations. The reasons fall mainly in two categories. First, the movement to African independence is by no means complete. Imperialism and race thus remain very highly charged questions. African nationalist leaders from dependent areas seek support and succor from the independent states, and sometimes play roles in African international relations very nearly equivalent to those of Africans in power in independent states.

Second, Africa is undergoing a renaissance. African

leaders know that their continent and their countries are entering a new world, and they are determined to seize the opportunity to fit new ideas and new techniques to Africa—and Africa to the new ideas and new techniques. Maps cannot display the human elements of hope and will and interest which accompany the movement to African independence.

The mood of Africa as the continent entered this climactic era of independence is the subject of Selection 8. Anthony Sampson notes the power of the idea of renaissance, with which are associated Pan-African ideas. However, he also points out the *reality* of many very different Africas without much comprehension of one another.

Selection 9 discusses, not the aspirations of Africans, but the tensions produced in Africans by their situation. Pressures on "Westernized" Africans, stemming from both their African heritage and their experience or awareness of Europe, produce different results. Peter Abrahams cites examples from Kenya, South Africa, and Ghana, but these are merely examples of a more general case. We may expect such pressures to influence both the outlooks and performance of African nations in international affairs at many times and in many places in the future.

Psychological and sociocultural factors such as these will usually function in the background. But nationalism takes its place in the forefront of any consideration of present-day international affairs, anywhere in the world. The reason is simple: the basic unit in the international system is the state. Once a political entity is recognized as a state, its membership in the international system is presumed to be permanent. This involves a further assumption that the political entity is stable and viable.

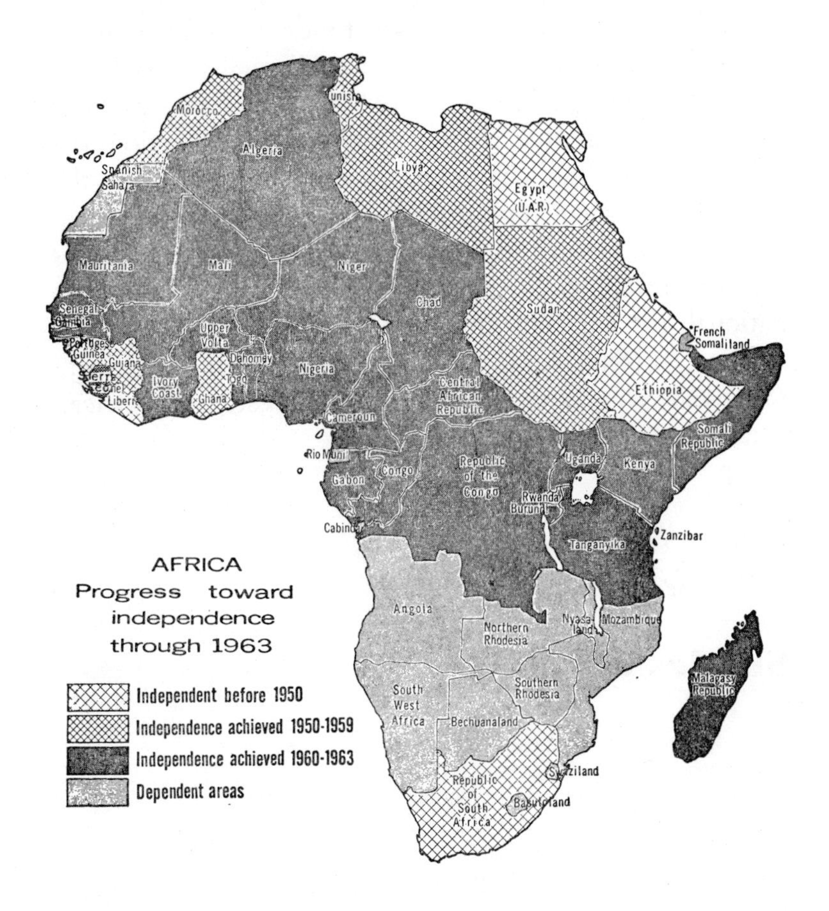

This map was adapted from Africa: Names and Concepts *by G. Etzel Pearcy, Department of State Publication 7298 (November 1963), African Series No. 23.*

Nationalism has in modern times proved a major guarantee of viability and stability. Virtually all political leaders encourage it, trying to ensure that their states will also be nations. Rupert Emerson (in Selection 10) wrestles with the character of nationalism within the swarm of African territories newly recognized as states and hence units in the international system. He suggests that out of the political ferment in Africa may emerge nationalisms not conforming to the present states within Africa. Granting he is right, we may perhaps anticipate some rude shocks to the international system as African states change in number or size.

Selection 8

Shades of Black*

ANTHONY SAMPSON

Anthony Sampson is a journalist in Great Britain and the author of several books on African topics.

"In the last century," Dr. Nkrumah said to a journalist the other day, "the Europeans discovered Africa. In the next century the Africans will discover Africa." He was talking, appropriately enough, at the conference of eight independent African States at Accra, which might be regarded as the first stage in the new African discovery. It was not, it is true, a very formidable gathering; there were only three black States—Ghana, Liberia and Ethiopia—none of which is very notable

* Reprinted by permission from *The National and English Review* (June 7, 1958), pp. 74–76.

for its interest in Africa beyond its own boundaries. But the very fact of their coming together to decide about the future of Africa (however ineffectual their decisions), as opposed to having it decided for them, is a fact that will find its echo throughout the bewildered continent.

For this idea of Africans discovering Africa, not only politically, but culturally, religiously, philosophically, is one that has been bubbling up in the noisy black townships from Cape Town to Accra. It is a recent thing; only in the last eighteen months, since the independence of Ghana and all the new confidence that spread from it, has the idea of an "African personality," as Dr. Nkrumah likes to call it, really begun to shape itself. But the idea of the African's Africa—of this new black self-consciousness, and self-confidence, together with the desire to re-think everything that the white man has taught—is something which will reverberate in the next few years. . . . there will no longer be something minor and comic about black men thinking about themselves.

Of course, the feeling about Pan-Africa at present is much more an ideal than a reality; there can be no simple picture of a united black people in a black continent. In spite of all the talk about liberating black brothers, and being the vanguard of African freedom, there are few states so parochial and introverted as Ghana; indeed, there are some in Ghana who say that the first thing that Nkrumah did when he achieved independence, like Napoleon in *Animal Farm*, was to come to terms with the hated White Government in South Africa (he made friendly noises, it is true, but he has hardly yet compromised himself). Black South Africans who have emigrated to Ghana and Nigeria, thinking them to be friendly Utopias, have been surprised by the ignorance and indifference about the Union, and the extent to which they themselves are treated as strangers, hardly less odd than Whites.

The whole white man's picture of Africa as being a network of interrelated countries, a distinctive continent whose common denominator is blackness, is a quite different map from that in African minds. The black African map is at least as multicoloured as that of Europe to Europeans; on top of the traditional enmities and loyalties of tribes and conquests, the different conditionings of white settler rule have produced quite different values and standards, and very different views of race. Nor is there any simple equation between freedom and achievement. A Ghanian visiting South Africa will be staggered by the sophistication and education of the African intelligentsia; black South Africans visiting Rhodesia are bored stiff by the African country bumpkins and their petty politics; and in Uganda they are appalled by the black *apartheid* between aristocracy and workers. Nyasas arriving in South Africa (for mining or domestic service) are cast for the same kind of role by the Johannesburg African "city slickers" as the "country gulls" in Elizabethan comedy.

There is no simple connection between these heterogeneous people; Europeans who speak of Tom Mboya wanting to set up a Ghana in Kenya, or Congress in South Africa being inspired by the Mau Mau in Kenya, might as well talk of setting up a Reichstag in Westminster. In practical influence the link between one country and another is extraordinarily slender. What is important is the *idea* of Pan-Africa, to which at the moment Ghana is the lightning conductor; and the idea can be more powerful than the reality. The cry of "Ghana!" which goes up in moments of crisis or celebration in the locations of Kenya, Rhodesia or South Africa is a very vague idea, which has little to do with the small State of the West coast; but it is an idea which is immensely evocative, for here is the beginning of the proud new Africa. Here is the awakening giant, late to find its feet, but profiting (so Africans will say) from its very lateness to avoid all the world's mistakes, and to face the 20th century free of the clutter and disillusion of a fumbled past.

This is the subject that you will now hear African writers, politicians and intellectuals discussing everywhere, however distant their prospects of power may seem; it is a discussion in which American Negroes and West Indians have joined, feeling at last that their African heritage is something to be proud of, something more than a background of servitude. What kind of new Utopias shall we build? What have we Africans got to teach the world? What shall we choose and reject from the West and the East? What do we look like as we preen ourselves in the mirror? It is a discussion conducted with all the boundless optimism of a twenty-first birthday.

It is, you may say, very much like the Asian awakening, an offshoot of Bandung. The same obscurantism, the same mystic talk about the "black soul," the same retreat into religious history and national traditions, leaving the white man confused and feeling unwelcome? It is too much, you may argue, to expect white men to take an interest in this new Africanism, to wave gaily as the African ship casts off its lines from the Western quay, for more remote and Eastern regions.

But it is very different from Asia. However much Africa is looking to her past—even in West Africa, where the sense of history and traditions are strongest—her eye is firmly set on the future; and it is, at the moment at least, a firmly Western future. The African intellectuals in whose hands this future will lie, are to a quite unusual degree the creations of the West; they have mostly undergone, at one stage in their lives, a period of obsession with Western ideas, forgetting all their own past, to an extent that no Asian leader would allow. However proud and confident Africans may sound when they talk of the old kingdoms of Ghana or Monomotapa, there is nothing that they would like less than to revert to the society in which Europeans first found them. The years of white mockery of black savagery (far different from the instinctive Western respect for Indian traditions) have left their deep mark on African minds. Though some Africans will justify a retrogressive movement like Mau Mau, they will justify it only as a desperate instrument of liberation, as necessary as the Stern gang to Israel.

Africans will not readily reject Western teaching, but they will reject the teachers. For many of them believe that they have, in their learning of Western thought, achieved something much purer and nobler than the West brought to them; and this is a thought which fascinates African intellectuals. Christianity without capitalism, education without privilege, government without arrogance, technology without inhumanity—these are the themes which run through African talk. In a recent essay called *Tradition and Industrialization*, the American novelist Richard Wright (inclined admittedly to over-romanticize the African predicament) suggests that the white men, by their very inhumanity, brought about an African revolution of rationality for which all black men must be thankful: "Thank you, Mr. White Man, for freeing me from the rot of my irrational traditions and customs, though you are still the victims of your own irrational customs and traditions."

The idea of the pupil teaching the teacher is one that recurs often in African writings about the White Man, and there is often an almost patronizing tone in their attitude to whites. "Technically he is in the atomic age, but spiritually he is retarded," says Marcus James, a West Indian writing about Christianity in the emergent Africa—a Christianity which is to cast off the accretions of Western dominance, and return to the simple humanity of Christ.

Humanity is a word which runs through any African conversation about their Utopia; sometimes, of course, it is overlaid with more sentimental Marxist idealization of the underdog, but at heart it is a very genuine African reaction. At some point in talking with almost any African politician there will be some sign of fear that, in gaining their freedom, they will lose their humanity. "To the absurd utilitarian agitation of the white, the black opposes the long authenticity of his suffering," says Jean-Paul Sartre in *Orphée Noir*, expounding the characteristics of *Négritude:* "The black represents himself in his own eyes as the man who has taken upon himself all human misery, and who suffers for all, even for the White."

There is nothing new, of course, about the idealization of suffering; an oppressed people must, after all, make the best of their predicament. What is new about the Africans is their complete absorption and digestion of the oppressors' ideas, at the same time that they are fighting them. They fight back with the same ideas, but fighting them with a new thought which, they believe, gives them a far broader humanity.

The new thinking shows itself in all kinds of forms, in each of which the white man's values are questioned in the white man's terms. I have before me a thesis on "The Non-European Character in South African English Fiction," written by one of the best black South African writers, Ezekiel Mphahlele, whose autobiography will soon be published in this country. It is basically a protest against the stereotyping of black characters in white men's books, as the powerless victims of their fate; he contrasts the two-sided awareness of *A Passage to India* or *An Outcast of the Islands* with what he regards as the flat portrayal of the bogus "African character" in a South African novel like *Cry, the Beloved Country*. But however critical Mphahlele is of South African writers, his models of fine characterization of Africans remain white models.

Mphahlele was protesting against an acceptance of white portrayals of Africans which was until quite recently unquestioned; the lack of African writing about Africans shows how undeveloped the African self-consciousness still is. It is one of the surprising ironies that the concept of the African personality, or *Négritude*, is most talked of among Africans who have become most assimilated, superficially at least, with white men. American Negroes, West Indians, and French Africans in Paris, are the leaders in the movement for African self-expression, and their chief organ, *Prêsence Africaine*, is published in Paris. It is an odd twist that French Africans envy their counterparts in British territories for the *apartheid* which (they say) enables them to develop a national consciousness; while in fact it is the assimilated "white" Africans, disengaged from the preoccupations of the struggle, who are the main spokesmen for that consciousness.

But the Africans' exploration of Africa is progressing all the time, and snowballing as it gathers confidence and the prestige of numbers. It is still comparatively inarticulate; all one can do is to take note of it, pick up a few hints of its direction, and watch for developments. But it is an exciting movement, which need not be observed by the West with despair; if it founders, it is partly the West's blame, for the educated African is essentially the Pygmalion of the West, rejuvenated and perhaps purified. The mixture of confusion and hope that makes up the modern African writer could be summed up in a poem by a Sierra Leonian writer, Crispin George:

> Let me play with the white man's ways
> Let me work with the black man's brains
> Let my affairs themselves sort out.
> Then in sweet rebirth I'll rise a better man
> Not ashamed to face the world.

Selection 9

The Conflict of Culture in Africa*

PETER ABRAHAMS

Peter Abrahams is a South African Negro who immigrated to the United Kingdom. He is well known as both a journalist and author.

Of the spate of books published on Africa in 1953, the most significant to my mind was a novel called *Blanket Boy's Moon*. It tells the story of Monare of Lomontsa, a member of the Basuto tribe. As a child he had lived in the old tribal ways. With other young boys he had herded cattle on the hillsides. He had gone to the tribal circumcision school. Then, later, he had become a Christian. Christianity allows a man only one wife: the tribal society as many as he can afford. Thus the first conflict, the first set of personal tensions come into play: the new ways against the old, the influence of the priest pulling one way and that of the tribal elders another. Still later Monare goes to Johannesburg, the city of gold, where the ways of the priest, which are the ways of the white man, are in full mastery over all. When he returns to his village after his spell in the city he is conscious of going from the present into the past. And then his chief orders him to participate in a ritual murder. Monare the Christian is revolted. By Christian standards ritual murder is a crime against both God and man. But tribal pressure wins in the end and Monare takes part in the murder. The personality of Monare, the man, is now split beyond repair. He leaves the tribe because it is responsible for the evil thing he was forced to do. He wanders in fear through the cities of the Union of South Africa finding no peace, no resting place because in serving his tribal chief he has put himself outside the law and ethics of the Christian present. When arrest and death finally come his fear is matched and mastered

* Reprinted by permission from *International Affairs* (July 1954), pp. 304–312. *International Affairs* is published by The Royal Institute of International Affairs.

by his relief. The long and terrible conflict is over at last. Now there can be peace.

Let us allow for the fact that Monare is a fictional creation and therefore more consciously articulate than a man in real life might be. Let us further allow that ritual murder poses the problem in highly dramatic form. But having made those allowances the book still retains its validity as a serious attempt to throw light on what is, to my mind, the most pressing problem of Africa today: the problem of the African's transition from the tribal past into the technological present. . . .

For the detribalized man this is essentially a situation of isolation. His rejection of tribalism places him outside the moral and psychological props of that society. He does not only lose its restraining and inhibiting influences, but also its comforting influences. Thus, his relations with his fellow Africans who still observe the tribal customs are, at best, uneasy. On the other hand the white administrator who could help and make life easier has very little, if any, time for him. Psychologically and emotionally he becomes an outcast to both the tribal ways of the past and the Western ways of the present. The two most obstructive forces in his life are the good tribal chief on the one hand and the colonial administrator on the other.

This is just the broad outline of a pattern. But it is a pattern that has repeated itself often enough in the unfolding of events in Africa for its validity to be accepted. For example, when the Mau Mau troubles started in Kenya one of the first victims was the "good" Chief Waruhiu who cooperated with the colonial administrators. This, however, is only one of a number of patterns. In some cases the detribalized man wins and exercises influence over the chiefs and tribesmen. This is seen in both the cases of Kwame Nkrumah and Jomo Kenyatta. In both cases this led to a head-on collision with the colonial administrators in their respective countries. Knowing both these men I am satisfied that the different results that came out of these head-on collisions are basically due to the fact that the one country has a white settler community and the other has not. But the achievement of a large measure of self-government in the Gold Coast has, to my mind, only underlined the seriousness of this conflict of culture between the tribal past and the Western technological present.

In Kenya one of the directions taken by the nationalists took the form of a rejection of Western institutions and habits. Africans who had been baptized and brought up as Christians renounced their Christian names. They rejected Western forms of worship and started churches of their own. I attended one meeting in Nairobi before the emergency where one of the leaders made an impassioned speech calling on his people to reject all European ways and institutions. They must, he asserted, go back to their own ways and institutions. This was a simple cry of renunciation. The fact that this call to reject all Western ways and institutions was made in the most excellent English (the speaker was not Kenyatta) made it all the more tragic and poignant for me. And when, later, I spoke to the man privately it seemed that he had adopted a course of desperation, that he did not really want to reject the West but that the West as represented by the settlers had rejected him. He had therefore countered their rejection of him by an attitude of rejection of all Western modes. Yet I was satisfied that he had evolved to a point where he belonged more to the Western, technological, present than to the tribal past. This man, and he is symbolic of many others, is a tragic victim of one of those torturing little traps of history. The fact that he had no recorded history of his own past, and that the white men around him belaboured this point by the way they talked of 'Western European civilization' as though it were something uniquely exclusive that owed nothing to non-European peoples such as the Chinese, the Indians, and the Egyptians, only gave point to his sense of tragic isolation. In the case of Kenyatta, it was the sense of isolation that compelled him to write *Facing Mount Kenya: the tribal life of the Gikuyu* (1953), his apologia for tribalism. For the need to belong somewhere, to have cultural roots, is one of the deepest of human needs. So, since the whites rejected him and set up colour bars to exclude him from those outward and visible symbols of the culture to which he aspired, he was forced, in his turn, to reject that which was his greatest need. The attitude of the white men around him, as well as the new sense of his individual worth as a man, which he had acquired on becoming no longer a tribal but a Western man, aware of the rights and dignity of Western man, compelled him to reject the inferior status which is his lot in the multi-racial communities today.

But rejection by itself was isolation. And it was not isolation he wanted but a place in the world: a place that would satisfy his deepest needs as a modern man with modern ideas on political, social, and economic relations. There was only one way out. He must fight for these things, he must wrest them from the white men who would not concede him an equal place in the multi-racial sun. So he set himself at the head of the tribesmen. In order to lead the tribesmen, however, he had to win their approval. He had to give the struggle a meaningfulness in terms that were significant and important to them. This meant that he had to go back to tribal ritual.

Freedom of choice is not a prominent tribal characteristic. The tribal society is inward, exclusive, and non-democratic. Power and authority are, ultimately, concentrated in the hands of a few. The binding oath, the secret ceremonial—these are important. He must make use of these. In order to gain the support and approval of those who have power and authority he must endorse and condone acts which under normal circumstances he would have frowned upon as a Western man. He must approve of instilling fear in men's minds in order to make them obey the more readily. He must encourage men's superstitions in order to exploit them. Fear and blood and darkness become his allies. To gain power over the tribesmen he must bring out the darker side of men's natures. Hitler has shown how successfully the darker side of even Western man's nature can be brought out: how much more easily could this apply to tribal man. And in doing all these things something happens to the detribalized man. One cannot bring forces of superstition and fear and darkness into play without being psychologically affected by them.

The Communist concept of the enemy as everything evil and malignant and beastly has come to be almost universally accepted in the West. To those holding this concept Kenyatta must be the embodiment of evil barbarity. I have had first-hand experience of the refinement of psychological and emotional torture of being a non-white Western man in the multi-racial societies of Africa, and mine was a situation of less isolation than Kenyatta's: so, although I disapprove strongly of the Mau Mau, Kenyatta is, for me, a victim of this tragic situation as well as of his own weaknesses rather than the embodiment of evil the white settlers would have him be. . . .

When he arrived back in his home country he was a Western man. He had spent long years as such in Europe. Had the colour climate of his country been different an easy integration with those who were his intellectual and cultural peers, and they would have been mainly white, might have taken place. He might then have participated creatively in the many problems that faced and still face his country. Indeed, when I was in Kenya an official told me that Kenyatta did, shortly after his arrival, become a member of a committee dealing with the land problem and that his contributions were quite valuable and constructive but that he then ceased attending the committee's meetings. The official did not know why he had ceased attending. Had he or any of the others any social contact with Kenyatta? No. . . . What struck me most when I saw Kenyatta was the terrible cultural isolation in which he lived. The whites around him were as inward and exclusive as the most inward tribal group I had ever met. And so this man was not given a chance to draw nourishment from the tap-roots of the culture which had now become his own. And so what happens to a plant in a desert happened to him. It is easy for those who have never experienced the reality of being excluded to talk about the villainy of such a man and piously to deplore the fact that he came to hate. It is not so easy to admit that they must themselves bear a measure of responsibility for frustrating him to a point where he turned against them. It is even less easy, in present circumstances, for them to comprehend the terrible and torturing conflicts which must have driven such a man to such action.

The reason for both the inward and exclusive nature of the whites on the one hand and the failure of Kenyatta on the other, stem to my mind, from a fundamental misconception about culture. In their dealings with the blacks the whites have justified their colour bars by saying that these bars were in defence of Western culture. Their arguments are very familiar so I shall not re-state them here. The key point is that all these arguments give Western culture an inwardness of appearance, an exclusiveness of character which are fundamentally false to its true sources and inspirations. The true motive forces of Western culture are to be found in the first place in the teachings of the Christ who taught a new concept of men's relations with their God and with each other, a concept that cuts across tribal gods and tribal loyalties and embraces all men in all lands, offering them a common brotherhood. From this primary source flow all its other motive forces in philosophy and the arts. The Kantian ethical theory, the Rights of Man, democracy and the uniquely new status it offers individual man, all form part of the non-exclusive sources of Western culture. From them stem the great advances in science and material prosperity, in man's mastery of the dark corners of his own personality as well as his mastery of the dark corners of the world in which he lives. To deny this fundamental outwardness in its nature is to deny Western culture itself. This denial has, I think, been largely made by the whites of the multiracial societies up to now. Their great problem is obvious. Any attempt at real democracy as we know it in Great Britain would place them in a minority position with all that that would involve. Materially and in terms of power they have very much to lose. It is a very real dilemma for them: they must either reject the moral and ethical bases of Western culture or else give up their position of power and privilege.

This dilemma has led to a unique position in the Union of South Africa. There, the whites represented by the Malan Government have rejected the values underlying Western culture rather than surrender any part of their power and privilege. The black élite of the Union, on the other hand, has accepted those values more completely than Africans in any of the other territories, with the possible exception of the Negro élite of the French African colonies. And because the Union is the most modern industrial State on the African continent its black élite is at the head of the largest group of urbanized and detribalized black men and women on the continent. The result is that it is the black leaders of the African National Congress who are today fighting in defence of the moral and ethical assumptions underlying Western culture. There is profound significance in this.

But Kenyatta's position was at once easier and more difficult than that of a man similarly placed in the Union. He had not experienced three hundred years of a physical occupation which was more complete and therefore more destuctive in its impact on the old tribal structure. The land allotted to the blacks in the Union was, man for man, less than that left to the Kikuyu. The result was that land-hunger was infinitely more acute in the Union's reserves than in those of the Kikuyu. But the Union had mines and secondary industries which offered alternatives to the land. These alternative means of making a livelihood led to other ways of living and thinking and looking at the world and, ultimately, to an adoption of the values of the culture of the cities. This did not make for black white men or 'imitation Englishmen,' but a new kind of black man with something to give to this new culture of the cities which historical necessity had forced on him. That this new black man has something to contribute to Western culture has been amply demonstrated by his output in music, art, and literature. Anyone really familiar with these knows that his output is anything but a slavish imitation of the output of white men. His African background and his unique and often devastating experiences as a black man in this modern world have given his output qualities that set it apart. His artistic contribution is and will continue to be different, but at the same time, an integral part of the unfolding world culture which is currently called 'Western'.

It is because of this historical background and their acceptance of 'Western' culture as a logical next stage in the unfolding pattern of world culture that the blacks of the Union have not allowed the whites to force them on to the psychological defensive about Western culture. Kenyatta did not have these historical sources of strength. He was alone. So he allowed himself to be forced on to the psychological defensive and then attempted his reassertion in exclusive, inward, tribal terms. I thus level the same charge against Kenyatta that I level against the whites. Both have rejected the moral and ethical assumptions on which Western culture is based. The fears of both have led them into an historic trap. The white man says: 'Must I serve Western culture at the price of my own interests? If I let down the barriers for one, even for a Kenyatta, it will only be a matter of time before others are clamouring at the door and then where will I be? No, I will make Western culture mean the same thing as being white. Thus I will have moral sanction in defending my interests'. And the black man says: 'I desire this Western culture, I am already a part of it. But yet they deny me. When I am not educated they say I am not fit for it. When I am, they still deny me, and mock me as trying to ape them. At every turn they outrage my self-respect. I will reject them and their culture. I have a culture too. I will say that tribal culture is superior to theirs. I will raise the tribesmen against them and we will drive them out and re-establish the old ways as they were before the white men came'. . . .

That this conflict of culture is not only confined to the multi-racial communities was clear to me when I visited the Gold Coast last year.

There, we are not faced with a settler community to complicate the issues. When Kwame Nkrumah went back after years in the United States and Great Britain he set himself at the head of a largely tribal people and challenged British authority. The slogan of 'self-government now' and the Western structure of Nkrumah's Convention People's Party (CPP) were new and dynamic, and welded the various tribes into a single political force. It carried Nkrumah to power. Nkrumah declared himself for democracy and the welfare State. The intention, thus, was clearly to bring into being a modern twentieth century State. But the power of the chiefs was more entrenched here than in most of the areas of East and South Africa, so Nkrumah had to accept the view on chieftaincy put forward by the Coussey Committee that 'the whole institution of chieftaincy is so deeply bound up with the life of the community that its disappearance will spell disaster'. But he warned the chiefs that their institutions should be adapted to the changing requirements of present times. That he regards this as a necessary expedient at present Nkrumah has made clear. He is politically shrewd enough not to want to engage on too many fronts all at once. I have very little doubt in my own mind that it is only a matter of time before there is a head-on collision between the government and the chiefs if the government are to carry out their intention of turning the Gold Coast into a modern efficiently run State. That the head of the party dedicated to this end should allow himself to be made 'life Chairman' of his party is disturbing. It is quite as disturbing as the superman myth that has been woven round the personality of the Prime Minister. I have heard stories of how Kwame can make himself disappear or go without food and drink for longer than ordinary men can.

But it is the currently publicized issue of bribery and corruption that can perhaps best illustrate my point about the conflict of culture. I was appalled by the extent of corruption when I was out there. In his book *The Gold Coast Revolution* (1953) George Padmore mentions the Dutch firm A. V. Schokbeton whose factory was to 'prefabricate up to 15,000 four- and five-roomed concrete houses fitted with running water, electricity, toilet basins, water closets', etc. When I asked about this and about housing generally I unearthed some distressing tales of corruption, and no houses.

The great and good thing about all this is that it has now come out into the open. What I want to suggest here is that in this case the conflict of culture has manifested itself in conflicting standards of public morality. In the tribal society the giving of presents to men in high positions is an accepted thing. If I know someone close to the chief, an elder or adviser, I approach the chief through him in the hope that my case or petition may be treated more favourably. It may be a matter of great importance to me, so I will be anxious that this person should do his very best on my behalf. In order that he should do his best I give him a present. The size and value of the present will depend on the importance of my case or petition. This has become the accepted practice. Everybody does it. There is nothing wrong or immoral about it in the tribal society.

Viewed in this light recent events in the Gold Coast are yet another illustration of the unfolding conflict of culture. The fact of a man becoming a minister or ministerial secretary does not of itself endow him with new standards of public morality. This same problem can be seen in other spheres. The tribal society is not tolerant to those in opposition to the established rulers of the day. This intolerance to opposition could, in modern government, lead to dictatorship and the suppression of views hostile to those of the government of the day. A case in point was the attempt of the CPP organ, the *Accra Evening News*, before Dr. Danquah had it closed down on a successful libel suit, to get the Liberian editor of the opposition *Daily Echo* expelled from the country. This man had lived in the country for well over a dozen years and had edited the paper long before the CPP came to power.

All that I saw in the Gold Coast led me to the conclusion that the political revolution so successfully led by Kwame Nkrumah had, so far, only succeeded in superimposing a twentieth century frame of government on an essentially tribal society. To do more than that, to bring the society itself into the twentieth century, is the task that now faces this government or any government that succeeds it. It seems to me that this task will be found far more difficult than the wresting of power from the Colonial Office. For the welfare State, which is the objective of the CPP, and the tribal State are fundamentally incompatible. A clean civil service is essential, therefore new standards of morality in public life must come into play. In Britain these standards of morality grew up over a long period. But in the historical position in which she finds herself the Gold Coast cannot allow herself the same time-period in which to evolve an honest and clean civil service. She must telescope the time-period. The ambivalent position of being both Western man and tribal man can, apart from creating severe personal tensions in the individual, harm work on projects like the Tema Harbour and the Volta River. A workman may be on the job for a period and then decide to go back home at a time when he would have become reasonably efficient. He would then have to be replaced by someone who has to learn the work all over again. Or, because of the nature of tribal loyalties as opposed to national loyalties, a man who is a Ga may be ambitious politically and build his campaign around the fact that the essentially Ga Accra is represented by Nkrumah who is a Nzima. For good measure he would attack the Tema and Volta schemes because they offer no prospect of immediate gain. I have actually seen this play on tribal loyalties and attack on the two schemes allied.

On a tribal basis, any central government that is dependent for office on the tribesmen may be called upon to appease so many conflicting interests in order to retain office as to become ineffective. I think the CPP government carries passengers for this reason. For a central government to be effective it must act for a nation whose individual members are conscious of being members of that nation. The creation of this sense of nationhood in each individual seems to me the most important question facing the leaders of the Gold Coast. It is, I think, an essential condition for the creation of a modern State in our time. And, to be truly democratic, the State must be founded on the underlying assumptions of Western culture. The tribal structure served the needs of tribal man. The moral codes of tribal man were adequate to his time. The needs of modern man, the conditions under which modern man lives, demand new structures and new values. The touching love of some anthropologists for the old ways should not blind us to their inadequacy for modern needs. Western culture is a world culture, not 'reserved for Europeans only'.

Selection 10

Nationalism and Political Development*

RUPERT EMERSON

Rupert Emerson is Professor of International Relations at Harvard University.

. . . Africa, south of the Sahara, offers a terrain in which a unique opportunity to bring nations into being is given to the nationalist and to the state, the latter appearing usually in the guise of a colonial administration. Elsewhere in the world the determinants of national allegiance can often be traced back to a remote past, and reasonably fixed landmarks of history, culture, and religion separate one nation from another. In Africa such national landmarks are at best much less evident and clearcut, and at worst have as yet not come into visible existence at all. The pre-colonial history of the continent had its quota of internal wars, conquests, and empires, but their effect in integrating large masses of people into potentially national communities was markedly more limited than in other parts of the world. The clan and the tribe, varying greatly in size in different parts, have been, and in large measure remain, the typical social and cultural units. If nations are to appear, they are still for the most part in the making. As to what the next decade or two ahead may hold in the way of unification and division of African peoples, I believe that a glance into any one crystal ball is about as good as another.

For the moment, however, Africa is the continent *par excellence* to sustain the thesis that colonial governments, given appropriate circumstances, may be the major instruments in shaping nations. In the first round political demands are directed to the colonial authorities, and

* Reprinted by permission from *Journal of Politics* (February 1960), pp. 14–17.

the implicit or explicit assumption is likely to be made that since "national self-determination" is what the contemporary world expects, anti-colonial movements assume the title of nationalism and are assumed to be serving as the agents of nations.

On the face of it, the current drift has unquestionably been toward a new territorial nationalism in Africa which takes the existing colonies as setting the frame of political reference. The caveat should, however, immediately be added that the cases on which we can generalize as to the relations between colonies and African nations are still so few in number, so limited in time, and so uncertain in their bearing, as to make any generalization immediately suspect. It is, in fact, nearer the truth to assert that there are as yet no coherent nations in sub-Saharan Africa than to claim that each of the political jurisdictions has shaped a nation within its ethnically arbitrary frontiers. Even among the whites of South Africa the Afrikaner has been by no means prepared to accept absorption into a single South African nation with his British-descended countrymen. As the oldest of the African states, Ethiopia embraces wide ethnic diversity and Liberia remains deeply divided between the Africans of the *hinterland* and the descendants of the settlers from America, even though significant efforts have been made of late to bring the two within a common framework. The Sudan and Ghana, in their different fashions, are likewise made up of heterogeneous elements which only much patience, time, and tactful labor can weld together. Nigeria is notoriously a precarious lumping together of peoples whose separate identity is at least as real a matter as their acceptance of national unity.

The French colonial territories present an even more baffling picture of national ambiguity. The British system, despite its fondness for indirect rule which maintains a particularistic tribal solidarity, tends to produce a measure of identification with the territory concerned. The French system has operated in a much more diffuse fashion. With Paris as its all-absorbing center and with central political institutions in which Africans were represented, the local territorial community and institutions tended to be lost from sight. Furthermore, the vast African holdings of France were divided into the two large federations of West and Equatorial Africa, the former of which had eight and the latter four provincial subdivisions. A substantial number of alternatives presented themselves. Was the unit of ultimate national allegiance to be the total Franco-African community, as some French spokesmen were given to assert, or the whole of French Africa, or each of the two federations, or the individual territories within the federations, or some other grouping of these territories based, perhaps, on still continuing tribal ties? A huge amount of jockeying for position and of more basic community formation obviously lies ahead, in the course of which the kinds of political allegiance which will dominate the future and determine the drawing of the new African frontiers will gradually become clear.

The uncertainties of the present situation can be illustrated on every side. The independence of Guinea, for example, suddenly asserted at the time of the referendum of the de Gaulle constitution, carried no necessary implication that the new state represented a national entity, and the decision to join forces with Ghana in some undesignated fashion again changed the terms of reckoning. At recent African conferences and in the pronouncements of leading spokesmen, much has been heard of the existence of an "African personality" and of pan-Africanism or of some merger of West African territories. The one constant factor in the situation is that Africa is caught up in a ferment of change and political upheaval, whose end is not yet in sight and whose ultimate form is still subject to a great measure of variation. Neither the older tribal units nor the present colonial boundaries are likely to furnish the full blueprint of the future, and it is even more unlikely that any grandiose conception of a consolidated Pan-African union will be created in any foreseeable future. The establishment of a number of separate and independent states, each of which will have its own body of vested interests and distinctive features, will work to make mergers increasingly difficult, but a number of present colonial jurisdictions seem palpably unviable and must seek to join forces with neighboring areas.

In Nigeria and Tanganyika, in the Congo, Guinea, and Equatorial Africa, the European powers have been engaged in a process which has a great bearing on the formation of nations, whether or not nations directly emerge from the colonial régimes which are now one by one vanishing. The work of the colonial administrators is actively supplemented by that of the nationalists who, in Africa even more than elsewhere, may claim the title of nation builders as well as political leaders. Everywhere the nationalists are by definition in the forefront of the national movements and are assumed to have a more acute awareness of its existence than the ordinary man, but it is also assumed that their rôle is not that of creating the nation but of rousing it to consciousness. The nation is something which is there as a great historical fact; it requires only the appropriate circumstances and the appeal of the leaders to swing it into political action. The task of the men of mid-nineteenth century Germany, Meiji Japan, or early twentieth-century Egypt was not to forge disparate elements into a hitherto non-existent identity but to give full expression to the deep underlying sense of national community which generations of living together had produced.

In Africa this approach to the national issue is in great part an illusion. It might, indeed, be argued with only slight exaggeration that the nations so far exist only in the persons of the nationalists themselves since they are the only people who have moved beyond the tribal horizons and have come to a broader sense of the society in which they live. The mass of the population in whose name they claim to speak continues to be divided into tribes which are bound together by little, if anything, in the way of language, religion, culture, or shared historical experience. The one common aspect of their lives has been the brief period of subjection to European rule, and this, for the bulk of them, has often meant virtually nothing in the way of a common life. Formally speaking they have been under a common government with its uniform economy and system of law and administration, but in practice they have lingered very largely within the framework of their traditional societies and have perhaps only recently been brought into any significant degree of association with their fellow colonials. As a random sample of what is involved one might cite the comment of James S. Coleman in 1956 that "Until the last five years the overwhelming majority of the peoples of northern Togoland were unaware of the existence of Togoland."* In the African setting the nationalists speak for nations yet to be born and themselves have a great responsibility for their emergence. Anti-colonialism may serve as a rallying-cry to build up a popular front of resistance, but the constructive work of bringing forth nations out of a motley colonial assemblage of tribes still remains almost wholly a matter for the future even after sovereign independence has been achieved. . . .

---

* *Togoland* (*International Conciliation*, September, 1956), p. 5, note 1:

II

BUILDING AFRICAN UNITY

The keynotes in African affairs are number and variety. As examples, one might cite the number of newly or potentially independent states, the number of languages, the number and variety of struggling, competing nationalisms and "tribalisms," the number and variety of tribes and cultures. The list could be extended.

Number and variety thus pose for African political leaders some enormously difficult questions concerning unity among Africans. The answers worked out will greatly influence Africa's role in the international system, since they will dictate the number, strength, and clarity of the voices Africa speaks with in international affairs, as well as the message or messages conveyed.

Part II of this book examines under four headings the problem of building African unity. The first section takes up the impulse toward unity—Pan-Africanism—recounting the history of the movement and discussing attitudes within it. The second section discusses pulls toward unity or separateness as demonstrated in various moves toward unification, regionalism, or federalism in various parts of Africa. The third section deals with the special problem of multiracialism as one aspect of the question of building unity. The fourth section contains some account of alignments among African states which have developed during the past several years largely in response to pulls or pressures in world politics.

AFRICAN UNITY—THE IMPULSE

The impulse toward African unity that we call Pan-Africanism has a long history. As Vernon McKay (Selection 11) indicates, it was at first a protest movement against oppression, then became a vehicle for the African nationalist drive against colonialism ("Scram out of Africa"), and finally, with the rapid spread of independence in Africa, has emphasized alignment of African states and peoples in a common front.

In this last guise, Pan-Africanism becomes particularly relevant to international relations, for each of the many African states is free to choose for itself the terms on which it will associate in common efforts with other African states. This situation of course gives rise to much international discussion, negotiation, and agitation over the purposes, principles, and mode of organization of any common front or Pan-African institutions.

A detailed discussion of the international politics of Pan-Africanism is reserved to Section Four of Part II. Presented in Section One are two of the major "philosophies" or approaches relating to the problem of Pan-African unity. Kwame Nkrumah (Selection 12) represents what is on the whole the more radical view—the impulse to unity is strong, and is justified on the ground of a need for a common front against colonialism, either existing or revived.

Nnamdi Azikewe (Selection 13) views more seriously the problems which African variety and number create for the Pan-African movement. In a sense the confrontation here is another skirmish in the perennial battle between idealist and realist in public affairs. Nkrumah, the idealist, regards diversity and differences among Africans not only as dangerous, but as mutable by an act of will, and calls for that act of will. Azikewe, although also committed to the ideal of unity, starts from the assumption that the facts will be difficult to change, that the acts necessary for mutation cannot simply be willed, and therefore adopts the gradualist, relatively conservative approach characteristic of the realist position.

Selection 11

The Concept of Pan-Africanism*

VERNON MCKAY

Vernon McKay is Professor of African Studies at the Johns Hopkins School of Advanced International Studies in Washington, D.C. He was formerly with the Department of State. He is the author of *Africa in World Politics* (1963).

The Sharpeville crisis of 1960 focussed world-wide attention on the new and uncompromising Pan-Africanists who precipitated it. Although there is today no substantial link between the Pan-Africanist organizations north and south of the Limpopo, the amorphous concept of Pan-Africanism arouses powerful emotions throughout the continent in varying ways and different degrees. Its potentialities for good and evil therefore merit the thoughtful consideration of all South Africans.

The enthusiasm of African leaders for the general principle of Pan-African unity was made abundantly clear at the two important international conferences held by Africans in Ghana in April and December, 1958. In the words of George Padmore, a leading theoretical exponent, "Pan-Africanism offers an ideological alternative to Communism on the one hand, and Tribalism on the other. It rejects both white racialism and black chauvinism. It stands for racial co-existence on the basis of absolute equality and respect for human personality."

This is indeed a high ideal which merits careful examination. Let us analyze it by defining its essential elements as they emerged at Accra in 1958; by looking back into history to see how the idea has evolved since its birth in the year 1900; by surveying the obstacles which hamper the realization of the ideal; by discussing some of the new

* Reprinted by permission from *Race Relations Journal*, Vol. XXVII, No. 3 (1960), pp. 112–126.

regional combinations in the Pan-African spirit; and finally, by pointing out the relationship between Pan-Africanism and the concepts of *negritude*, "black power" and "blackism."

The essential elements of Pan-Africanism are evident in the collection of emotionally and loosely worded omnibus resolutions adopted by the 200 delegates from twenty-eight states and territories at the All-African People's Conference in Accra in December, 1958. The ultimate goal of Pan-Africanism is the establishment of what is variously termed a Commonwealth of Free African States, a Pan-African Commonwealth, or a United States of Africa. As an interim goal, however, Pan-Africanism calls for the amalgamation of independent African states into regional federations or groupings on the basis of geographical contiguity, economic inter-dependence, and linguistic and cultural affinity, with the caveat, however, that the establishment of such regional federations should not be prejudicial to the ultimate objective of a Pan-African Commonwealth.

The Conference committee which drafted this resolution is said to have had in mind five regional groupings—North Africa and West Africa at an early date, and East Africa, Central Africa and South Africa later, when these areas are controlled by Africans. The delegates drew little distinction between black Africa and the multiracial areas in the South. Tom Mboya from Kenya, the chairman of the Conference, told the delegates that even in Central and South Africa, it is not a question of whether Africans will win: "It is how and when." And Dr. Gikonyo Kiano of Kenya said, "Bogus theories of multi-racialism, partnership or Bantustanism are essentially devices to deflect the African from his rightful goal of governing his country." White and Asian residents, he added, "will have to accept African citizenship first if they want to live there as citizens."

Numerous observers at the conference, however, reported that it was not anti-white in tone. Mboya, they point out, declared that Africans will not practice "racism in reverse." And Prime Minister Kwame Nkrumah said at the opening session " . . . we are not racialists or chauvinists. We welcome into our midst peoples of all other races, other nations, other communities, who desire to live among us in peace and equality. But they must respect us and our rights, our right as the majority to rule. That, as our Western friends have taught us to understand it, is the essence of democracy."

In the view of an American Negro observer the Conference gave birth to a new concept of "residential Pan-Africanism," that is to say the rejection of racialism, in favour of the idea that all persons born or naturalised in African states, irrespective of race, creed or colour are "Africans" provided they believe in absolute economic and social equality and the principle of one man, one vote. In the actual resolutions adopted, this rational approach sometimes disappears in favour of sweeping condemnations of such things as the "pernicious system of racialism and discriminating laws, especially as expressed in its extreme and most brutal forms" in South Africa, Rhodesia and Portuguese territories. To what extent the rational or the emotional element will dominate the Pan-African spirit in the future, only time will tell. In the beginning, however, Pan-Africanism did not call for driving the white man into the sea.

In fact, another essential element of Pan-Africanism is its rejection of violence as a systematic and deliberate revolutionary weapon in favour of "non-violent positive action," that is to say, strikes, boycotts and civil disobedience. When the Egyptians and Algerians at the Accra Conference objected to this view, they forced clarification from Mr. Mboya to the effect that although he believed in non-violent methods, "this does not mean that if Africans are struck, they will not hit back." This clarification of the non-violence principle was incorporated in the Conference resolution on imperialism and colonialism which declared "full support to all fighters for freedom in Africa, to all those who resort to peaceful means of non-violence and civil obedience as well as to all those who are compelled to retaliate against violence . . . "

Another important aspect of the Pan-African spirit is that it is modernist rather than traditionalist, that is to say, it condemns those aspects of tribalism, religious separatism, and traditional institutions, especially chieftaincy, which obstruct the African march to unity, freedom and democracy.

Finally, although the conference adopted no resolution on the subject, it is clear that Pan-Africanism is socialist in its economic outlook. It welcomes the assistance of private enterprise and capital but believes that a high degree of government enterprise and ownership is essential to regenerate African society.

In summary, the spirit or ideal of Pan-Africanism is federationist, non-racial, non-violent, modernist, and socialist, and favours non-alignment in the cold war. The extent to which this ideal can be realised in practice remains to be seen.

To deepen our understanding of Pan-Africanism it is now essential to look back at its sixty years of history. The first striking fact about it is that it originated, and found its earliest support and leadership, not in Africa but among Negroes in the West Indies and the United States. A West Indian barrister named Henry Sylvester-Williams organized a Pan-African conference in London in 1900. It was attended by about thirty Negro intellectuals, mostly from England and the West Indies, along with several American Negroes. The conference attempted to arouse British reformers to take steps to protect natives in African areas from abuses. Thus the idea of Pan-Africanism first arose as a "manifestation of fraternal solidarity among Africans and peoples of African descent" in other areas. Sylvester-Williams died soon afterwards, however, and little was heard of the movement for another generation.

The second phase of Pan-Africanism developed out of the idealism aroused by the First World War. It is identified with the forceful personality of W. E. B. DuBois, an eminent American Negro Ph.D. from Harvard whose later disillusionment turned him to Communism, and who retired to live in Russia at about the age of 90. Unable to attend the Accra conference in December, 1958, he sent his wife to read an emotional speech recounting the history of Pan-Africanism and exhorting the delegates to awake and "put on the beautiful robes of Pan-African Socialism," and to realise that their bond with the white world is closest to the Communists and not to the West.

DuBois had attended the 1900 conference and also a Races Congress in London in 1911. In 1919 he seized the opportunity presented by the Paris Peace Conference to organize what is called the first Pan-African Congress. When Clemenceau was persuaded by a Senegalese leader named Blaise-Diagne to approve such a meeting, fifty-seven persons met in Paris to voice African complaints during the peace conference and to petition the Allied Powers to place the former German colonies in Africa under international supervision.

Two years later a second Pan-African Congress held three sessions in London, Brussels and Paris in August and September, 1921, to adopt a moderate "Declaration to the World," drafted by DuBois, which demanded, among other things, the recognition of civilised men as civilised, despite their race or colour. They also elected a delegation headed by DuBois to present a petition to the Permanent Mandates Commission of the League of Nations asking that a Negro be appointed to the Commission as soon as a vacancy occurred.

In 1923 a third Pan-African Congress met in two sessions in London and Lisbon, and four years later, in 1927, 208 delegates from eleven countries, predominantly Americans, attended a fourth Pan-African Congress in New York. DuBois planned to hold a Fifth Congress, in the continent of Africa for the first time, but the depression which struck the United States in 1929 killed his chances for financial support and put a damper on the Pan-African movement for sixteen years years until the end of World War II.

DuBois' efforts during the 1920's had also suffered from the meteoric rise and fall of a rival Negro leader whose inflammatory "Black Zionism" enabled him to build up a mass following of perhaps two million Negroes in thirty branches of an organization called the Universal Negro Improvement Association. Marcus Garvey was of West Indian origin, a spectacular showman, who was named "Provisional President of the African Republic" at an International Convention of the Universal Negro Improvement Association in Harlem in 1920.

Garvey's "Back to Africa" movement called for the establishment of a great Negro state in Africa as the homeland for all Black people. He also campaigned for the establishment of Negro-owned and run commercial and industrial enterprise throughout the world. In keeping with the latter idea he sought to establish the Black Star Line—a steamship line to be owned and operated by Negroes. It got him into financial difficulties, however, which jailed him in 1923 and undermined the Garvey movement. It is worthy of note that Nkrumah named his new steamship line the Black Star Line, and in his autobiography Nkrumah writes: "I think that of all the literature I studied (in the United States), the book that did more than any other to fire my enthusiasm was the *Philosophy and Opinions of Marcus Garvey*."

The failure of Garvey's scheme for a Black Star Line was accompanied by another blow when the Liberian Government refused to support his plan for a Negro state in Africa to which any Black could return. Long under attack by DuBois and other American Negro leaders, the Garvey movement split apart in 1929, and withered away by the time of Garvey's death in 1940.

The essential difference between DuBois and Garvey has been summarised as follows by George Padmore:

> "Where DuBois differed from Garvey was in his conception of the Pan-African movement as an aid to the promotion of national self-determination among Africans under African leadership, for the benefit of Africans themselves. Marcus Garvey, on the other hand, looked upon Africa as a place for colonising Western Negroes under his personal domination."

If Garveyism is considered something of an aberration, it may be said that the third phase of Pan-Africanism did not begin until 1945 when a Fifth Pan-African Congress was held in England. In the previous year a number of coloured organizations had formed a Pan-African Federation, and in February, 1945 the World Federation of Trade Unions was established by trade unionists who included African delegates from British West Africa and the West Indies. These two groups, the coloured organizations in England and the colonial trade unionists, with the encouragement of DuBois, made the preparations for the Fifth Pan-African Congress which met in Manchester in October, 1945 with more than two hundred delegates and observers present.

The Fifth Congress was a milestone in the Pan-African movement. Although DuBois was in the chair, the initiative and leadership had passed for the first time into the hands of Africans rather than American and West Indian Negroes. Kwame Nkrumah, Jomo Kenyatta, Peter Abrahams and other future African leaders played prominent roles. Reports on African areas were presented to the delegates by the Africans themselves rather than by Western scholars.

Another important change was the more radical and militant approach adopted by this younger and more African generation of political, labour, farmer and student leaders, in contrast to the moderate approach of the small intellectual elite which had guided the movement in the past. By 1945, the demand for positive political action to obtain self-government had risen to the top of Pan-African aims. The new militance is evident in the Declaration to the Colonial Peoples adopted at the 1945 Congress:

> "We affirm the right of all colonial peoples to control their own destiny.

All colonies must be free from foreign imperialist control whether political or economic. The peoples of the colonies must have the right to elect their own governments, without restrictions from foreign powers. We say to the peoples of the colonies that they must fight for these ends by all the means at their disposal. The object of imperialist powers is to exploit. By granting the right to colonial peoples to govern themselves that object is defeated. Therefore, the struggle for political power by colonial and subject peoples is the first step towards, and the necessary prerequisite to, complete social, economic, and political emancipation. The Fifth Pan-African Congress therefore calls on the workers and farmers of the colonies to organize effectively. Colonial workers must be in the front of the battle against imperialism. Your weapons—the strike and the boycott—are invincible.

"We also call upon the intellectuals and professional classes of the colonies to awaken to their responsibilities. By fighting for trade union rights, the right to form cooperatives, freedom of the press, assembly, demonstration and strike, freedom to print and read the literature which is necessary for the education of the masses, you will be using the only means by which your liberties will be won and maintained. Today there is only one road to effective action—the organization of the masses. And in that organization the educated colonials must join. Colonial and subject peoples of the world, unite!"

As will be noted, many of these ideas sound like those which emanated from the December, 1958 Conference in Accra, which is sometimes referred to as the Sixth Pan-African Congress. Pan-Africanist declarations were still so amorphous that one might argue that the movement was neither "Pan," nor "African" nor an "ism." By 1945, the concept of an "African personality," which Nkrumah was later to popularise, had only begun to take shape. The objective of the movement was more nationalist than Pan-African, that is to say, its emphasis was on the fight for independence in each colony rather than on inter-territorial association. Co-operation among colonial peoples the world over was called for as a method of obtaining this objective. This nationalist emphasis is quite understandable since it is difficult to arouse any enthusiasm for federation when there are no independent states to federate. Consequently, for more than a decade after World War II, the nationalist aspect continued to dominate the movement, while its Pan-Africanist aspect remained as an ideal in the background.

During this period, however, two important developments prepared the way for the Pan-African ideal to attain greater strength. One of these was the emergence of new states in Africa. The other was the rise of the Afro-Asian solidarity movement which began with the formation of the Afro-Asian block in the United Nations, and was followed by the Bandung conference of 1955 and the Afro-Asian Peoples Solidarity Conference in Cairo at the end of 1957.

The Afro-Asian bloc developed in the United Nations in December, 1950, during the Korean crisis, and continued to meet thereafter to discuss problems of mutual interest. Thirteen of its sixteen members (excluding Liberia, Ethiopia and Thailand) joined in a successful endeavour to get the Moroccan question, the Tunisian question and the item on race conflict in South Africa onto the agenda of the General Assembly. In addition to their hostility to colonialism, these states shared a common and related interest in fighting racial discrimination against peoples of colour, and in seeking ways and means for the economic development of their underdeveloped countries. Through bloc politics in the United Nations, they found that they gained additional strength, influence and prestige, and were able to win membership for a larger number of their members in various United Nations organs and offices. They thus found that the advantages of maintaining this solidarity outweighed the differences and rivalries which sometimes divided them.

The advantages in this new relationship were one of the factors which induced the Asian-African countries to hold the historic conference in Bandung, Indonesia, in April, 1955. Twenty-nine states were represented by top officials at Bandung, including six African countries—Egypt, Ethiopia, the Gold Coast, Liberia, Libya and the Sudan. Like the Pan-African Congresses, Bandung created no specific political organization, but was psychologically important as an assertion of Asian and African personality in world affairs. As Indonesian President Soekarno said at Bandung: "The peoples of Asia and Africa wield little physical power, but they are 1,400,000,000 strong and can mobilize all the spiritual, all the moral, all the political strength of Asia and Africa on the side of peace." And, in his closing speech, Prime Minister Nehru of India made a special appeal to Africans: "I think there is nothing more terrible, there is nothing more horrible than the infinite tragedy of Africa in the past few hundred years . . . it is up to Asia to help Africa to the best of her ability because we are sister continents."

The Afro-Asian movement took a new turn during the last week in 1957 at the first Afro-Asian Peoples Solidarity Conference, held in Cairo. This was an unofficial conference of peoples rather than an official conference of governments, which explains why its pronouncements were more emotional and unrestrained. A second important fact about it was the presence of a 27-man Soviet delegation, in contrast to Bandung where the Russians had been deliberately kept out. These two facts explain why the Cairo conference adopted not only a battery of anti-colonial resolutions but also numerous anti-Western resolutions condemning NATO, the Eisenhower doctrine, the Baghdad Pact, and nuclear weapons. The Communist influence in the movement was even more prominent at its second conference in Conakry, Guinea, in April, 1960.

In addition to these meetings of political leaders, two other Afro-Asian efforts have been made to organize cultural and economic activities. At a conference of nearly 200 Afro-Asian writers, which was held in Tashkent, capital of Soviet Uzbekistan, for five days at the beginning of October, 1958, it was decided to establish a permanent bureau at Colombo, Ceylon, and to hold another conference in 1960 in Cairo. And in December, 1958, an Afro-Asian Organization for Economic Co-operation was created at a conference held in Cairo by delegates from 38 countries.

Now, what relationship does this Afro-Asian solidarity movement have to the development of Pan-Africanism? In one sense it might be regarded as a stage on the road to the concept of an African personality. When the new states of Africa were not yet numerous enough to give adequate voice to their own desire for self-expression they found psychological satisfaction in unity with Asia. As they gained numbers and experience, however, the desire to emphasize their own uniqueness grew stronger. They found that the voices of Bandung and even Cairo were predominantly Asian. The need for Asia's help in support of African aims in world politics will no doubt induce African states to maintain solidarity with Asia, whenever it is advantangeous to do so. At the same time Africa, particularly south of the Sahara, has its own unique qualities, and differs from Asia in many ways. African leaders therefore began to look for better ways of asserting a distinctively African personality in world affairs.

A second reason for the new emphasis may have been African uneasiness at Communist influence. Communist China had played an influential role at Bandung, and the Soviet Union had scored a propaganda coup at Cairo. African delegates at Bandung were impressed by the sharp attack on Soviet colonialism made by Ceylonese and other Asian delegates. At Cairo, delegates from Ghana, Tunisia, Ethiopia and the Sudan had tried to moderate the anti-Western tone of the conference. Even President Nasser is said to have cautioned Egyptian delegates about the manoeuvres of the Soviet delegation. Meanwhile, Soviet brutality in suppressing Hungarian nationalists in 1956 had startled African leaders. Anxious for Western aid, the new states of Africa perhaps foresaw a practical value in developing their own international posture.

Finally, the ambitious designs of President Nasser probably helped to crystallise the rival ambitions of Prime Minister Nkrumah of Ghana for leadership in Africa. Nasserism was also becoming increasingly irritating to the chiefs of state in Ethiopia, Libya, the Sudan, Morocco and Tunisia. The latter three states, it should be recalled, had become independent only in 1956, while Ghana did not attain its independence until March 6, 1957.

By 1958, therefore, the way was prepared for the fourth phase of the Pan-African movement. During that year a remarkable series of seven precedent-setting international conferences were held *in* Africa *by* Africans for the first time. All seven of them were in one way or another Pan-African in spirit, indicating possible new combinations of African states. Many new ideas for regional combinations varying from political unions to loose economic organisations grew out of these meetings.

The most significant of the Africa conferences of 1958 were the two meetings in Accra in April and December. Like Bandung and Cairo, the Accra conferences differed in that the first was a meeting of governments and the second a meeting of peoples. The ambitious Pan-African programme already described, it should be recalled, emanated from the unofficial peoples conference in December, and not from the meeting of responsible government officials in April.

The more limited aim of the April Conference of Independent African States, as outlined by Prime Minister Nkrumah at the inaugural session was to forge "closer links of friendship, brotherhood, co-operation and solidarity . . . " among the eight participating countries. The resolutions adopted by the conference were naturally anti-colonial, but their tone and substance was far more moderate than either the Cairo resolutions or those of the later All-African Peoples Conference. No mention was made of any form of Pan-African Commonwealth. Instead, the Conference developed the concept of a "distinctive African personality which will speak with a concerted voice . . . "

To give meaning to this concept, the eight states agreed to constitute their Permanent Representatives at the United Nations in New York as a body of informal but permanent machinery for consultation and co-operation. In addition, it was agreed that the Conference of Independent African States should meet every two years, and that interim meetings of ministers or experts should be held from time to time.

The idea of using the African Permanent Representatives to the United Nations as the machinery of Pan-Africanism was a notable development in international relations, and a further illustration of the impact of the United Nations on Africa. The eight representatives met in New York soon after the Accra Conference and set up a Co-Ordinating body, chaired by each African state in turn, to meet once a month or at the request of any member. Four of the members were elected to a Secretariat to meet every two weeks, and the representative of Ghana was made Executive Secretary. One of the group's first steps was a quite unique bit of all-African diplomatic technique. It appointed three delegations, each composed of three African diplomats, to visit Europe, South America and Central America, to win support for Algerian independence. Their efforts probably had some effect because in the U.N. debate on the Algerian question in December, 1958, a resolution favouring Algeria's right to independence and calling for negotiations failed by only one vote to gain the required two-thirds majority.*

In 1959 and 1960 there were indications that this Pan-African diplomatic technique might be further employed, particularly against the *apartheid* policy of South Africa.

Meanwhile, the exuberant All-African Peoples Conference held its first meeting in Accra in December, 1958. Prime Minister Nkrumah

* Joan Gillespie, "Africa's Voice at the U.N.," *Africa Special Report*, June, 1959, 13–14.

appeared in a brilliant Ashanti cloth robe instead of the Western dress he wore at the earlier conference of official delegates. Addressing the opening session, however, he said: "Do not let us forget that colonialism and imperialism may come to us yet in a different guise, not necessarily from Europe. We must alert ourselves to be able to recognize this when it rears its head and prepare ourselves to fight against it." Despite the ambiguity of this declaration Nkrumah apparently had in mind Communist and possibly Egyptian intrigues as manifested at the Cairo conference. He is reported to have said in private that he omitted any reference to Bandung because Nasser had corrupted its principles of non-interference by intruding Asian and Communist influences into African affairs.

Nkrumah's opposition to Communist influence was evidently shared by George Padmore, who served in Ghana from 1951 till his death in 1959. As Nkrumah's adviser, he was the main theorist of Pan-Africanism. He was a Negro journalist of West Indian origin who was educated in the United States at Fisk and Howard Universities and joined the American Communist Party in the late 1920's. He said that he quit the Party in 1934, when he finally realised that "Russia wanted to use Africa for her own purposes." After 1934 he repeatedly attacked the Communists and called for a dynamic concept of Pan-Africanism, combined with Democratic Socialism, as "the only force capable of containing Communism in Asia and Africa . . ." His ideology of Pan-Africanism is set forth in a valuable book published in 1956 called *Pan-Africanism or Communism? The Coming Struggle for Africa.*

Nkrumah and Padmore had been the joint secretaries of the organizing committee of the Fifth Pan-African Congress at Manchester in 1945. Their Pan-Africanist efforts and successes at the two Accra conferences of 1958 were thus the partial realisation of a long-standing dream.

Meanwhile, although nine African states continued to participate in the twenty-nine state Afro-Asian block in the U.N., there was growing friction between the African and Asian members. This was particularly evident in a French Cameroons issue in the U.N. early in 1959, when Indian and other Asian members joined the Western powers to defeat an African proposal for new elections in the French Cameroons before it became independent on January 1, 1960. There was also disagreement between Africans and Asians over tactics to be used in the U.N. on the South-West Africa problem, and on French nuclear testing in the Sahara. It was reported on one occasion that the African delegates not only failed to appear at an Afro-Asian bloc meeting, but held a separate meeting of their own.* In general it seemed that the Asians were beginning to view controversial issues more calmly than the Africans. In reprisal, the Africans failed to support India in the 1959 Economic and Social Council elections, which enabled Japan to win a post.

The year 1959 also witnessed further efforts to expand the machinery of Pan-Africanism. Prime Minister Nkrumah of Ghana, President W. V. S. Tubman of Liberia, and Prime Minister Sékou Touré of Guinea, at a "summit" meeting of their own in Liberia on July 20, 1959, decided to call a conference in 1960 to prepare the formation of a Community of Independent African States. Six months earlier, on January 26, President Tubman had published a Liberian proposal to establish a loose organisation called the Associated States of Africa. Evidently he had in mind something more like the Organisation of American States than the Ghana-Guinea Union already established by Prime Ministers Nkrumah and Sékou Touré.

By 1959 other new entities in the Pan-African spirit included the Mali Federation of Senegal and the French Sudan; the Sahel Benin Entente, an economic arrangement in which Ivory Coast and Dahomey made their port facilities available to the interior territories of Upper-Volta and Niger; and the Equatorial Africa Customs Union and Common Transport System of the four former colonies of French Equatorial Africa.

In addition to these new regional combinations already in existence, a number of others had been proposed, including a Maghrebian Confederation of Morocco, Algeria and Tuninsia; a Greater Morocco integrated with Mauritania; a Greater Egypt; a Greater Somalia including the three Somalias plus the Ogaden province of Ethiopia and the Northern Province of Kenya; a Big Uganda united with the Sudan from Malakal South, plus the Nyanza province of Kenya, and Ruanda-Urundi; a United States of East and Central Africa comprising Kenya, Uganda, Tanganyika, Nyasaland and Northern Rhodesia;

---

* Thomas J. Hamilton—*The New York Times*, Nov. 8, 1959.

and a Capricorn Africa of all British East and Central African territories.

This confusion of overlapping proposals and counter-proposals raises the problem of obstacles to Pan-Africanism. The barriers in the way of a successful United States of Africa are indeed so numerous and so high that they are even obstacles to nationhood, let alone Pan-Africanism. They may be summarised as follows, although not all of them are necessarily a barrier to unity in every instance:

Different languages. Africa has not only 800 or more vernaculars, but at least five European languages, plus Arabic and Afrikaans. West Africans, when confronted with this problem, like to cite the example of Canada as proof that the problem is not insurmountable for English- and French-speaking Africans. And the December, 1958 Accra conference of peoples adopted a resolution calling upon all states and countries in Africa which are in a position to do so, to provide for reciprocal teaching of the English and French languages in the secondary schools of each territory.

Differing histories and cultures of the African peoples, even before the advent of Europe, particularly between Africa North and Africa South of the Sahara, but also among peoples South of the Sahara.

Differing colonial heritages in the territories ruled by different powers, which includes different cultural traditions of the modernized elites, as well as differing political traditions, and differing economic links such as trade and investment patterns.

Transportation and communication barriers, which are still enormous.

Differing religions, particularly Christianity and Islam.

Frontier difficulties such as the border which separates Ethiopian Somalis from the people of the three Somalilands.

Competing agricultural economies such as the potential competition for markets between Ghanian cocoa and the expanding cocoa production of the Ivory Coast and the French Cameroons.

Differences between black Africa and the multi-racial areas, such as South Africa and Southern Rhodesia.

Rival ambitions of African leaders such as Nkrumah and Nasser, Nkrumah and Tubman, Nkrumah and Awolowo, Nkrumah and

Houphouet-Boigny, Sékou Touré and Houphouet-Boigny, Nasser and Haile Selassie. When asked about this rivalry of leaders, George Padmore made the optimistic reply: "We have the spirit of adventure. We will not be bound by previous constitutional formats. If necessary we will have a rotating presidency, perhaps even a collective one. We hope to do something new and through the genius of our own people."

Finally, the potential barriers in African nationalism itself. As Thomas Hodgkin has commented in his fine book on *Nationalism in Colonial Africa*, African "nationalism" tries to operate at a variety of levels: first, at the level of a particular language group or greater tribe such as the Yoruba or Ewe; secondly, at the level of a particular territory such as Ubangi-Shari or Nigeria; thirdly, at the regional level of West Africa or the French *Afrique Noire*; and finally at the Pan-African level. The nationalisms of the first three levels all tend to conflict with Pan-Africanism in its widest meaning.

In conclusion it is evident that Pan-Africanism means different things to different people. Between 1900 and 1960 it evolved from the concept of a brotherhood of Negro blood into the idea of new political and economic entities of regional scope. The United States of Africa may be almost as much a dream as ever, but other regional combinations on a lesser scale are already emerging.

One of Ghana's intellectuals believes that the common people of British and French West African territories "feel" a sense of unity despite the personal rivalries of some of their leaders. A variation on the same idea has been expressed by an American Negro living in Paris, who was an observer at the first International Congress of Negro Writers and Artists in Paris in September, 1956. As the Congress debate wore on, he has written, it became clear "that there *was* something which all black men held in common, something which cut across opposing points of view, and placed in the same context their widely dissimilar experience. What they held in common was the necessity to remake the world in their own image, to impose this image on the world, and no longer be controlled by the vision of the world, and of themselves held by other people. What, in sum, black men held in common was their ache to come into the world as men. And this ache united people who might otherwise have been divided as to what a man should be."*

* James Baldwin, "Princes and Powers," *Encounter*, January 1957, pp. 52–60.

French African intellectuals have developed the related concept of *negritude* in recent years, meaning the distinctive qualities of their Negroeness. The International Writers and Artists Congress just mentioned was a cultural conference at which the declaration of political views was supposedly out of order, but the opening speaker referred to it as a kind of second Bandung. And the questions discussed revealed some of the emotional political undertones of Pan-Africanism. For example: "What are the essential qualities and enduring values of our Negro-African inheritance? How can it best be developed and renewed? How can we be ourselves? How can we make use of European ideas, institutions, and techniques, without becoming their prisoner—without ceasing to be African?"

The idea of *negritude* was conceived by Aimee Cesaire, a Negro poet from Martinique. It became something of an intellectual battle-cry as well as a literary movement in French West Africa. Its chief exponent is Leopold Sedar Senghor who, in his poem *New York*, found only "artificial hearts paid for in hard cash," except in Harlem. Western culture is a "world that has died of machines and cannons," and can be saved only by the natural vitality and life force of the black peoples.†

By 1960 the Pan-African concepts of a brotherhood of Negro blood, and the related concept of *negritude*, were evolving in the minds of certain Negroes into the more chauvinistic concept of "black power." In his book, *Black Power*, Richard Wright admonishes Prime Minister Nkrumah to be hard, to enforce social discipline and militarise the Ghanaian masses in order to force them to make the sacrifices necessary to project Ghana immediately into the twentieth century. In a volatile attack on French atomic testing in the Sahara made in the Nigerian House of Representatives on August 11, 1959, Mr. R. A. Fani-Kayode of Ife declared: "This is the opportunity we have been looking for to show that black men all over Africa must stand or fall together. I have said it often and often in this House that *blackism* is the answer to our problems."

The most eloquent voicing of the concept of "black power," however, has come from another American Negro, Paul Robeson. In a

---

† On *negritude* see Simon Biesheuvel, *Race, Culture and Personality*, Johannesburg 1959, pp. 35–37; Ulli Beier, "In Search of an African Personality," *The Twentieth Century*, April 1959; and Paul-Marc Henri, "Pan-Africanism: A Dream Come True," *Foreign Affairs*, pp. 443–452.

fascinating interview with the Negro journalist, Carl Rowan, Robeson said:

> "I think a good deal in terms of the power of the black people in the world. That's why Africa means so much to me. As an American Negro, I'm as proud of Africa as one of those West Coast Chinese is proud of China. Now that doesn't mean I'm going back to Africa, but spiritually I've been a part of Africa for a long time. Yes, this black power moves me. Look at Jamaica. In a few years the white minority will be there on the sufferance of black men. If they're nice decent fellows they can stay. Yes, I look at Senator Eastland and say, 'So you think you are powerful here. If only I could get you across the border.' Although I may stay here the rest of my life, spiritually I'll always be part of that world where the black man can say to these crackers, 'Get the hell out of here by morning'. If I could get a passport, I'd just like to go to Ghana or Jamaica just to sit there for a few days and observe this black power."

The element of chauvinism in the concept of "black power" was repudiated by African leaders at the two Pan-African conferences in Accra in 1958. There is, however, a significant common denominator in the concepts of the brotherhood of Negro blood, *negritude*, the African personality, blackism, and black power—they all have a powerful emotional content which is productive of both good and evil. And that, perhaps is the greatest significance of Pan-Africanism. The idea of a United States of Africa faces too many obstacles for realisation except in limited forms. But the feelings behind it are a powerful force which policymakers can ignore only at their peril.

Selection 12

African Affairs*

Kwame Nkrumah

One of the earlier and most eminent African nationalist and Pan-African leaders, Kwame Nkrumah is now President of the Republic of Ghana.

Address delivered to the National Assembly by Osagyefo Dr. Kwame Nkrumah, President of the Republic of Ghana, on August 8th, 1960.

. . . Throughout the whole continent of Africa colonialism is in confusion and retreat. The retreat of colonialism, however, is of no value unless the peoples of Africa are mobilised to advance and occupy the positions from which the colonialists have retreated. Nothing could be more dangerous than a Power vacuum in Africa.

The new African nations must from the very nature of the conditions under which they became independent, be in their early days weak and powerless when contrasted with the great and older established nations of the world. Potentially, however, an African union could be one of the greatest forces in the world as we know it. One of the most encouraging things which have taken place within the last six months or so is the growing realisation among African statesmen that we must unite politically and that, indeed, in the words of the Prime Minister of Northern Nigeria, a United States of Africa is inevitable. As I stated elsewhere, there are three alternatives open to African States. Firstly, to unite and save our continent. Secondly, to disunite and disintegrate. Or, thirdly, to sell out. In other words: either to unite, or to stand separately and disintegrate or to sell ourselves to foreign powers. . . .

* Reprinted by permission from *Ghana Today*, Supplement, August 31, 1960.

The duty of African politicians is to explain, patiently, continuously and persistently, to the outside world the essence of African nationalism and its problems.

In the first place, whether any particular continent is backward or developed, is a pure question of the moment in time when one happens to study the continent in question.

Civilisation probably dawned contemporaneously in Africa and in China. Certainly, the origins of European culture trace their roots back to the ancient civilizations of the Nile Valley.

An English writer thus compared the conditions in the ancient kingdom of Ghana with those of England of the same date:—

"In 1066 Duke William of Normandy invaded England. In 1067 an Andalusian Arab, El Bekri, wrote an account of the court of the West African King of Ghana. This king, whenever holding audience, 'sits in a pavilion around which stand his horses caparisoned in cloth of gold; behind him stand ten pages holding shields and gold-mounted swords; and on his right hand are the sons of the princes of his empire, splendidly clad . . .' Barbarous splendour, perhaps; but was the court of this African monarch so much inferior, in point of organised government, to the court of Saxon Harold? Wasn't the balance of achievement just possibly the other way round?"

Why was it that Ghana, which was in the eleventh century, at least equal in power and might to England, disappeared as it did? The answer is obvious. It was through the disunity of the African continent created by serious external influences and internal disharmony and discord.

Throughout the Middle Ages great African States existed and indeed the culture and traditions of the ancient world were preserved not in Europe, but in the countries of Africa. The fatal error of the North African States of that day was that they were engaged in conflict not only in the north with the powers of Europe, but also in the south with African States of the day.

We have, however, now overcome this ancient disunion. The Sahara no longer divides us; it is no longer a physical or a political barrier between us.

One of the greatest achievements of the Conference of Independent African States is to bring together in one organisation the African States north and south of the Sahara. We have all of us come to realise that our interests are not conflicting but that we all have a common interest in preserving the unity and independence of Africa.

DANGER OF BALKANISATION

Perhaps the greatest danger that Africa faces today is what I call balkanisation.

The term is particularly appropriate for describing this danger since it arises from the action of the then great powers when they divided into a number of small and competing States the colonial possessions of the Turkish Empire in Europe.

At the very time when these great powers were splitting up the Balkans in Europe into a number of States, they were also engaged in partitioning Africa amongst themselves. In Europe the political situation had developed to an extent which made it impossible openly to apportion the Turkish Empire among the other great powers. Already there were small independent States in the Balkans and therefore all the great powers could do was to ensure that whatever happened no Balkan State should be created which was strong enough to stand on its own feet.

The great powers at the end of the 19th century established their domination over one or other of the little States which had been created. The effect was to produce a political tinderbox which any spark could set alight and involve the whole world in flames. The explosion came in 1914 when in one part of the old Turkish Empire an Austrian Archduke was murdered by a Serbian from another former part of the same colonial empire.

This murder involved the world in the greatest war which history had ever seen up to that time. The war occurred primarily because Serbia, from whence the murderer came, was a Balkan State under the protection of the then imperialist Russia, while Bosnia, where the murder took place, was a colonial possession taken over from Turkey by the Austro-Hungarian Empire. Russia came to the aid of Serbia, Germany to the aid of the Austro-Hungarian Empire. France then joined in support of Russia. In order to attack France, Germany invaded Belgium, and in order to defend Belgium, the Government of the United Kingdom declared war upon Germany on behalf of all members of the then British Empire. . . .

I have given this account of the history and effect of balkanisation in Europe to illustrate the extreme danger of a similar policy being applied by the colonial powers to the African continent. In the same way as defensive alliances by the Balkan powers with rival powers outside the Balkans resulted in a world war, so a world war could easily originate on the African continent if African States make political, economic and military alliances with rival powers from outside Africa. The new colonialism creates client States, independent in name, but in point of fact pawns to the colonial power that is supposed to have given them independence. When an African balkanised State concludes a pact with its colonial power, then that State has lost control over its foreign policy and is therefore not free.

On the other hand, if Africa is converted into a series of tiny States, such alliances are inevitable. Some of these States have neither the resources nor the personnel to provide for their own defence or to conduct an independent foreign policy. They will, in their weak position, rely on the armed forces and the diplomats of another country both for their security and their external policy. Nor can they become economically independent. They have not the resources to establish their own independent banking systems and they are compelled to continue with the old colonial framework of trade. The only way out is to stand together politically.

Political freedom is essential in order to win economic freedom, but political freedom is meaningless unless it is of such a nature which enables the country which has obtained it to maintain its economic freedom.

The African struggle for independence and unity must begin with political union. A loose confederation of economic cooperation is deceptively time-delaying. It is only a political union that will ensure a uniformity in our foreign policy projecting the African personality and presenting Africa as a force important to be reckoned with. I repeat, a loose economic co-operation means a screen behind which detractors, imperialist and colonialist protagonists and African puppet leaders hide to operate and weaken the concept of any effort to realize African unity and independence. A political union envisages a common foreign and defence policy and rapid social, economic and industrial developments. The economic resources of Africa are immense and staggering. It is only by unity that these resources can be utilised for the progress of the Continent and for the happiness of mankind.

We must learn from history. The genius of the South American people has been to a considerable extent frustrated by the fact that when the Spanish and Portuguese colonial empires dissolved they did not organise themselves into a United States of South America. At the same time, when South America became free, the colonial States which acquired their independence were potentially as powerful as the United States in North America. Their failure to come together resulted in one part of the American continent developing at the expense of the other. Nevertheless, there is only one country in South America, namely Paraguay, which has a population of less than three million.

At the moment independent States in Africa are being established with populations of less than a million. Territories in Africa which have become independent or are likely to become independent in the near future, and which have populations of less than three million, include the Central African Republic, Chad, the former French Congo (which has a population of only three-quarters of a million), Dahomey, Gabon with a population of less than half a million, the Ivory Coast, Niger, Sierra Leone and Togoland.

"TERRIBLE FRAGMENTATION"

It is impossible to imagine that the colonial powers seriously believe that independence could be of much value to these African States in such a terrible state of fragmentation. Surely this is only in pursuance of the old policy of divide and rule. . . .

I have frequently emphasised that imperialism in the present stage of African nationalism will employ many feints. With one hand it may concede independence, while with the other it will stir up the muddy waters of tribalism, feudalism, separatism and chicanery in order to find its way back in another guise.

What is going on now in Congo is a typical example of this latest kind of imperialist and colonialist manoeuvre. And there are very good reasons why we should have expected something of the kind to happen. The interests that are engaged in Congo are empires in themselves, and those in Katanga especially have fabulous advantages which they are loath to abandon.

Foremost among these is the immensely ramified Societe General de Belgique, whose pyramidal structure covers the Comité Speciale du Katanga. This Comité holds property of a size which is breath-taking.

That a single concern could hold property of the size of one hundred and eleven million one hundred and eleven thousand and one hundred and eleven acres is a staggering thought. But this is the size of the empire of the Comité General du Katanga, and it contains some of the world's most valuable mineral rights.

A subsidiary in this giant structure is the Compagnie du Haut Katanga, which is linked to the Union Miniere du Haut Katanga. The Union Miniere has procured for itself in the Katanga area a concession of seven thousand seven hundred square miles; that is, a territory more than half the size of Belgium itself. This concession was not due to expire until 11th March, 1990. The independence which passed to the people of Congo on the 30th June this year they feared could cut across the privileges enjoyed by the Union Miniere to exploit the riches of this vast region in the interests of its shareholders and the Belgian Government, which has two-thirds interest in the Comité Speciale du Katanga, the organisation owning 25 per cent of the Union Miniere.

Here are interlocking connections which are of considerable importance, and it is easy enough to understand what there is at stake when we realise that the Union Miniere produces out of its Katanga concessions 7 per cent of the total world production of copper, 80 per cent of cobalt, 5 per cent of zinc, as well as substantial quantities of cadium, silver, platinum, columbium, tungsten and many other important minerals. It also operates the uranium mine at Shinkolobwe, which provides the raw material for some nuclear weapon nations. The amount of this production is a closely guarded secret, as is also the price paid for it.

MILLIONS OF POUNDS PROFIT

The Union Miniere produces at least 45 per cent of all Congo exports, and these are so profitable that its net profits, that is, its profits after all reserves and allocations have been made, are well over twenty million pounds per annum.

When we consider these facts in relation to the present serious situation in Congo, it is not at all difficult to appreciate the efforts that are being made to separate Katanga from the Republic of Congo. With the present fiercely Congolese nationalist movement, this can only be done through puppets who are willing to be used. Thus we have the apparent willingness of the Belgians to comply with the United Nations resolution and to withdraw their troops from Congo being counteracted by the threat of secession by Tshombe, the Chairman of the Provincial Council of Katanga, a province of the independent Republic of Congo, and through him the Union Miniere and the Belgian Government defying the United Nations troops from entering Katanga. . . .

Capital investment from outside is, of course, required in Africa. But if there is real political independence the profits from the investment of this capital can be shared in a way which is fair both to the outside investor and to the people of the country where the investment is made.

The evil of balkanisation, disunity and secessions is that the new Balkan States of Africa will not have the independence to shake off the economic colonial shackles which result in Africa being a source of riches to the outside world while grinding poverty continues at home.

There is a real danger that the colonial powers will grant a nominal type of political independence to individual small units so as to ensure that the same old colonial type of economic organisation continues long after independence has been achieved. This in itself is a source of the gravest potential danger for the whole world. The peoples of Africa do not seek political freedom for abstract purposes. They seek it because they believe that through political freedom they can obtain economic advancement, education and a real control over their own destiny. If there is a grant of independence to a State which is so small that it cannot mobilise its own resources and which is tied by a series of economic and military agreements to the former colonial power, then a potentially revolutionary situation is at once created. These are the situations facing the new Africa of today. . . .

Selection 13

The Integration of Africa*

NNAMDI AZIKEWE

Nnamdi Azikewe is President of the Republic of Nigeria and for many years has been a leading Nigerian nationalist and Pan-Africanist.

From an address delivered by Dr Nnamdi Azikewe, Premier of Eastern Nigeria and National President of the National Council of Nigeria and the Cameroons, on July 31, 1959, at the Carlton Rooms, Maida Vale, London W.9 under the auspices of the London Branch of the NCNC with Dr T. O. Elias, LL.M., Ph.D., Teaching Fellow in Law at Oxford University, in the chair.

In connection with the relationship between Nigeria and the other African States, the need for economic, social and political integration has been mentioned. Since many views have been propounded on how the free African States can be linked the situation is rather confusing. Perhaps it may be pertinent for me to pursue this matter further in order not to leave any room for doubt or confusion.

Nigeria should co-operate closely with the other independent African States with the aim of establishing unity of outlook and purpose in foreign policy. The pursuing of this objective should make for better understanding among the African States and a realization of identity of interest among them. Moreover, it would advertise the importance of Africa in world affairs and help to heal the wounds that have been inflicted on this continent and which can be a basis of a revanche movement.

There are many schools of thought on how the African States should

---

* Reprinted by permission from *Zik: Selected Speeches of Nnamdi Azikewe* (Cambridge, England: Cambridge University Press, 1961), pp. 70–73.

be aligned. One school favours a political union of African States now. Another school favours an association of African States on the basis of community of interests. Still another school favours an alignment of a rigid or loose character on a regional basis. Other schools develop this splendid idea further and there can be no doubt that more will be heard from other quarters.

My personal opinion is that there is great need for close co-operation between Nigeria and the other African States. The nature of such close co-operation need not delay sincere efforts to attain such a desirable goal, but we must be realistic in pursuing this matter lest we plunge the continent of Africa in a maelstrom of conflicting personal ambitions and interests.

I would suggest that Nigeria, in the first instance, should explore with its nearest neighbours the possibility of a customs union. This would lead to the abolition of tariffs between the two or more countries and would encourage "free trade" in areas which might ultimately turn into a common market. With a free flow and interchange of goods, Nigeria and its neighbours would come closer in their economic relationship which is very fundamental in human relations.

I would also suggest a gradual abolition of boundaries which demarcate the geographical territory of Nigeria and its neighbours. The experience of Canada and the United States has been encouraging and should be explored. Once travelling is freely permitted, other things being equal, people will forget about physical frontiers and begin to concentrate on essential problems of living together.

I would suggest further that Nigeria should interest its neighbours in a joint endeavour to build international road systems which should link West African countries with East African territories, on the one hand, and North African countries with Central African territories, on the other. By encouraging the construction of *autobahn* systems across strategic areas of Africa, and by providing travelling facilities, in the shape of hotels, motels, petrol-filling stations, we should be able to knit the continent of Africa into a tapestry of free-trading, free-travelling, and free-living peoples.

I would finally suggest cultural exchanges on a wider scale than is practised at present. Students, dancers, artistes, traders and holiday-makers should be able to cross the frontiers of Nigeria and its neighbours with full freedom. They are usually the ambassadors of goodwill and they can help to produce the sense of one-ness which is so lacking in most of Africa at present. Given official support these ordinary folk would become the harbingers of a new era in Africa, because once a sense of one-ness has permeated the social fabric it facilitates the crystallization of common nationality, as the experience of Nigerian history vindicates.

I believe that economic and social integration will enable Nigeria and its neighbours to bring to pass the United States of Africa, which is the dream of African nationalists. It would be capital folly to assume that hard-bargaining politicians who passed through the ordeal of victimization and the crucible of persecution to win their political independence will easily surrender their newly-won political power in the interest of a political leviathan which is populated by people who are alien to one another in their social and economic relations. It has not been possible in Europe or America, and unless Africa can show herself different from other continents, the verdict of history on this score will remain unchallenged and unaltered.

Lest there should be any mistaken notion of my stand on the alignment of interests of African States, may I reiterate that I firmly believe in the attainment of an association or union of African States either on a regional or continental basis in the future. I would regard such a future as not within the life-time of the heroes and heroines who have spearheaded the struggle for freedom in Africa, these four decades. But I honestly believe that social and economic integration would so mix the masses of the various African territories into an amalgam of understanding that the objective might be realizable earlier than we expected.

In other words, the prerequisites of political integration in Africa are the economic and social integration of African peoples. Otherwise, we shall be precipitating a crisis which will find African leaders jockeying among themselves for leadership of peoples who are not only alien to each other but are unprepared for such a social revolution. This would be disastrous to the ideals of Pan-Africanism which all of us, as sincere nationalists, have been propagating all these years. It means going the way of Europe, which gave top priority to political integration before social and economic integration, only to disintegrate into unimportant nation-states after the Peace of Westphalia in 1648. . . .

UNITY VERSUS SEPARATISM

The African continent is very much fragmented, politically, socially, and also culturally. Proponents of African unity have therefore had to contend at every level, from the continental to the purely local, with separatist tendencies. Possible outcomes of the contention were outlined by Rupert Emerson in Selection 10. The readings in this section develop this discussion by suggesting some of the motivations and issues involved in the confrontation.

European conquest contributed to African unity by amalgamating tribes into larger political units. One question raised by the coming of independence is whether or not the former colonies can survive the revival of "tribal nationalism," now partially released from the fetters of foreign rule. In Selection 14, numerous examples are cited to show that the question is not an idle one. Yet a paradox exists, it is suggested, for African leaders, struggling with such problems at home, at the same time exhibit great confidence in the possibilities for African continental and regional unity. The author seems to imply that African hopes for greater unity are not entirely realistic when viewed in the light of domestic political difficulties.

A fuller examination of internal problems of nation-building in Africa must be left aside; we can only note the paradox of politicians representing at Pan-African conferences states which themselves are torn by centrifugal forces, and then turn (rather paradoxically) to the role of these states as "building-blocks" of an African international system.

Here the basic question is whether the political units put together by the colonial powers might not assume national identities and pursue separate policies which then handicap efforts to establish even more inclusive units? There is impressive evidence that this is the case. Almost all attempts at federal union in Africa, for example, have foundered. Impatient and energetic African leaders, ambitious for themselves and their countries, apparently tend to react to federal arrangements as intolerably obstructive to their own economic planning and political leadership.

Much African thought has been devoted to the separatist tendencies thus seemingly inherent in the post-colonial situation. Selection 15 is a broad and balanced consideration of the problem. Obviously a convinced Pan-Africanist, Mr. Rashidi Kawawa is particularly interesting for his rejection both of the "radical" argument against regional federations as divisive of continental unity, and of the "gradualist" view of the route which must be followed to achieve eventual unity.

Selection 14

Tribe and Nation in East Africa: Separatism and Regionalism*

THE ROUND TABLE

It is a paradox of present-day African politics that new rulers who live in such constant fear of separatism, and the splitting of their newly independent States into their tribal components, should yet be so hopeful

* Reprinted by permission from *The Round Table* (June 1962), pp. 252–258.

about the possibilities of building up regional federations which are, by European standard, of immense size and of very heterogeneous populations. District and tribal rivalries complicate the anxious months of constitution making for each Colony or Protectorate which is fighting its way to Independence. Uganda could presumably have celebrated this event four or five years ago if it had been possible to satisfy the ambitions of the Ganda who were, and are, the dominant tribe in the Protectorate, consistently with those of the three other lesser kingdoms—Bunyoro, Toro and Ankole—and the twelve or so less centralized tribes who live in the west, north and east of this territory. A newly tailored constitution has been accepted at long last and the date of Independence day has been mentioned, but some tribal groups are still trying to change their status under the new deal. The day this article was written Bunyoro, Toro and Ankole were demanding a new kind of federal status and the Chief Minister of the interim government was asking to postpone the date of the first elections. The negotiations over the Kenya constitution have already lasted six weeks because nine or so tribal groups, which are afraid of being dominated by the pushing and successful Kikuyu and the Luo, are asking for a federal and not a centralized constitution; Somalis on the coastal strip want separate status. These are small groups. In Uganda there was an estimated African population of 6½ millions in 1959, of which the Ganda accounted for nearly 2 million but the fourteen other largest tribes numbered on an average 300,000 each. In Kenya there are reckoned to be nearly two million Kikuyu and 800,000 Luo; but some of the other groups are very much smaller, such as the Kamba (600,000) and the Bantu Kavirondo (300,000). European observers can be forgiven for feeling irritated that new constitutional arrangements should be held up by jealousy and suspicion between the members of such small ethnic groups.

In view of the difficulties which African leaders evidently have in building up a viable State from groups which have long been administered as part of one political system, it is at first sight surprising that these politicians should apparently see no insuperable obstacles to the much more delicate task of creating a Federation of East African territories or even a "United States of Africa." On the home front their attention seems to be riveted on the importance of cultural differences between neighbouring tribes and on the difficulty of securing any measure of constitutional balance between so many different traditional polities—kingdoms, chiefdoms, societies based on age-grades, or on locally rooted lineages; but in the context of the world situation these same leaders are claiming that there is a common African personality which is sufficient to unite the inhabitants of the vast continent of Africa. Mr. Nyerere, lately Prime Minister of the newly independent Tanganyika, is known to favour a Federation of Kenya, Tanganyika and Uganda with the possible inclusion of Nyasaland and Ruanda-Urundi. He was the Chairman of the first conference of PAFMECA (Pan-African Freedom Movement for East and Central Africa) held in 1960. This conference is now attended by representatives from Ethiopia, Kenya, Northern Rhodesia, Nyasaland, Somalia, Tanganyika, Uganda and Zanzibar. Mr. Mboya, a leader of KANU, one of the two political parties in Kenya which have been unable to settle tribal differences in order to agree on a new constitution, flew to Addis Ababa to act as Chairman of the second PAFMECA Conference in February of this year. Although it seems likely that any new flag accepted by Kenya will strain at the seams as it runs up the mast-head, yet PAFMECA seemed to find no difficulty in including among its members the Emperor of an ancient Christian State, the Kabaka of Buganda, the Moslem Sultan of Zanzibar, Tanganyika with its 120 separate tribes, as well as the Africans in white-dominated countries such as South Africa and Northern Rhodesia. The name of the conference was in fact changed to PAFMECSA to include the southern territories. In spite of this large alliance of dissimilar cultures and constitutions, the conference was rebuked by Mr. John Tettegah, an observer from Ghana, for narrowness and regionalism and told that "As long as we remain balkanized regionally or territorially we shall be at the mercy of Colonialism and Imperialism."

It is true that no central secretariat or council was set up for the PAFMECSA countries, such as was proposed but not finally implemented by the Lagos conference of twenty African countries which met in January this year; but such a step seems to have been contemplated. Here again countries which are woefully short of trained administrators at the territorial level, and are plainly conscious of this shortage, are yet able to consider with equanimity the provision of the much more experienced administrative staff which would be required for the conduct of the business of such a large and heterogeneous Federation.

CONDITIONS MAKING FOR TRIBALISM

The conditions which make for the persistence of militant tribalism are becoming clearer with the trials and errors of each new African State, although it must be admitted that our knowledge has generally been acquired through the painful process of helplessly watching the birth pangs of each newly independent country and is hence often of historical rather than practical interest. It becomes clear for instance, as probably could have been predicted, that tribal rivalry has been greatest in territories in which one or more tribes have acquired a dominant position, either through a tradition of successful conquest over surrounding peoples, through having achieved a more or less centralized government, or through having been in a position to exploit the new economic advantages brought by Europeans such as a profitable cash crop or some industrial development. In the last case it has often happened that the people in question have achieved a jump ahead, so to speak, of the other tribes in the territory and have become the object of envy and dislike. The Ganda of Uganda, the Kongo, Lunda and Luba of the Congo are examples of peoples with historical traditions of conquest and superior political organization on the basis of which they claim special privilege. The Kikuyu in Kenya, or again the Ganda and the Luba, are instances of peoples which have become richer, more skilled and better educated than their fellow countrymen owing to earlier participation in European economic developments. Nairobi with its industrial possibilities was built in Kikuyu country; Ganda became rich through the introduction of cotton in 1905 and later of coffee and through the building of a railway through their country; the Kongo were the Congo peoples who responded most quickly to the new economic opportunities in the mines and the railways. Luba travelled widely to become skilled technicians, mechanics and lorry drivers. Tanganyika with its enormous area, its widely dispersed population and its 120 or more small tribes has not had to face the problem of the self-consciously independent African kingdom, or of the single dominant and hence hated tribe; and separatism has not been such a problem for Mr. Nyerere.

The unequal economic development of different areas which has been so conspicuous in African territories has led to very sharp contrasts in educational facilities. Independence inevitably means a struggle for posts in the Central administration—posts formerly filled by expatriates and highly paid in relation to the rest of the bureaucracy. Members of the economically favoured tribes are naturally best fitted to hold such posts. It is almost impossible for the Ganda to accept the position that Ministers and heads of Government departments should be selected from members of what are, to them, savage tribes, and just as difficult for these latter tribes to watch the power in the Central government being wielded by the Ganda. Studies of the tribal composition of African *élites* and their educational qualifications in different territories are only now beginning. They show in a revealing way the differential access of members of different tribes to higher posts in the Central government, in political party leadership and in legislative assemblies. . . .

PAN-AFRICANISM AND NEGRITUDE

We return then to our paradox. Tribal jealousies and suspicion are all too inevitable under present conditions. How are they combined in the politician's mind with the excessively ambitious forms of African regionalism which have been described? First, it must be remembered that Pan-Africanism was originally an emotional protest, a creed or a crusade: it was not a practical plan for a United States of Africa as a political entity. So also Regionalism began as a movement of like-minded African militants fighting for independence in neighbouring territories, and not as a scheme for political, military or economic co-operation. The dream of a mighty world alliance of peoples with black skins could give comfort to those who had not achieved centralized government in their own territories. A true political federation would not have been a possibility in these circumstances. . . .

These Pan-African movements were clearly very far from political alliances in any ordinary sense of the term. One has only to instance the fact that though Indians attended these conferences and joined in the talk of common brotherhood, yet those Indians who actually settled in large numbers in Kenya, Uganda, Tanganyika and South Africa have not made common cause with African politicians in these territories, except for the isolated instance of the short-lived Passive Resistance movement organized in South Africa in 1952. Indians in Uganda and Kenya have sometimes sided with Europeans as the two civilized communities in league against the barbarian Africans. At other times Africans have joined Europeans in their dislike of the Indian settlers. African students at Makerere College in Uganda have been heard exclaiming to their Indian fellow students "It isn't even as though you fellows were Christians like us"!

Even anti-colonialism, which developed later than Pan-Africanism, and came much nearer to a political objective, has so far been in the main a rallying cry, a movement of sympathy from the newly independent States to those still under foreign domination, and a focal point for joint voting at U.N. meetings, rather than the basis of any military or economic alliance. It is true that at this year's meeting of PAFMECSA some militant pronouncements were made as to the determination of the Powers represented to free the Africans in Portuguese territory and the Union by 1970. It is also true that Dr. Verwoerd has warned his countrymen that they should take defence measures against possible military action by well-armed and independent African States farther north, but such a planned offensive has not yet been launched.*

Thus the new African politicians face the problems of Regionalism and Pan-Africanism with long traditions of a time when Pan-African conferences provided a get-together for African and New World negro militants rather than meetings of working diplomatists. It would not be surprising if such conferences as PAFMECSA were considered as stimulating and heartening interludes in the long struggle with local politics. The quasi-philosophical concepts of brotherhood evolved by negro intellectuals of other countries, who show little knowledge of or even interest in African administrative problems, must have a strong attraction for African politicians although they provide little help in present constitutional or economic difficulties.

NEED FOR ALLIANCES

In the new conditions it is natural that African leaders should feel suddenly defenceless as Independence is proclaimed and that they should immediately look for alliances. English-speaking Ghana and French-speaking Guinea sign a treaty of Union in 1958; Senegal, the Sudan and Upper Volta form the Mali Federation in 1959. Dahomey

* *Editor's Note:* This is no longer so. The Organization of African Unity has created a committee to coordinate the African drive against the white-dominated territories and states of Southern Africa.

offers to join but the union breaks up in 1960. The Ivory Coast, Upper Volta, Dahomey and Niger form an Entente in 1958. Twelve ex-French States set up a common Secretariat at Brazzaville in 1960—the so-called "Brazzaville group." Such alliances may be more difficult to form in East Africa with its long history of white settlement, but a union of Nyasaland and Tanganyika has often been mooted.

If we accuse African politicians of being over-ambitious about their regional schemes we must remember that they have come into power in an age of planning, and that they are constantly visited by economists who tend to under-emphasize the administrative difficulties of territorial union and who tell them their newly independent States are too small to support major industries. Indeed all short-term "visiting firemen" tend to underestimate the importance of linguistic and cultural differences. American advisers are impatient of the smallness of some of the new States, as they are of European subdivisions. International finance prefers to give loans to big countries. Even Africans, not so far mainly swayed by economic considerations, now begin to desire union with other States in order to be able to build up better armament industries, and they clearly realize the advantage of including a wealthy mining area like Katanga in their federations. At the PAFMECSA conference the chief delegate for Ethiopia said that political union was necessary if the countries of East Africa want to diversify their economies, integrate their development programmes, exploit mineral resources and river potential. This is a sentence straight from the economic textbooks and a far cry from the mysticism of the idea of "negritude."

East African politicians also consider the wider Pan-African links. They realize they are behind West Africa in wealth, experience and numbers of university-trained citizens. They fear West African domination and patronage, but know it is only through an East-West union that they can obtain a position of world power on a level, or so they hope, with the USA, China, the USSR.

It is important too to remember that African politicians import their constitutions and do not hammer them out by trial and error in the do-it-yourself fashion that is all that was open to our own forefathers. We fought our way through to something like a centralized government by the tenth century A.D., but twentieth-century politicians in Africa think it their right not only to read about other constitutions but to go and look for patterns abroad. An African Minister from a small East African kingdom, encountered in Victoria Street with swinging cane and hat jauntily acock, explained that he was on his way to America "to have a look at their Federal system to see if it would suit us." Many Africans have now been educated in America, and it is difficult for them to believe that what America has federated they cannot federate as well! We live after all in an age of expanding politics. Even England, with boundaries that seemed so fixed, is a member of NATO and standing on the brink of a common market. If African politicians dream of a mighty United States of Africa while struggling to keep tiny tribal groups united within their own small boundaries we cannot criticize them too harshly.

Selection 15

A Tanganyikan View on Pan-Africanism*

RASHIDI KAWAWA

Rashidi Kawawa is Vice President of Tanganyika. This selection is from a speech delivered by Mr. Kawawa before the East, South, and Central African Seminar held in late 1963 and early 1964 in Dar es Salaam, Tanganyika.

One of the most important facts about the campaign for African Unity is that there is no-one in a responsible position in Africa who now questions the need for such unity. . . .

This means that psychologically we are much further advanced towards unity than any other continent. No public figure can come out openly and oppose the principle of unity, because this is now part of our philosophy; it is an unquestioned assumption that unity is good, and that African Unity must come.

---

* Reprinted from *The Student*, Vol. VII, No. 4 (April 1964), pp. 13–17, 29. *The Student* is published on a monthly basis in English, French, and Spanish by COSEC—the Coordinating Secretariat of the National Unions of Students—on behalf of the International Student Conference.

WHY UNITY?

. . . Africa's freedom struggle took the form of nationalism because the 19th century scramble for Africa had resulted in the partition of Africa between different colonial powers. Had Africa been colonized by one European power—as India was—then our freedom movement would have been a continent-wide one; it would have been the African National Congress, or the African National Union, without the prefix "South Africa," Tanganyika, Congo, or anything else.

The "nations" which now exist in Africa are really the product of the nationalist movements. The people of Sukumaland are conscious of being in Tanganyika because they were organized into the Tanganyika African National Union, which covered a particular colonial administrative area. Had the colonial powers drawn the map differently, the people of that area would still have taken part in the freedom movement, and would have thought of themselves as "Kenyans" or as members of some other nation.

The freedom movements of the different parts of Africa were—and are—simply the local organizations of a continent-wide peoples' movement. They had to operate separately and adopt different tactics only because of the colonial organization. Basically, they were all part of one movement. The leaders of the different areas were really more like Divisional Commanders in one army. It is, therefore, logical that, once the colonial powers have been expelled, the resulting "nations" be integrated into the one unit they really are, with the administrative decentralization which is necessary for effective government.

BOUNDARIES ARTIFICIAL

But, of course, unity is not simply a question of logic. Because the national boundaries we inherit from colonialism are completely artificial, it is essential that we reduce their importance to the minimum. Within Africa, there is not a single border which has been drawn on the basis of dividing different races, tribes, or peoples with contrasting ways of life. Neither are there many border lines which run along the natural geographical divisions of the land. We find the Ewe people living in Ghana and Togoland; the Masai in Kenya and Tanganyika; the Yao in Nyasaland and Mozambique; and so on. We find rivers in one country, and their natural hinterland in another; mountain ranges separate one part of the country from another while the border between two nations runs across an indivisible plain. The list is endless.

With the success of the freedom movements these absurd boundaries become a very real danger to the separate nations of Africa, and to Africa as a whole. We have already seen border conflict between Morocco and Algeria, and have the immediate threat of it between Somalia and Kenya. Such conflicts did not arise before independence because the boundaries were then unimportant; they were administrative divisions. What did it matter to the French colonial administration whether a particular village was in the colony with its headquarters at Rabat or in the one centred in Algiers? The District Officers of the areas concerned probably sent protests to each other, and the people preferred to be in one or the other colony according to which was governed by the more humane or sensible individual. But there was no question of people losing their lives or their homes because of this dispute; it was not an international issue.

When those same boundaries become divisions between different sovereign "nations," however, an entirely different range of issues enters into consideration. Question of "national pride"; of different forms of government; of free movement; all these things become important, and conflict between nations can very easily arise. Once that happens, the people of Africa will find that instead of being in different divisions of one army, they find themselves killing each other in opposing armies.

I do not need to emphasize this point; the danger is real. To us in Tanganyika it now seems absurd to think of fighting with our brothers in Kenya over border issues or anything else. But while we remain separate sovereign states this possibility can never be ruled out. Or take Nyasaland; the boundary between us is drawn in such a way that the moment a Tanganyikan enters the waters of Lake Nyasa, he is technically entering another country. If there is a dispute between two fishermen, one from the Tanganyika shore and the other from the Nyasa shore, then an international incident is created.

Of course, international incidents do not necessarily lead to international conflict when the nations are friendly and strong. But they do inevitably provide an opportunity for anyone who wishes to stir up trouble between the two countries. The dangers of neo-colonialism are never so present as when questions of this sort enter the discussion. If an outsider is interested in selling armaments, destroying a government, diverting a particular economic policy, or anything of this sort, then a "border incident" gives him an opportunity to pose as a defender of his "friends'" country. And so we could easily drift into a position where different African countries are armed by different world powers, and are fighting on African soil the conflicts of those world powers—at the cost of African blood and African sacrifice.

For this reason alone unity is essential. The borders which now separate us must become the lines which link one part of Africa to another. They can then resume their proper importance as administrative conveniences hallowed only by custom, and left as they are simply because there are more urgent things to do than re-draw them.

THE FREEDOM OF AFRICA

Then there is the question of freedom, of defence against outside aggression—however unlikely this now appears. The fight for freedom in Africa really got under way after the end of the world war in 1945. It is still going on, and it will continue until the whole of Africa is free. As long as there remain colonies in Africa, and as long as racial oppression continues there, our freedom struggle must be maintained. Freedom for Angola and Mozambique, for Spanish Guinea, and for South Africa is not a matter for the people of those countries alone; the struggle there is part of the same fight which has been waged in countries now free. The freedom of Africa is indivisible. How can one man claim to be free while his brother is in bondage? But unity is needed to deal with this question of liberation.

And even when all Africa is free from alien rule, how will we defend our freedom if we remain separate nation states, pursuing separate foreign and defence policies, perhaps providing bases for different outside powers, or depending on them to equip our military forces? As separate nations, we have no alternative but to build separate armies, obtaining our munitions from the sources available to us. Yet none of us can really afford to spend money on these things, so we find that one small nation gets military assistance from one powerful country while its neighbour receives counter military assistance from the enemy of that powerful nation. How long shall we be able to live in peace on that basis?

The way to avoid this danger does not lie in having an inter-African

Armaments Convention; armaments are a symptom, not a disease. The reason that there are no wars between one section of Tanganyika and another is not an absence of weapons; it is the existence of one government over the whole area. Similarly, the only way in which disputes can be prevented from becoming inter-African wars is by having one government over the whole of Africa.

ECONOMIC NECESSITY FOR UNITY

Quite apart from these political questions, the economic arguments for unity are overwhelming. It is not accident that causes the United States of America to be so rich and powerful while Latin America remains listed among the underdeveloped parts of the world, or while Europe lags behind. The U.S.A. is a single economic market of 180 million people, incorporating many natural resources and wide variations of climate and soil. Modern technology can be used there to the fullest; the movement of its products is not inhibited by tariffs and customs barriers. But we in Africa have independent nations of less than half a million people; "countries" which are about 30 miles across. And when goods move from one part to another, they pay tax, or wait for hours while border formalities are completed.

This is nonsense. We complicate the daily lives of the people who live near one of these "borders," we make development more difficult than it already is, and we rule out economic means of producing the goods we need because our market is too small to make the capital investment worth while. As long as we remain so separate, we shall remain poor. Our individual development plans will make an improvement upon the recent position, but they will never lead to Africa's assuming its rightful place in the world as a prosperous economic unit. For this, we must have an African Development Plan, and that requires unity. No plan can ever be drawn up properly or administered, while unanimous agreement of more than thirty separate authorities is required. There must be one authority—an authority which is responsible to all Africa.

WHAT A UNITED AFRICA MUST BE ABLE TO DO

I have spent some time discussing the reasons for African Unity because they must affect the form a United Africa will take and the steps which will be necessary to achieve it.

The Government of a United Africa must be able to do three things. It must be able to speak for the whole of Africa to the outside world; it must be able to defend Africa against any attack or subversion from the outside world; and it must be able to plan and co-ordinate the development of Africa as a whole so as to ensure the well-being of every part of the continent.

In order to do these three things there must be one authority in the continent which has exclusive powers over foreign affairs, defence, currency and external trade relations. It must be able to control inter-African trade, and secure internal peace for the continent. And it must also have considerable powers as regards economic development and be able to work towards ensuring the social and economic, as well as the political, equality of all the peoples of Africa.

THE PROBLEMS TO BE OVERCOME

Within this broad framework the details of the institutions established and the detailed division of powers between the States and the Centre, are matters which can be worked out, discussed and compromised on. The important thing is that the African Government should have powers to deal with the major problems which require it to be established.

For there will have to be discussions and compromise. The unity of Africa is not going to come as a result of an intervention from heaven saying, "Let there be unity." The moment sovereign states with representative governments exist, then unity becomes difficult to organize. This is not because of the personal vested interests of the different leaders of Africa. Talk about "stooges" or "power-hunger" on the part of leaders is much too easy. There are, of course, some personality problems in any conference which has a purpose; there are always people who fear a change because it might have an adverse effect on their own status. But in Africa, these are very minor issues; they could complicate the working out of united institutions, and they might even be able to delay unity for a short while. But they could certainly not stop the movement; the problems are more difficult than that.

The real problem is that each of the separate nations has the fear that in a United Africa, it might become a backward and neglected area, exploited for the benefit of another part of this great continent.

This is not a stupid objection, nor a selfish one. Even in the United States of America, there have been areas which have remained poor and undeveloped despite the general prosperity, and it is the duty of the elected leaders of each part of Africa to look after the interests of the people they represent. Of course, it is possible to answer that even the poorest part of the U.S.A. is infinitely richer than the richest part of Africa; but this theoretical answer is not enough by itself. The leaders of every present-day sovereign state have to think of the short-term advantages which might accrue to the people of their area by remaining separate, as well as the long-term advantages of unity. It is not an easy question to deal with at all, and any discussions about achieving unity have to take this problem into account.

And finally, there is the sheer problem of time and opportunity. Every national leader in Africa has enormous problems to face within his own country. Every day he must make decisions on matters affecting the welfare of the people who elected him—and in doing so, he is often making decisions which affect the rest of Africa too. But he cannot long delay the development of his own country in the hope that African Unity will make it possible for African needs to be looked at as a whole. He has immediate responsibilities and, in fact, the pressure of work for the nation makes it difficult for anyone really to devote enough time to working out long-term projects for Africa as a whole.

THE STEPS TOWARDS UNITY

These are the real problems which have to be overcome before there can be African Unity. They will take energy, enthusiasm and patience on the part of all concerned. Because once the decision is made and unity effected, there can be no reconsideration of it. Real African Unity involves the surrender of sovereignty by the separate States to the African Authority.

When we built our nationalist organizations, and when we began to operate the fight against poverty on a national basis, so at the same time we built up a pattern of loyalty to our respective nations. The establishment of African Unity means transferring that loyalty to Africa, just as we transferred tribal loyalty to national. And every day that passes makes this more difficult. Our people know their own leaders, and trust them; in a United Africa, they will have to accept that their particular leaders are not any longer the ultimate authority, and will have to get to know other people—of whom perhaps they have only vaguely heard, or read about in unsympathetic newspapers.

There are already 35 separate independent States in Africa. Is it likely that every one of these States will be ready at the same time to make this surrender of power to another Authority? For there can be no question of forcing any particular area to come under a United African government. Its problems are going to be great enough without having an area of internal disaffection to cope with, and the Central African Federation is a very recent lesson (if we needed it) that only unity based on the will of the people can last.

Leaving questions of unity to be taken all at one step means waiting until everyone is ready to make all the surrender of powers which is necessary. This might take a long time. But unless we begin to move towards unity now, we shall find that the separate development which each country has to undertake in the meantime will make the ultimate step more difficult.

Therefore, although there are good theoretical arguments for having one all-African Conference and achieving unity all at once, practical questions make this only a dream. It is a pity, but it is a fact. The important thing is getting unity; how we get it is a secondary matter and depends on the facts of the situation. And the facts of Africa are that we have 35 separate independent States—with more to come—each of which has its own peculiar constitutional and economic difficulties. For some the need for economic cooperation with others is obvious, and clearly advantageous immediately; for others, fear of losing an important export market or having infant industries overwhelmed causes hesitation over proposals for economic union with neighbouring African States. Similarly, in some cases political identification with the rest of Africa is easy; in other cases it is for historical reasons more difficult to achieve quickly.

These facts mean that our way to unity is most likely to require a step by step advance from our present separateness. In some fields, joint consultation between African states is all that can be achieved; in others, joint action may be possible. But whatever can be done to reduce our isolation one from another is a contribution towards the total goal.

There is one way in which we can move forward; until we have unity, we should try to act as if we had it, because that will bring it nearer. By this, I mean that even while joint action can be vetoed by any one State, each State should try to avoid exercising that veto; on each occasion that it disagrees with the majority it should weigh very carefully the comparative disadvantages of breaking our united front and appearing to support policies of which it really disapproves. Similarly, it is necessary for us to remember always that when African nations quarrel, unity is put in jeopardy—and it takes two to make a quarrel! One of the most difficult things to do is not to answer a verbal attack upon your own policies or upon a favourite project, yet the self-discipline of saying nothing in cases of provocation can frequently do more to serve the real cause of unity than a dozen speeches of brotherly love!

I do not wish to be understood as advocating a "gradual policy" towards unity. I am advocating that we should take whatever steps are open to us at a particular time. There will be occasions when an All-Africa advance is possible; we should seize such opportunities with both hands. It is for this reason that the Addis Ababa Conference was so important. It did not establish unity; sovereignty was not surrendered by anyone; but it did state quite clearly the African objective, and it established All-African machinery for cooperation and for the settlement of disputes between African nations. It also laid down the principles which should be observed by all States in their relations with each other and the outside world. It dug the foundations for the edifice of a United Africa, and it dug them deep.

PROBLEMS OF REGIONAL GROUPINGS

This, however, was only the first step, and it does not preclude others, nor require that they shall all wait until the next meeting of Heads of State. What the Organization of African Unity does demand is that every other step towards inter-African cooperation should be consistent with over-all unity. It therefore called for a very severe examination of the regional groupings which had begun to grow up, so as to ensure that they did not become exclusive cliques which could stand in the way of total unity.

This requirement has to be looked at very carefully. I do not myself believe that the Charter means that no two or more States can get together to plan a joint economic venture across their boundaries; nor does it preclude consultation over problems which are common to some states but not to all. What it does demand is that there should be no exclusiveness about such consultations or joint arrangements, and that none of them should enter into undertakings liable to harm other African States.

The Addis Ababa Charter does not preclude the formation of new Federations within Africa. In fact, of course, establishing a Federation is a very different thing from entering into a new grouping or alliance. A new Federation formed out of separate sovereign states means that one state exists where before there was more than one.

The essential difference is that sovereignty is surrendered by nation states which enter a Federation; the sovereignty is transferred to the Federation. The new State—the Federation—then replaces all its constituent parts in the Organization of African Unity, in the United Nations and elsewhere. A new Federation is in the same position as Federations—like Nigeria—which were formed before independence. Its representative is able to take decisions for the whole area, because there is one authority for the whole area.

There is no inconsistency between working for a Federation of a small number of States, and working also for total African Unity. On the contrary, if a Federation can be formed successfully, it will demonstrate that the greatest difficulties facing the formation of an All-African government can be overcome. For the problems are essentially the same; both demand the surrender of sovereignty, both demand arrangements which ensure the development of the poorer areas as well as the continued expansion of existing economic centres. The only way in which a new Federation could be an obstacle to total Unity is if it is not a Federation at all but simply a regional grouping called by that name. Provided the new Federation is "real"—in other words, provided the transfer of sovereignty is effected—it can only contribute to the final objective.

These considerations apply to a Federation anywhere in Africa. But historical factors probably make a Federation in East Africa the easiest to achieve. . . .

IN CONTEXT OF AFRICAN UNITY

These are the reasons why we in East Africa are working for a Federation without waiting until it is possible to begin consideration of the problems of a Federation of all Africa. But, I repeat, these two things are not incompatible. It may be indeed that this is the way in which Africa will progress to total unity. Not through the continual expansion of an East African Federation until it absorbs all other countries; we have no ambition to create an octopus which gathers all others to itself, nor do we claim that an East African Federation would be a nucleus of an African Federation. We do not want to be exclusive, but neither do we want to drag other countries unwillingly into our new State.

No, I am merely suggesting that it is possible that the large number of small nation states which now exist will form themselves into a smaller number of Federations, and that the Heads of these Federations will be the ones who take the final step of creating an all-African Sovereign State. It might be easier this way; small committees and conferences often make more progress than large gatherings in dealing with thorny problems and coming to a decision.

But this is conjecture. In throwing out this suggestion, I am not advocating particular policies nor really making prophesies based on the realities of African politics. In fact, it is more likely that different parts of the continent will take different steps towards unity, and at different times. And it does not matter. The only important thing is that the ultimate goal shall always be kept clearly in sight, and that our attitude to each other should always be one of understanding and sympathy. Any means of reducing the present disunity of Africa which does not end in an insurmountable obstacle to total unity should receive the support of the rest of Africa. . . .

UNITY—"THE WHITE TRIBE"?

A certain African public figure once delighted in calling the European settlers in Kenya "that white tribe." The jibe has a point. If one ignores the connection of the white minority with the imperial power, it becomes merely another distinctive sociocultural group—another tribe among many—although admittedly one with peculiarly unfortunate antecedents and pigmentation.

Viewed in this light, the issue of white versus black in

Africa becomes merely a special case of the general clash between "tribalism" and nationalism. The position of the settler community resembles that of the Ganda or other African tribe rather thoroughly committed to the idea of political separateness. If this were the whole sum of the matter, the question of the white man in Africa would be one just of separatism versus unity.

But it is not the whole sum of the matter. The problem is complicated by differences in race, by the settlers' connection with imperialism, and by the fact that the white communities are the bearers to Africa of things modern. As one commentator put this last point: "The settler's case thus must ultimately rest on his functions"—what he contributes to the evolving communities and states of Africa.

It is this last argument upon which Michael Blundell, a moderate white leader in Kenya, bases his case for multiracialism and the political devices which, in his view, are necessary to make it possible (Selection 16). A moderate African nationalist, Ndabaningi Sithole, in Selection 17 aims some sharp shafts at the doctrine and the political devices. He sees them as hypocritical, and shows by implication how race and the background of imperialism affect multiracialist aspirations. In Selection 18 B. T. G. Chidzero, a prominent African political scientist, suggests the difficulties of multiracialism as a political policy for either black or white leaders. Selection 19 offers the African extremist at white heat—contrast this with Selection 5 to understand better why neither black nor white leaders find moderation and multiracialism a very easy policy to advocate.

If multiracialism is a sham and/or a political delusion, what then is to be the fate of the "white tribe"? This is a question of some importance in African international relations, being particularly pertinent to the white-dominated southern portions of the continent. Selection 19 is, for example, not only radically racialist in orientation, but also reflects the sense of increasing power to deal with southern Africa which the spread of independence has given Africans. We can predict that, to the extent Africans express this sentiment by bringing power to bear on southern Africa, we will find ourselves living with yet another highly active international issue.

Selection 16

Making a Nation in Kenya*

MICHAEL BLUNDELL

Michael Blundell is a farmer and politician in Kenya, and has played a leading role in efforts to create political cooperation among races in that country.

The address that follows was given by the Hon. Michael Blundell M.L.C., former Minister of Agriculture, Kenya, at a joint meeting of the Royal African Society and the Royal Commonwealth Society on May 7, 1959. Mr. Brian Macdona, Vice-Chairman of the Council of the Royal African Society, took the chair.

Many years ago the leaders of political thought in Kenya, indeed almost the only producers of any constructive political thought at all, were the European settlers led by Lord Delamere. Their political objectives were simple and in terms of those days realistic. Nothing less than the creation of a self-governing white Dominion within the Com-

* Reprinted by courtesy of The Royal African Society from *African Affairs* (July 1959), pp. 221–225.

monwealth. Indeed I remember early in 1955 being bitterly attacked by an older colleague of mine in the Legislative Council for the concept of multi-racialism for which I was fighting on the grounds that I had destroyed everything for which he had worked throughout his life. I asked him what were his ambitions and he answered simply "A White Dominion of East Africa." Looking at the Continent of Africa today, observing the emergency of States such as Ghana and Nigeria and measuring the powerful waves of human emotion piling up against the embankments of Colonialism, how unrealistic such a remark seems. Yet such an intent gave to the country of Kenya a continuing and long term policy which achieved stability of purpose and a sense of service which overcame the dictates of race. The early settlers, strongly imbued with the political philosophy of Conservatism, believed in the happiness of the people and consistently presented policies which in their view were in the best interest of all and not solely of a minority section. Recently we have been adrift, mainly because that clear and simple image of the country which it was sought to build has been lost, blurred by the emotions of colour and race sweeping the world since the war and the strident and contending voices of rival racialisms. . . .

. . . we have the distinction of representing within our small boundaries most of the peoples of the Commonwealth—European, Indian, Muslim and African. I believe we (the leaders of all communities) would be wise in Kenya to keep this image of our future clearly in mind and in building our political and human structures to take no step which will distort it. If we would do so, much antagonism and fear would depart. Africa today is a Continent in a hurry and measured in terms of human needs and happiness we can't afford to hurry—there is still so much to build from the human material which is still so ignorant and immature. Yet I believe the general acceptance of the intention to build a self-governing country within the Commonwealth might well help us in reducing the urge of speed and remove the fear of being left behind in comparison with neighbouring territories which acts as a spur to racial emotions and ambitions. Stated in the simplest terms—what is the alternative? There is none—we can't put a stop to the increasing maturity of our country; we can't stand still, and above all we can't avoid each other. Such a decision would clearly indicate the steps that we should take to achieve our objective. First the continuing control of Her Majesty's Government in regard to our affairs needs examination in regard to its purpose. Too many people regard it as a protective device which will insulate them from unpleasant decisions; for instance for the Africans that their hope of advance lies in the economy and financial stability which European, Indian and Muslim energies bring. For the other races the fact that our self-governing country will largely consist of Africans. Far from pure protection we need the colonial system primarily for three things. One the building up of an economy which will enable us eventually to provide most of the services and administrative machinery of a modern State. Secondly, the creation of a local Civil Service which will give us stability within that administrative machinery, and lastly, the evolution of a system of government which will enable us to take the necessary steps to independence. I don't intend to say much about the building up of an economy which will stand the test of time. To us it seems so obvious, to the African racialist it is just another device by the European to prevent him seizing the levers of power. At least we should do our utmost to see that it—the economy—is spread as far as possible across the racial field and not concentrated in single racial columns. Again I am convinced that the more the emerging African leader can see it working in local government and central government so that he is made to realise the vital part which finance plays in any decisions the better. I do wonder whether we might not be wise to bring African leaders in contact more with business men and financiers both in Kenya and Great Britain with a view to explaining to them the basis upon which investment is made and the estimates on stability in any country which influence investment. So many things which we take for granted (or which we have learnt by bitter experience) in the financial field are dismissed by the African as so much hoodlum to prevent him entering into his real estate. . . .

The group which I have the honour to represent believes in the evolution of a parliamentary system suitable to the needs of Kenya. There are today two schools of thought in regard to these matters. Those who advocate undiluted democracy and those who dismiss democracy as undesirable for Africa anyway. In Kenya we must never forget however much it may displease the liberal economist that a small minority of people from the European, Indian, Muslim and Arab communities generate by their enterprise and energy the economy upon which the hope of advance of 5½ million Africans rests. Not only that, but these efforts by minorities have raised the whole field of endeavour before the eyes of the African population from the limited horizon of an obscure and undeveloped tropical country poor in natural resources to the fair prospect of a modern State, the centre and hub of the activity of a region the size of Western Europe. A government based on undiluted democracy in its fullest sense must mean today and for many years to come the complete elimination from political influence of the elements of society in our country which generate the wealth upon which our advance depends. In our immaturity today, such a development would be most dangerous. To some African leaders, democracy is a cry particularly attractive to political thought in Western Europe, a cry which is designed not to the orderly development of the idea of contrasting governments based on the changing opinions of the people but to the grasping of power with little intention of relinquishing it later.

I have been disturbed by the constant reiteration of such phrases as "the paramountcy of the will of the majority" in a purely racial sense by some of our African leaders. This seems to deny completely the whole essence of a true parliamentary system—respect for the views and rights of the minority of the moment in the knowledge that it may well become the majority of tomorrow. At the present moment among our African people the gap between the few educated leaders and the ordinary mass of the people, in training, education and experience, is so wide that one of the essential features of a democratic system is lacking. I refer to sustained, informed and responsible criticism upon which alternative views can be built and upon which democratic leaders can be made sensitive to the movement of public opinion. In other words, our educational field is still so largely untouched that the few who have had the benefits of it are regarded as oracles of wisdom, and until that field can be immensely extended, I do not think that it is wise or possible for us to embark in the condition of our country upon universal franchise.

I have referred earlier to those people who feel that democracy is not suited to the problems of our Continent. As I have indicated, it is often regarded merely as a vehicle for power and both in Ghana and in the Sudan we have seen total or partial withdrawals from the full implementation of the parliamentary system as we know it in the United

Kingdom. . . . In so far as the progress of Kenya is concerned, I believe that much of the thinking in regard to the unsuitability of a parliamentary system in Africa is largely academic, because it is difficult—indeed, almost impossible—for the people of Great Britain, who accept the ultimate responsibility for our country, to transplant anything else.

As a Group, we feel that further extension of the franchise based on racial electorates should be avoided. Indeed, we feel they are unwise, because they crystallize and underline the differences of race between us. . . . We feel that we want to build an electoral system in which common interests and the acceptance of common responsibilities predominate over the individual interests of race. Any such system must allow for the further development of our country, which will take place as the years go by.

Secondly, it must take into consideration the increasing education of the African people generally in the future and, above all, it must eventually reflect the increasing number of responsible Africans who, by reason of that development and education, are capable of taking part in the full affairs of our country.

I must issue a warning that anything that is designed to shut out the African people from their reasonable expectations of taking a fuller responsibility in our affairs as the country expands and develops must be doomed to failure.

Some time within the next year, we shall be meeting in a conference convened by the Secretary of State to seek a solution to some of our constitutional difficulties. I believe that it would be unwise today to outline in detail the lines upon which we think that Conference might proceed. I would merely like to say that too often discussions in Kenya on constitutional matters develop into racial tugs of war with no clear picture on either side of what we are trying to do. I think it would be wise for all parties to enter these discussions with the firm intention of moving on the lines of a parliamentary system which is suitable to the needs and conditions of our country. It should neither attempt to exclude the views of the great mass of our people, the African, nor should it attempt to eliminate the proper expectations of the minorities, upon whom so much depends, that their views will be respected. It should, however, set us quite firmly upon the path towards creating a self-governing country within the Commonwealth. If this is done, we have a reasonable chance of success. . . .

Selection 17

The Majority Mind of Europeans*

Ndabaningi Sithole

Ndabaningi Sithole is an ordained minister and a prominent African nationalist leader in Rhodesia.

. . . An examination of the various political doctrines prevalent in Africa will show clearly how the European mind works in relation to the African people. In British East Africa, for instance, a new type of government policy is being hammered out, and this is the so-called multiracialism. The avowed intention of this policy is that all races in a multiracial society shall participate fully in the central government of the country. In other words, multiracialism is an effort to do away with the already unacceptable exclusive European policy, and an effort to bring about an inclusive policy. The argument against an exclusively white government and in favour of an inclusive policy is that a multiracial society should be reflected in the multiracial composition of the government. This is to say that only a multiracial government can truly reflect a healthy multiracial society. In accordance with this doctrine, therefore, the principle of direct racial representation has been fully accepted and implemented. Although this policy has its glaring shortcomings it is definitely an advance on the previous policy which excluded the African from any participation in the government of the country.

On the other hand, however, a closer examination of this policy reveals that politics in multiracial British East Africa run on racial tracks, and that its real intention is to bypass adult universal suffrage in the sole interest of white supremacy. In Kenya, for example, in the Legislative Council, there are 14 Europeans, 14 Africans, 6 Asians

---

* Reprinted by permission from *African Nationalism* by Ndabaningi Sithole (Cape Town: Oxford University Press, 1959), pp. 123–126.

and 1 Arab who make up the unofficial members. The gist of this multiracial set-up is that the number of non-white members shall not exceed that of the whites. Out of 32 official members there is provision for only 2 African members, so that in the entire Legislative Council of 67 members (32 official and 35 unofficial members) there are only 14 Africans who represent 5,000,000 Africans whereas the non-African members represent less than a quarter of a million non-Africans (whites and Asiatics). Tanganyika, which has a 10-10-10 parity (whites, Africans and Asiatics), shows the same political trend, i.e. 10 Africans represent 7,000,000 Africans whereas the rest represent less than a quarter of a million people. Multiracialism accords to all races a say in the government of the country but it also clearly shows serious defects as a permanent solution to the present problems.*

While multiracialism allows group participation, and recognizes group rights, it denies individual citizenship rights. Multiracialism as practised in British East Africa means that other races are allowed to participate in governmental affairs so long as they are satisfied with a secondary place in the whole scheme, while the first place is reserved for whites only. In the final analysis multiracialism as an instrument of government is a subtle entrenchment of white supremacy, a domination of one race by another, a rule by minority and not by majority, and a refusal to create a common electorate. This is the fatal weakness of multiracialism. It is a political solution based on the principle of ignoring the legitimate claims of the majority of the people in favour of those of a minority.

The Kenya settlers put it more openly when they said:

"We are opposed to any scheme of provincial independence which might go so far as to deprive Europeans of leadership and control of the colony as a whole."[1]

At the bottom of multiracialism we see European autocracy at work, and it is this that often puzzles the African when he is called upon to distinguish between Russian communists and European powers in Africa. These two seem to be blood-brothers. They are both for ever seeking domination of other people. With both of them

---

* *Editor's Note:* Details given for Kenya, Tanganyika, and Federation of Rhodesia and Nyasaland are out of date and should be regarded as illustrative only.

[1] *Africa South*, vol. 1, no. 3, April-June 1957, p. 73.

the will of the majority does not count, but only that of a minority. To refuse adult universal franchise is to refuse the granting of some of the basic human rights to the majority of the people. The triumph of multiracialism, therefore, if it remained as it is at present, would be the triumph of white supremacy and the perpetuation of African subjection.

In the Federation of Rhodesia and Nyasaland we find another policy by a different name, but fundamentally the same as multiracialism. This is the policy of partnership. The principle of direct African representation has been accepted and implemented. According to the federal constitution of Rhodesia and Nyasaland only twelve Africans represent 6,500,000 Africans and the rest (except for three Europeans specially elected to represent African interests) represent less than 300,000 whites.

When the Federation was pressed to define the meaning of partnership, the white politicians found it expedient to do this in terms of senior and junior partners—the former being whites, and the latter, of course, Africans. But when more political pressure was exerted, the government came out with a bolder statement that "the government must remain in the hands of civilized and responsible people." This was as good as saying that, at least for the present, "racial equality will bring about black domination over whites, and this must be resisted." Such a construction is justified by the fact that this standard of civilization and responsibility can only be determined by the white man himself who is unwilling to abdicate power over Africa. It is clear then that even in the Federation of Rhodesia and Nyasaland, whose policy is midway between the apartheid policy of the Union of South Africa and that of adult universal franchise, we find entrenched deeply the desire to maintain white ascendancy over the black man.

It was Cecil John Rhodes who coined the dictum, "Equal rights for all civilized men" in reference to British-occupied Africa. This dictum, as it did not promise to give these rights immediately to the African, was easily accepted by Europeans because at that time there was hardly any African who possessed sufficient externals of Western civilization. But today the situation is different, and the white man, in view of the present large number of "civilized" Africans, is confronted with redeeming or dishonouring his promise. The idea of equal citizenship with the African is to him abhorrent. And so the European finds himself engaging in a faith-shaking occupation of manufacturing countless ingenious definitions of "civilized" so that he can exclude, with a semblance of legality, most eligible Africans from qualifying as registered voters. The political battle raging in British East Africa and the Federation of Rhodesia and Nyasaland is one of forestalling the creation of adult universal franchise in favour of racial group participation. Bluntly stated, the white man insists on being the first citizen of Africa. The African also wants to be one, and anything less than this is unacceptable since it involves being discriminated against. "Racial discrimination," to borrow the Rev. George Gay's words, "has no meaning apart from degradation." It is this European-inflicted stigma which the African now seeks to remove. While the African accepts multiracialism or partnership, he views this as an interim measure because both policies have a tendency to perpetuate this European-inflicted stigma which has subjected the African to the ridicule of the rest of mankind. . . .

Selection 18

African Leaders and Parties*

B. T. G. Chidzero

A political scientist well known for his writings on African politics and government, Mr. Chidzero is a Southern Rhodesian at present working with the United Nations Economic Commission for Africa in Addis Ababa.

In all this, there remains one vital consideration, namely, that in multi-racial societies, because of the strong position of the European community in particular and (where these exist, as in the Rhodesias)

---

* Reprinted by permission from "African Nationalism in East and Central Africa" by B. T. G. Chidzero, *International Affairs*, Vol. 36, No. 4 (October 1960), pp. 474–475. This reprint comprises only the latter part of the article.

the predominantly European electorates, political moderation is difficult. The only African leader who can impress his followers and arouse the masses is he who bids highest, and the leader who collaborates with Europeans, because he is dependent on the European voter, soon loses. It is only where the substance of power is in the hands of the African, or where an African leader can appeal to an African electorate, as in Tanganyika, that some co-operation between races becomes possible and constructive. Equally, political parties tend to be exclusively European or African, and the latter to be revolutionary. The nationalist party has in most cases no electorate except the disenfranchised masses, and it could not be otherwise than revolutionary. On the other hand, the minority communities tend to regard nationalist leaders and parties as political vermin, thus rendering moderation even more difficult. A further difficulty is that in the multi-racial societies African leadership is often divided and forced to waste its energies in impotent multi-racial associations. Where, of course, you have a Mboya or a Dr Banda or a Julius Nyerere or a Kenneth Kaunda, the situation takes on a different complexion. Leadership becomes more or less polarized, recognizable, and effective; strong nationalist parties emerge, and there is a distinct force to reckon with. But, equally, the success of such parties sounds the death-knell for European-controlled parties. These multi-racial parties, such as the Central Africa Party in the Rhodesias, or the now dead United Tanganyika Party, or the beleaguered New Kenya Party led by Mr Blundell, all sooner or later cease to hold much influence over the Africans. They fail to meet the African case.

Until and unless there are large mixed electorates, it is difficult to see any future for multi-racial parties. But it is equally difficult to see any future for multi-racial parties once the electorates are predominantly African. It is to be hoped, however, that it will be the individual and not his racial origin that will matter, so that Governments controlled by African parties may be expected to rule in the national interest and to safeguard individual rights.

The subject of African nationalism is necessarily a difficult one to handle, particularly in such wide and differing societies. But it can be said with fairness that the essence of African nationalism lies in its egalitarian and democratic aspirations. Whether in fact, however, triumphant African nationalism will serve the cause of individual freedom and protect democratic institutions is anybody's guess. But it does appear that for a long time to come democracy will be subjected to rigorous forces in Africa as elsewhere, and that there is much to suggest the emergence of centralized and authoritarian regimes. It seems also fair to say that while there is not in African nationalism any real racial bitterness, the intransigence of the minority communities could easily turn it into racialism. For Britain and the world at large, the time has probably come when the choice must be clearly made between propping up European-controlled Governments in the multiracial societies and so running the risk of wholly alienating Africans and forfeiting their good will and co-operation, or moving expeditiously to support the emergence of majority rule and so to influence the new African Governments to deal fairly with the minorities. Quite clearly this is a matter of crucial importance in the problem of the world balance of power, and particularly in the struggle between the West and the Soviet bloc. Africa can be won for the West, but it will be necessary for a just price to be paid. This may sound like so much blackmail, but it is more probably a hard, realistic, and constructive appraisal of the situation, the only constructive solution of the dilemma, and the only way to render the minorities acceptable to the African majorities.

Selection 19

The Right and Might in the Liberatory Struggle*

ANGRY PAN-AFRICANIST

For fourteen years India had been seeking a peaceful solution over Goa, but as usual the Portuguese imperialists refused to negotiate. Finally India made up her mind to exercise force, being the only lan-

* Reprinted by permission from *Voice of Africa*, Vol. 2, No. 2 (February 1962), pp. 32–33.

guage that imperialists can understand. In less than thirty-six hours India liberated Goa from the decayed yoke of colonialism and imperialism. For that brave action we in Africa and other countries (who sympathise with Africa's struggle for freedom) sincerely congratulate Prime Minister Nehru and the entire Indian people.

AFRICA'S HIGH COMMAND

Goa should be a typical example, sufficient enough to justify the need for the African High Command which Osagyefo the President Dr Kwame Nkrumah and other Heads of Casablanca States have been trying to achieve.

The colonial powers want to consolidate their imperialist and colonialist positions for their common objective of spreading neo-colonialism, pressing the cause of imperialism and of the merciless exploitation of the entire African people. Their chief aim is to degrade African dignity in Africa and in the outside world to keep Africa in ignorance, and to reserve poverty for the African people so that they may remain in hunger, disease, and perpetual slavery.

THE BIG GIANT

Is the big giant fully awake? Has he really broken the chains of slavery and set himself free from the yoke of colonialism and imperialism? If not when is he to awake? And how are we to unchain him?

Africa's Giant is awake. It only remains for him to unchain himself from the political servitude of the colonialists. *That can only be* achieved *if all the Independent African States unite for the liberation of the oppressed African States.*

One united Africa is essential to the maintenance and consolidation of freedom and independence. It is the only means of enabling us to make good use of our land together with its mineral wealth and human labour which are for the time being, greedily exploited by the imperialists. A united Africa can within a short time abolish colonialism and imperialism and establish a very highly civilized society.

HOW CAN UNITY BE ACHIEVED?

It will be noted that all the colonial powers namely Britain, France, Belgium, Portugal and Spain have fully approved and appreciated the dreadful actions of one another and also impuniously determined to massacre, torture and enslave the entire African people. Yet some Independent African States flatly ignore the necessity for joining the African High Command.

Simultaneously, they underestimate the immediate effect it will produce towards the total liberation of the African people. Wherever the colonialists have to satisfy their insatiable greed no sacrifice is too great.

Only force liberated Goa, and the threat of force liberated New Guinea. Only force will liberate Angola, Katanga, Algeria, South Africa and all places that are now dominated by the colonialists and the puppets.

How and when will the French colonialists say peacefully and friendly say to Algerian people: "You are now independent. We are leaving your wealth in the Sahara, because we believe we have sufficient. Thank you very much. Good-bye."?

When and how will the Portuguese colonialists vacate the rich lands of Angola for the Angolans or the British colonalists Zambia (N. Rhodesia) for and Zimbabwe (S. Rhodesia) for the Zambians and Zimbabwans? In all these places they came by force and stay by force and only force will push them out.

In Angola, South Africa, Mozambique and Rhodesia where the Africans are kept most backward in every respect, the imperialists went further. They illegally legalised their illegal occupation of these states and unashamedly claimed these areas as their own.

Shame! How can you expect such shameless bloodthirsty vampires to quit peacefully? Beside the countries they have been grabbing, the imperialists have struck yet another blow in a desperate attempt to snatch Katanga from Congo in order to debar the Africans from enjoying the wealth of their own country. What a shameless monopoly!

LACKEY TSHOMBE THE SHAMELESS

. . . Tshombe the shameless, Tshombe the quisling, Tshombe the stooge, Tshombe the number one enemy of the African people has agreed to the colonialists to murder his fellow Africans. Tshombe has agreed with the colonialists in their attempts to undermine the Congo's independence and her territorial integrity.

Tshombe invites the white Boers from South Africa and all other white colonialists to join his treacherous army to exterminate the African people.

Tshombe obeyed the orders of his Belgian masters to murder the legally elected first Prime Minister of the Congo, the martyred Patrice Lumumba of saintly memory. If left unchecked Tshombe will negotiate with colonialists to merge Katanga with the "Federation." . . .

Let Tshombe and his associates stop deceiving themselves. They should know by now that colonialists came to Africa not to help the Africans but to exploit them.

The Katanga war is not between the United Nations and the Africans. It is United Nations versus the white mercenaries who were imported to volunteer for the cause of taking away the rich province of Katanga for the imperialists and colonialists. All colonialist powers supply arms for this perfidious deed . . .

The Western colonialists have their NATO, their European Command Market and many similar organs. The socialist countries have their WARSAW pact. We do not see why in Africa we should not have our own African High Command!

Colonialists and imperialists came to Africa by force and maintain themselves by force and only force will push them out. Only the African High Command will effectively counter the fresh colonialist aggression in Africa.

PROGRESS TOWARD UNITY

What headway, if any, is being made toward African unity? Is it mere aspiration, or is it becoming reality? The following chart (page 134) is designed not only to supply data on membership of various groupings of African nations, but also to show trends in the relationships among African nations.

As independence spread in Africa, the independent states met at Accra (1958) and Addis Ababa (1960). A breakdown in relations then led to subcontinental regroupings (for example, the "Casablanca," "Monrovia," and similar groupings shown in the chart). When the *Organization of African Unity* (OAU) was established, however, these major groups dissolved themselves. Shading on the chart indicates this; unshaded groupings still exist. For example, the main "Brazzaville" grouping, the *Afro-Malagasy Union* (UAM), was dissolved, but the association with the *European Economic Community* (EEC), and the economic counterpart, the *Afro-Malagasy Organization for Economic Cooperation* (OAMCE), remain.

Patterns of participation appear in greater detail under the "Miscellaneous" heading in the chart. (For the *All-African Trade Union Federation* [AATUF] and the *African Trade Union Confederation* [ATUC] see also Selections 31, 32, and 33.) The columns on the right, dealing with the *Commission for Technical Cooperation in Africa* (CCTA), and the *United Nations Economic Commission for Africa* (UNECA), demonstrate the changing situation of the European powers and the relations of the United Nations with Pan-Africanism. The CCTA, founded by the colonial powers to cover sub-Saharan Africa only, still has European membership, but none from North Africa. If it should become an arm of the OAU, as now suggested in Africa, its metamorphosis would presumably be completed. Beginning in 1964, the European members of UNECA were dropped from full participation.

Some brief notes will clarify the chart. The Algerian Provisional (insurgent) Government has been shown as independent since 1960, although in fact independence came in 1962. Trade unions, not governments, are members of AATUF and ATUC, although in Africa the association is usually close. The chart is designed to show Libya, Sudan, and Tunisia in an intermediate position between the strongly Arab "Casablanca" group and the greater, sub-Saharan mass of the "Monrovia" grouping.

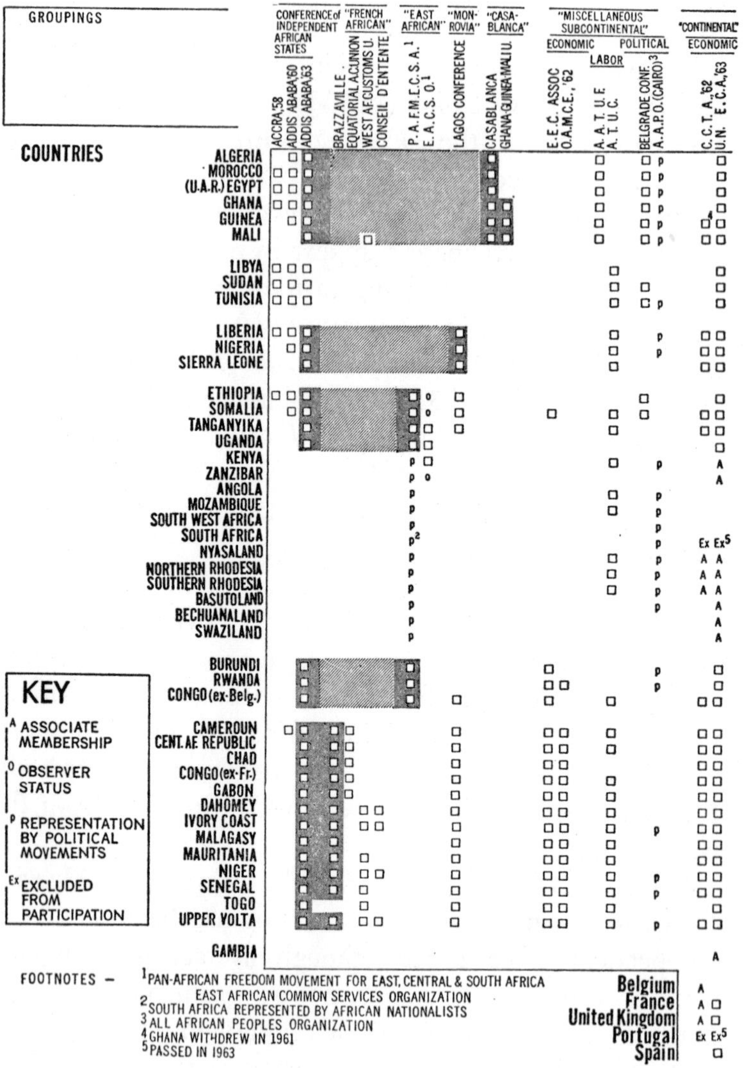

GROUPINGS	CONFERENCE of INDEPENDENT AFRICAN STATES			"FRENCH AFRICAN"				"EAST AFRICAN"		"MONROVIA"	"CASABLANCA"		"MISCELLANEOUS SUBCONTINENTAL" ECONOMIC		LABOR		POLITICAL		"CONTINENTAL" ECONOMIC	
COUNTRIES	ACCRA,'58	ADDIS ABABA,'60	ADDIS ABABA,'63	BRAZZAVILLE	EQUATORIAL AF.CUNION	WEST AF.CUSTOMS U.	CONSEIL D'ENTENTE	P. A. F. M. E. C. S. A.[1]	E. A. C. S. O.[1]	LAGOS CONFERENCE	CASABLANCA	GHANA-GUINEA-MALI U.	E. E. C. ASSOC	O.A.M.C.E., '62	A. A. T. U. F.	A. T. U. C.	BELGRADE CONF.	A. A. P. O. (CAIRO)[3]	C. C. T. A.,'62	U.N. E. C. A.,'63
ALGERIA		□	□								□				□		□	p		□
MOROCCO	□	□	□								□				□		□	p		□
(U.A.R.) EGYPT	□	□	□								□				□		□	p		□
GHANA	□	□	□								□	□			□		□	p		□
GUINEA		□	□								□	□			□		□	p	□[4]	□
MALI			□			□					□	□			□		□	p	□	□
LIBYA	□	□	□													□				□
SUDAN	□	□	□													□	□			□
TUNISIA	□	□	□													□	□	p		□
LIBERIA	□	□	□							□						□		p	□	□
NIGERIA		□	□							□						□		p	□	□
SIERRA LEONE			□							□						□			□	□
ETHIOPIA	□	□	□					□	o	□							□			□
SOMALIA		□	□					□	o	□			□			□	□		□	□
TANGANYIKA			□					□	□	□						□			□	□
UGANDA			□					□	□											□
KENYA								p	□							□		p		A
ZANZIBAR								p	o											A
ANGOLA								p								□		p		
MOZAMBIQUE								p								□		p		
SOUTH WEST AFRICA								p										p		
SOUTH AFRICA								p[2]										p	Ex	Ex[5]
NYASALAND								p								□		p	A	A
NORTHERN RHODESIA								p								□		p	A	A
SOUTHERN RHODESIA								p								□		p	A	A
BASUTOLAND								p										p		A
BECHUANALAND								p												A
SWAZILAND								p												A
BURUNDI			□					□					□					p		□
RWANDA			□					□					□	□				p		□
CONGO (ex-Belg.)			□					□		□			□			□			□	□
CAMEROUN		□	□	□	□					□			□	□		□			□	□
CENT. AF. REPUBLIC			□	□	□					□			□	□		□			□	□
CHAD			□	□	□					□			□	□					□	□
CONGO (ex-Fr.)			□	□	□					□			□	□		□			□	□
GABON			□	□	□					□			□	□		□			□	□
DAHOMEY			□	□		□	□			□			□	□		□			□	□
IVORY COAST			□	□		□	□			□			□	□		□		p	□	□
MALAGASY			□	□						□			□	□		□			□	□
MAURITANIA			□	□		□				□			□	□		□			□	□
NIGER			□	□		□	□			□			□	□		□		p	□	□
SENEGAL			□	□		□				□			□	□		□		p	□	□
TOGO			□			□				□			□	□		□				□
UPPER VOLTA			□	□		□	□			□			□	□		□		p	□	□
GAMBIA																				A
Belgium																			A	
France																			A	□
United Kingdom																			A	□
Portugal																			Ex	Ex[5]
Spain																				□

KEY

A ASSOCIATE MEMBERSHIP

O OBSERVER STATUS

P REPRESENTATION BY POLITICAL MOVEMENTS

Ex EXCLUDED FROM PARTICIPATION

FOOTNOTES –

[1] PAN-AFRICAN FREEDOM MOVEMENT FOR EAST, CENTRAL & SOUTH AFRICA; EAST AFRICAN COMMON SERVICES ORGANIZATION

[2] SOUTH AFRICA REPRESENTED BY AFRICAN NATIONALISTS

[3] ALL AFRICAN PEOPLES ORGANIZATION

[4] GHANA WITHDREW IN 1961

[5] PASSED IN 1963

AFRICAN INTERNATIONAL GROUPINGS

Libya in fact participated in conferences of both groups. As name and membership indicate, the *Pan-African Freedom Movement of East, Central, and South Africa* (PAFMECSA) laid emphasis on terminating white domination of southern Africa. In dissolving itself, it turned over this function to the nine-member "Liberation Committee" of the OAU. Finally, note that although most of the participants under the "Lagos" heading are not shaded, these members and the entire grouping were absorbed into the OAU.

Selection 20 is intended partially as a guide to understanding the chart. In it, G. Mennen Williams describes some of the major groupings—in particular the Casablanca and Monrovia blocs—and attempts to assess their relationships to one another and to the future of the Pan-African movement. A further giant step toward understanding is provided in Selection 21, which discusses political attitudes rather than political groupings as such. Through discussion of the Congo crisis, we are introduced to the living issues in Pan-African politics, and thus are shown indirectly the nature of at least some of the differing alignments described in the chart.

Selection 20

Aids and Obstacles to Political Stability in Mid-Africa*

G. Mennen Williams

Mr. Williams is at present Assistant Secretary of State for African Affairs. Prior to appointment to that position by President Kennedy in 1961, he was for several terms (1949–1960) governor of Michigan.

The emergence of a broad band of sovereign nations in mid-Africa is part of one of the major events of the 20th century—the dissolution of the great colonial empires that were built during the age of exploration. . . .

. . . Mid-Africa is not a term in common use, and I would like to define it for the purpose of these remarks. As I use the phrase, it includes all of Africa south of the Sahara to the northern boundaries of Angola, Northern Rhodesia, and Mozambique.

Mid-Africa today embraces 23 independent nations, 21 of which became sovereign states within the last 6 years. It also includes several areas that are in various transitional stages on the road to self-determination.

More than twice the size of the United States, this area encompasses a wide range of geographical conditions. It comprises the belt of sand and grassland states running across Africa below the Sahara; the Horn of Africa, composed of the Ethiopian highlands and the coastal lowlands; the rain-forest states of the west coast, extending from Senegal through the Congo; and the east African lands of Kenya, Uganda, Tanganyika, and Zanzibar.

---

* Reprinted from *The Department of State Bulletin*, Vol. XLVI, No. 1195 (May 21, 1962), pp. 841–846.

Within this vast arc of old, new, and emerging nations there are readily recognizable diversities in peoples, economies, languages, politics, and ways of life. Some of these factors are divisive forces and obstacles to political stability in the mid-African section of the continent.

These forces are balanced, however, by a series of cohesive forces—a large number of factors that tend to unite the entire region spiritually and aid in its desire for political stability. These include a common love of freedom and independence, a determination to improve standards of living and education, an insistence on personal and national dignity, a reluctance to be drawn into the maelstrom of the cold war through political alinements with either East or West, and a strong interest in unity, both regional and Africa-wide. I would like to concentrate on this last aspect today.

AFRICAN DESIRE FOR UNITY

The desire for unity—either pan-Africanism or regional cooperation—is dear to the heart of every African leader. Yet even within the body of this unifying factor, which carries the seed of healthy coordination and cooperation, there is also the seed of disunity, which can bear bitter fruit in terms of unstable political relationships among mid-African states. On balance, however, the solidarity of purpose and belief that some form of mutual cooperation is necessary and proper to Africa's political, economic, and social development is the predominant force. . . .

PROGRESS TOWARD REGIONAL GROUPINGS

Thus, while there is a common desire for some form of unity among Africans in all parts of Africa, there are not enough other points of mutual interest to sustain immediate continent-wide groupings. On the other hand, there is considerable activity in Africa in terms of regional political, economic, and social consultations and groupings. These are welcome developments because we believe that some form of mutual effort is necessary if a number of new African states are to become economically and politically viable.

Although we view such associations with pleasure, we do not propose to tell Africans which groupings we consider good, bad, or indifferent. This is a matter for Africans to decide upon for themselves. As President Kennedy has said, we want for the Africans what they want for themselves, and we intend to hold to that position. In a sense this is the opposite side of the coin of African nonalinement in the cold war—a development in which we choose not to aline ourselves with one or another of the various associational movements that are taking place on the African Continent.

Some of Africa's progress toward regional groupings is the outgrowth of patterns set by former colonial regimes, which usually were administered on an area or regional basis. After the first blush of independence wore off, the reestablishment of old relationships with African neighbors commenced among the new African states and has continued through a series of shifting patterns. The motivation for such regrouping is both political and economic, stemming from realization on the part of most new nations that they are too limited in size, in population, in wealth, or in defense capabilities to make their way without cooperating together.

MAJOR REGIONAL ORGANIZATIONS

Because there is a constant process of change in African groupings, they present a kaleidoscopic picture to an outside observer. At the moment there are four major regional groupings in mid-Africa.

First, there is the Union Africaine et Malgache—the African and Malagasy Union—composed of 12 states of French "expression." The UAM contains two subgroups—the Conseil de l'Entente (Ivory Coast, Upper Volta, Niger, and Dahomey) and the Conference of Equatorial States (the Republic of Congo [Brazzaville], Gabon, Chad, and the Central African Republic)—and Cameroon, Senegal, Mauritania, and the Malagasy Republic.

A second group is known as the Casablanca powers, which are five in number—Morocco, Guinea, Ghana, Mali, and the United Arab Republic. This is the only group combining north African with mid-African states. The Casablanca group meetings also have been attended by the Provisional Government of Algeria.

A third group is the East African Common Services Organization. This grew out of the common services performed by the East African High Commission, which includes Kenya, Uganda, and Tanganyika. At the recent Conference of the Pan-African Freedom Movement for East and Central Africa, it was agreed that Somalia and Ethiopia should negotiate to become members. This group one day may become the East African Federation.

Fourth, there is the new Lagos group of 20 nations which cuts across the continent and unites nations that speak both French and English. The Lagos grouping includes the 12 UAM states, Togo, Liberia, the Republic of the Congo (Léopoldville), Ethiopia, Somalia, Nigeria, Sierra Leone, and Tanganyika.

From Angola north to the Sahara, then, the only independent mid-African country not participating in one or more of the new African regional organizations is the Sudan.

SIMILARITY OF ORGANIZATIONAL PATTERNS

Apart from the east African group, which includes countries not yet independent, these original groupings have patterns of organization so similar that they are almost stereotypes. Generally, they are composed of a council of chiefs of state, which makes all political and administrative decisions; a defense council; an organization for economic and cultural cooperation; a customs union; and an organization for postal communications, telecommunications, and transport. None has a central capital, and the various secretariats are scattered among the members' capitals. The meetings of the council of the chiefs of state rotate among the capitals, and there is a fixed rotation for the council presidency. Methods of operation depend on the motivating political ideology, the area covered, and the degree of similarity of members' institutions.

UNION AFRICAINE ET MALGACHE

The most recent meeting of any of these four groups took place only a few weeks ago, when the Union Africaine et Malgache held its second formal conference of chiefs of state at Bangui, Central African Republic. This really was the sixth meeting of the group known as the Brazzaville states since early 1960, although the group was not organized formally as the UAM until it met at Tananarive in the Malagasy Republic in September 1961.

The cohesion of this grouping is favored by common traditions and, to some extent, common administrative arrangements inherited from the French colonial period. They take pride in their French cultural "expression." They are members of the franc zone, are associate members of the European Economic Community, and continue to receive large French economic (and to some extent military) support. Although they shun any formal alinements with Western powers, most of them consider themselves part of the West in many ways.

The Council of the UAM meets twice a year and is the group's organ for determining overall internal and external policy. To make foreign policies effective, the charter of the UAM provides for the establishment of a corresponding group at the United Nations and makes it obligatory for the group to meet there on all important issues. This has led to the 12 UAM states' voting together on most issues. As they represent about one-eighth of U.N. membership, their posture in the U.N. is extremely significant. The Council also has shown definite interest in the development of wider African groups.

A Defense Council and a secretariat were created by the defense pact of the 12 UAM states. There is, however, no intention to create a single command or a single army. Emphasis is on military cooperation only to help check externally supported subversion. This Council could provide members with a useful means of cooperating in the suppression of Communist subversion. Establishment of a defense organization also may help to reduce pressures for large national arms buildups and their consequent drains on national budgets.

OBJECTIVES OF OAMCE

The Organization for African and Malagasy Economic Cooperation, OAMCE, is the economic arm of the UAM. Its objectives are to establish common policies relating to currency, customs, and investments. The committee structure of the OAMCE illustrates its broad program:

a. The Committee of Foreign Commerce is working on harmonizing customs classification procedures and nomenclature leading toward the establishment of an Afro-Malagasy free trade zone. It also is studying the organization of African markets.

b. The Committee for Study of Monetary Problems plans to propose measures to coordinate the activities of the three existing banks of issue, to study methods of transferring funds, and to examine annually the balance of payments of each state and propose measures to eliminate deficits.

c. The Committee of Economic and Social Development is geared to study and coordinate the development plans of the member states to harmonize their investment codes and to study the possibility of a common price stabilization fund. It presently is considering the establishment of a development institute and bank.

d. The Committee of Scientific and Technical Research is coordinating documentation relating to the development of member states and the possibility of setting up technical institutes at African universities in member states. It also has under consideration a plan for pooling African technicians, who are in short supply in UAM and other mid-African countries.

e. The Committee for Post and Telecommunications has the complicated function of coordinating existing systems of communication, establishing networks, and drafting codes for intraregional postal and telecommunications services. Among the first questions to be considered by this unit were the issuance of stamps, transport of mail, and uniform postal rates.

f. Air Afrique is a joint airline enterprise that serves all member states except Madagascar. It also serves Paris and Nice and has arranged reciprocal service between Dakar and Conakry with Air Guinea. Organized in close association with Western commercial airlines, Air Afrique represents a constructive alternative to a number of small, uneconomic airlines established for prestige purposes. Although Air France and Union Aero-Maritime de Transport are minority shareholders in Air Afrique, UAM member governments have the controlling interest in the line. Air Afrique has a permanent secretariat answerable to the UAM Committee of Transport Ministers, which is presently considering both additional internal air links and links with the outside world.

CULTURAL EMPHASIS IN CASABLANCA AND LAGOS GROUPS

The Casablanca and Lagos groups have laid more emphasis on cultural relations than the UAM. This is not surprising because the UAM states have a common background of French culture. The Casablanca group desires to develop a purely African culture as part of its tradition. The Lagos group, composed as it is of both French- and English-speaking Africans, who cannot communicate without translators, is determined "to promote and accelerate the consolidation of our African cultures and traditions in the interests of preserving our heritage." To speed this development, the Lagos group is forming an educational and cultural council to:

1. break down language barriers among African and Malagasy states;
2. harmonize the group's various educational systems;
3. adapt school curricula and general educational policies to the needs and experience of the African and Malagasy states;
4. develop and use rationally university resources;
5. promote the revival of African and Malagasy culture and traditions;
6. establish an African and Malagasy organization for educational, cultural, and scientific cooperation;
7. develop the education of women.

NEED FOR REGIONAL PLANNING

In examining the physical and cultural fragmentation of Africa today, the need for regional cooperation is apparent. This is a strategic moment to begin such a task, as the field is virgin and available funds have to be channeled carefully for most efficient use. Transportation and communications facilities are generally poor in mid-Africa, and it would be wise to plan for improvements on a regional, as well as on a national, basis.

Larger markets are essential to attract modern industrial investment, and these can be achieved only by breaking down political boundary lines to form a common market-at least among small neighboring countries. Within a common market, there can be cooperation in development planning to secure the benefits of industrial specialization, and agreement can be reached on legal means and ways to provide an attractive investment climate.

In the field of higher education a single center financed from combined resources could make possible the establishment of better institutions for professional, scientific, and medical training and research. Diseases—human, plant, and animal—do not respect borders and can only be held in check by the combined efforts of neighbors.

Although many development plans are in the blueprint stage, they give strong assurances that Africans are thinking through their problems. The principal problems and greatest needs are professional cadres and investment capital, and these have to be built rapidly to implement the many unborn plans.

DIFFERENCES AMONG MAJOR GROUPS

In the area of pan-Africanism interest on the part of mid-African states is very much alive, but predictions on future developments are precarious. The Conference of Independent African States (CIAS), now favored by the Casablanca group, held its first meeting in Accra, Ghana, in April 1958, with 8 states present, and met again in Addis Ababa, Ethiopia, in June 1960, with 12 states represented. It originally was scheduled to hold its third session in Tunis this month. This meeting, to which all 29 independent African states were invited, has been postponed until late fall in the hope of attracting the 20 Lagos powers.

Although all of Africa's independent states were invited to the Pan-African Monrovia Conference in June 1961 and the Lagos Conference in January 1962, the Casablanca powers boycotted both conferences. Although the charter of the Lagos group, which is now in the final drafting stage, is designed for an all-African organization, the possible attendance of Lagos group members at the next CIAS conference is a matter yet to be resolved by the members. The question was debated by the French-speaking members at the recent UAM conference at Bangui and will be a major agenda item at the next meeting of the Lagos chiefs of state, which will probably take place before the CIAS Tunis meeting is scheduled.

Aside from their outspoken "nonalinement" position, the deepest split between the Casablanca powers and the other groups lies in the Casablanca group's militant anti-imperialist and anticolonialist philosophy. This group considers the UAM members to be "neocolonialist" because they have remained associates of the European Economic Community and are negotiating to renew that association. The Casablanca group claims that regional groups "Balkanize" Africa. For their part, the UAM and the Lagos group feel that they are deeply anticolonial and anti-imperialist and believe they have developed an evolutionary concept of decolonialization. Instead of making a radical break with the former colonial powers when they became independent, these groups have been content to loosen ties gradually and to accept economic and military aid for support and services they cannot yet afford.

U.N. ECONOMIC COMMISSION FOR AFRICA

The United Nations Economic Commission for Africa and the Commission for Technical Cooperation in Africa South of the Sahara, known as the CCTA, also are part of the mainstream of pan-Africanism. Mid-African nations are very active in these organizations.

The U.N. Economic Commission for Africa in one sense is becoming an African parliament, to which delegations from all of Africa come to debate issues of continental interest. Although the watchword is African unity, the free expression of political differences frequently puts the spirit of such unity to severe test. Agreement is frequent, however, and at the last session of the Commission one of the most important items agreed upon was the establishment of an African Institute of Economic and Social Development at Dakar, which will be established this year. The Commission's greatest service lies in the technical studies which the secretariat undertakes on Africa-wide social and economic problems and in the technical committees set up to study them.

WORK OF THE CCTA

The CCTA, which was established in 1950 by France, Britain, Belgium, Portugal, and South Africa, by 1961 included 19 independent African states. Its object is to insure technical cooperation between all the countries south of the Sahara in four main fields:

a. problems related to the physical background of the continent, such as geology, geography, cartography, climatology, hydrology, and pedology;

b. problems related to biological subjects—plant life, forests, ecology, agriculture, plant industry, and animal industry;

c. human subjects—health, medicine, nutrition, and science of man, including problems of education, labor, and statistics; and

d. technology, such as housing, road research, and treatment of waters.

Much important work has been accomplished by this group. At its last meeting in February of this year, the European members either withdrew or were expelled, and membership is now purely African, directed by Africa for the benefit of African development.

Among the items of urgent consideration at the CCTA's most recent meeting was the creation of a specialized training fund to establish regional training centers for middle-level personnel. Three such centers have already been set up for customs officers, hydrology agents, and port guards. An audiovisual language center has been established to assist in developing bilingualism in French and English.

This organization presently is carrying out projects such as rinderpest eradication, research to combat bovine pneumonia, and oceanographic and fisheries research in the Gulf of Guinea. The United States has made a substantial contribution to the latter.

The CCTA and the U.N. Economic Commission for Africa are the only two organizations supported by members of both the Casablanca and Lagos groups. As instruments of inter-African cooperation, they may serve not only to develop highly important technical projects but also to bring currently competing African political groups closer together.

COMMON INTEREST AMONG ALL GROUPINGS

Although this picture of the many and various mid-African groupings may seem confused and overlapping, there is a considerable body of common interest throughout. The need for cooperation to develop Africa is found at all levels, from a small cluster of neighbors through an all-Africa grouping. As the small units blend into the larger, they bring to the latter valuable practical experience. At such times both groups reevaluate the functions they have been performing. Some functions are discarded in the merger, while others of a purely local nature are retained.

These groups are all fiercely proud of maintaining the purely African personality of their various entities. Yet they well realize, however, their dependence on outside assistance, especially in the form of capital and expertise to accomplish their plans and projects.

How these various interests are resolved will hold the key to Africa's rate of development and to the future peace and stability of the continent.

Selection 21

Four African Views of the Congo Crisis*

ROBERT C. GOOD

Mr. Good has been a research associate with The Washington, D.C., Center of Foreign Policy Research.

Mario Cardoso, the Congo's representative at the UN, once complained that Western capitalism had provoked Katanga's secession, while Communism had fomented the secession of Orientale. "It is not the Congolese that are divided, it is the world that is divided. Therefore, leave the Congo alone. . . . " There is enough truth in this plea to make it poignant. But it is a half-truth. The other half relates, of course, to the perfectly obvious dissensions among the principal actors in the Congo—and just as important, among the African states.

A review of UN debates and recent African conferences discloses three clusters of African attitudes concerning the Congo. For want of better labels, it has become customary to call their exponents "radicals" (Ghana, Guinea, Mali, Morocco and the UAR), "conservatives" (the former sub-Saharan French states excluding Guinea, Mali and Togo) and "moderates" (Ethiopia, Liberia, Libya, Nigeria, Togo, Tunisia, Somalia and the Sudan).

WHO IS THE ENEMY?

The basic issues in the Congo crisis, around which these attitudes have formed, are four: Who is the "enemy"? What is the Congo?

* Reprinted by permission from *Africa Report* (June 1961), pp. 3–4, 6, 12, 15. (This article is an abbreviated version of the conclusions reached in "Congo Crisis: The Role of the New States," published as part of a symposium by The Washington Center of Foreign Policy Research in 1963.)

What role for the UN? And what about the problem of unilateral aid —or intervention, depending on one's point of view?

One or two warning flags must be posted immediately. The following summary represents broad positions. Differences within each camp, admittedly important, are not adequately explored. Also, each position represents an orientation that obviously affects, but does not preclude, tactical maneuver. Moreover, we are examining "declaratory policies" which are often exaggerated for impact. Still, within these limitations, the following survey does illustrate broad differences in African analyses of the Congo crisis. These differences, I think, reflect some of the forces that will help shape political developments on the continent in the opening years of the postcolonial era.

I. THE RADICALS

To understand the position of the radicals concerning the Congo, and African developments in general, one must first understand the word "neo-colonialism"—for a complete world view attaches to it. In the radical ideology concerning neo-colonialism, there are three tenets that especially concern us. The first is the notion of "pseudo-independence," or what Ghana's President Kwame Nkrumah has called "clientele-sovereignty." This, he explained, is "the practice of granting a sort of independence by the metropolitan power, with the concealed intention of making the liberated country a client-state and controlling it effectively by means other than political ones."

The second tenet is capsuled in the term "Balkanization," which the radicals believe is the basic strategy of neo-colonialists for maintaining pseudo-independent regimes. The colonial power fragments an area—the Congo, for example—into a number of small states. None is viable, so all must remain "clients" of the former mother country. Balkanization is practiced not only on a country-basis, but regionally and even continentally to divide the new states from one another. "We know the objectives of the West," Lumumba once said. "Yesterday it divided us at the level of tribes, clans, and chiefs. Today—because Africa is freeing itself—it wishes to divide us on the level of states. It wishes to create antagonistic blocks and satellites and from that state of cold war accentuate the divisions with a view to maintaining its eternal trusteeship." If the African block has been fractured, it is the result, not of genuine, internal divisions, but of "sabotage" carried on by the colonial powers in order to wreck African "solidarity."

In the radical view, the saboteurs have accomplices recruited from the colonized population. These are the "stooges" of the imperialist powers. A third tenet of the radical view deals with this "enemy within." Often, he is an unwitting puppet, the victim of a colonially-corrupted mind. After a bitter exchange in the Security Council, the delegate from Guinea said to his opposite number from the former French Congo: ". . . it is with great sadness that I have listened to the man that I . . . call my brother—sadness to see to what point colonization can change the very nature of the colonized. . . ." Whether knowingly or unwittingly, the stooge or the puppet is the instrument of the neo-colonialists; he is the enemy within the gate. He was Bao Dai in Vietnam, Baccouche in Tunisia, El-Glaoui in Morocco, and now Tshombe, or Mobutu, or perhaps even Kasavubu in the Congo.

The Neo-Colonialist Threat

Neo-colonialism is the "enemy." From this notion, the radical's position on the other issues follows logically. Thus, the proper definition of the Congo: it is an embryonic state threatened with extinction by the Belgians and their neo-colonialist allies who have "set Congolese fighting Congolese."

To void the imperialist's plot demands rapid consolidation against every attempt at Balkanization. ". . . let me assure you that Tshombes do not exist in Mali," the delegate from that country told the Security Council. It demands decisive reduction of reliance on the former metropole, for a foreign-controlled economy means domination every bit as effective as outright political control. It demands the unity of the postcolonial states ("pan-Africanism"), not just because there resides in unity that strength which is the only ultimate answer to imperialist designs, but also because a setback anywhere along the nationalists' front line may cause a break-through of neo-colonialist forces which would utterly overwhelm the fragile new states. This is why the neo-colonialist assault on the Congo must be defeated conclusively, for if it succeeds, said the delegate from Guinea, "the entire world would undoubtedly be a spectator to the destruction and breaking up of Africa to the satisfaction of the colonial Powers . . . As far as we are concerned, Guinea could well be the Congo, and the Congo, Africa. . . . "

For the radicals, the legitimacy of a postcolonial regime relates in part to its legal mandate; but even more, legitimacy relates to the regime's credentials as a representative of genuine nationalism fighting against the intrigues of neo-colonialism. This is why Lumumba was so extolled—this "best son of Africa," this "Lincoln of the Congo," this "black Messiah," whose struggle was made noble by his unswerving demand for centralism against all forms of Balkanization and rendered heroic by his unyielding resistance to the forces of neo-colonialism which finally killed his body, but not his spirit.

In this situation, the United Nations has only one possible function. It must place its resources at the disposal of the nationalist regime. The doctrine has been stated most clearly by Guinea: ". . . the United Nations must acquiesce in all requests of the [Lumumbist] Central Government . . . " That the United Nations did not do so can only be explained by the fact that the organization came under the domination of neo-colonial forces. It lost its legitimacy and became an added cause of the crisis rather than the cure. Under these circumstances the UN ought to withdraw from the Congo.

If the UN fails to thwart neo-colonialist ambitions, action must be taken outside the world organization. "We cannot be passive spectators," said the Moroccan ambassador to the United Nations, ". . . [watching] the rebirth of colonialism and its return to the Congo. . . . "

The radicals have been accused of "intervention." But intervention, which is an illicit involvement of one sovereign state in the affairs of another, is meaningful only in the context of true international relations—relations, that is, between sovereign and equal members of international society. It is central to the radical view of African politics that no such international society now exists in Africa, nor can it come into existence until the plots of the neo-colonialists have been exposed and defeated. Rather, Africa is seen as composed of a few "beachheads" of genuine independence struggling to consolidate against an implacable foe. Surrounding these enclaves are vast areas, nominally independent to be sure, but still controlled in varying degrees by neo-colonialist forces. These are what Ismael Toure of Guinea has called "regimes of surveillance" as opposed to "regimes of pure liberty."

Pseudo-Independence Cited

Under Lumumba, the Congo had a fighting chance to frustrate the plots of imperialism. But the imperialists overwhelmed Lumumba. The Congo, except for Gizenga-land, came under the control of neo-colonialist forces. A state controlled by neo-colonialism is not a sovereign member of the international community at all. This being the case, one cannot speak of "intervention" in the Congo. Rather, one must speak of the continuation of the struggle of nationalism vs. colonialism on a new front. Pseudo-independence may change the form of the problem, but not the reality. On the same day (February 21, 1961) that the Security Council passed a resolution calling for "the solution of the problem of the Congo . . . without any interference from the outside"—a resolution co-sponsored by the UAR—President Nasser announced that he was giving unilateral aid to the Gizenga government in Stanleyville! This is a contradiction only to those who do not share the radical view of African politics.

The questions raised by all this are intriguing, the more so because they would appear to apply to relations between the radicals and the many "conservative" states of the former French empire. When does the postcolonial era really begin? When do the rules of the game change? Obviously the rules that obtain during the struggle for independence are one thing; the rules that govern relations between sovereign and equal members of international society are another. There is a tendency on the part of the radicals to assume that the rules do not change until Africa has established a position of strength independent of the former colonial powers; has thus annulled the plots of the neo-colonialists; and has brought into being a true pan-African State. Until that end has been reached tactics that less radical minds might condemn as intervention or subversion remain perfectly fair game.

II. THE CONSERVATIVES

Unlike the radicals, who want to upset the *status quo* in emerging Africa, the former French sub-Saharan territories (barring Guinea,

Mali, and Togo) want to preserve it. Rather than disrupt the ties with the former metropole, the conservatives wish to maintain them. Instead of developing Africa as an autonomous continent, beholden to no external force, they want their states to develop, at least for the present, in close cooperation with Europe. In place of the radicals' notion that the state system inherited from the colonial era is a form of Balkanization which does not provide an adequate or even a legitimate basis for relations among true African nationalists, the conservatives insist on the legitimacy of present boundaries—again, for the present.

These conservative states have achieved independence in amity with France. For the most part they do not question the propriety of maintaining civil order and technical services with extensive French help. One supposes therefore that the animus of the radical toward the former metropole is difficult for them to comprehend. (Only Ghana among the radicals does not share this animus.)

As the conservatives' approach to the problem of organizing the postcolonial world differs markedly from that of the radicals, so too is the entire problem of the Congo structured differently for the conservatives. Belgium may be an "enemy," but for many conservatives she is not the only enemy nor even the major one.

For the conservative extremists (Cameroun and Congo-Brazzaville are the clearest examples), the real "enemy" in the Congo situation is not Western imperialism but Communism—the fountainhead of a new imperialism. Frequently these states simply take over the categories of the radicals but fill them with opposite content. It is Mr. Gizenga who is scored as a "colonialist puppet," with Soviet imperialists handling the strings. It is the radical state that suffers "independence on parole," having sold itself to the "rapacious" Communist master. While the radicals speak of the conservatives as "imperialist stooges," the conservatives refer to the radicals as "Soviet satellites," Russia's "African colonies," and "crypto-Communists." Thus does the Cold War infiltrate African squabbles despite the best intentions of the new states to keep it out.

The "Myth" of the Congo

For the radicals' doctrinaire assertion that the Congo is, or must be made, one nation indivisible, the conservatives tend to stress its diversity. In place of the "inviolable principle" of unity, they have emphasized "reality." After recording the enormous diversity lying beneath the "myth" of the Congo, Mr. Thiam of Senegal noted how complex were the problems of achieving unity even among countries long exposed to modern life, like those of Europe. How much more difficult, then, in Africa! "We accused France of having Balkanized Africa. But who knows if we would not have found ourselves in a Congo-like situation if independence had been granted to us, not on the basis of each territory being one State, but the basis of a united territory." Added to the Senegalese sense of "reality" is French Equatorial "realism." The Congo's near-neighbors in former French Africa are hardly enthusiastic about the emergence of a unitarian Congolese state susceptible of control by a "radical" government.

Concerning the governmental crisis in the Congo, the conservatives, while proclaiming a "hands-off" attitude, have supported Kasavubu and his Prime Minister, Joseph Ileo, as the carriers of the Congolese nationalist tradition and have dismissed Lumumba as a "newcomer." When Mr. Lumumba was assassinated, the conservatives politely participated in denunciations of "political violence." Some noted, however, that the event created a greater sensation outside the Congo than within. ". . . when a member of the family dies," said the Central African Republic delegate, ". . . wakes are organized during which people weep. . . . It is improper [however] for neighbors and friends to weep more loudly than the deceased person's own relatives."

If the radicals scored the UN Congo mission because it would not intervene enough, the conservatives have criticized the world organization because it intervened too much. While acknowledging the usefulness of the UN in preventing foreign intervention in the Congo, the conservative states have stressed that the United Nations must not practice "pro-consulship" (Senegal), that it "should keep its hands clean in respect of the problems of African internal politics, which are a family matter" (Central African Republic), that it "can take no stand in the institutional crisis" (Ivory Coast), and that it must take no action tantamount to disarming the troops of a sovereign state member of the United Nations as "this would be a grave precedent indeed" (Congo-Brazzaville).

Most conservative states would probably agree with an observation made to Marguerite Higgins by a Cameroun official who drew a parallel between divisions in the Congo and the radical-supported, Bamileke rebellion in his own country: "We are lucky. Think of the terrible situation if the United Nations had ever come in here . . . they would have interposed themselves between us and the rebels, restraining us from trying to wipe them out. This would have given them a chance to consolidate themselves."

Both Sides Obstruct UN

Of course, the radical Lumumba said much the same thing. But that is just the point. Both the radicals and the conservatives have lined up against the UN. Both have said that the UN should get out of the Congo, or at least be restricted to a minimal role. The difference between radical and conservative denunciations of the UN Congo Mission is this: the radicals are against the world organization because they believe it defends a wholly unsatisfactory *status quo*; the conservatives are hesitant about the UN because they believe it may act to upset a *status quo* that will permit a slow movement toward a settlement favorable to conservative interests. ". . . it is necessary . . . to wait patiently until the obstacles are overcome one by one," said Malagasy's Louis Rakotomalala, capturing the conservative mood nicely. External intervention, whether unilateral or multilateral, would only complicate the process. This is one of the reasons why Mr. Thiam of Senegal has called the principle of non-interference in the domestic affairs of other states "the Golden Rule of international relations."

III. THE MODERATES

The African "moderates" are the in-between group—whether for historical, ideological, or political reasons. Historically, Ethiopia and Liberia have remained aloof, though admittedly that is changing rapidly. For reasons of ideology, French-speaking Tunisia and Togo cannot identify with the French-speaking conservative groups; nor can the Sudan and Somalia for historical reasons. At the same time, political considerations (and possibly ideological ones as well) prompt Tunisia, Togo and the Sudan to keep their distance from the radicals. Togo's delicate relationship to Ghana demands this, as do the relationships of Tunisia and the Sudan to the UAR. Somalia has not as yet been drawn into the larger African arena mainly because its border problem with Ethiopia is its preoccupation. Nigeria is self-possessed, content with its size and its potential, and intent thus far on playing an independent role. Libya, like Morocco, is radical in its diplomatic discourse, but conservative at home. There is a tendency to reflect the UAR line, but Libya, unlike Morocco with its claim to Mauritania, has no compelling interest in sub-Saharan politics.

As compared with the two extremes, there is less emotional content to the judgments of the moderates about the Congo and greater inclination to deal with the problem in terms of institutions and procedures rather than personalities and symbols. For the moderates, the problem of achieving order in the Congo presses slightly more heavily than does the concern to establish this group in power or prevent that group from ascendancy. The foregoing are not bald distinctions; they are nuances, but important nonetheless.

For the extreme radical and the extreme conservative, the "enemy" in the Congo crisis has been defined simply—neo-colonialism in the one case and Communism in the other. The moderates, though there are great variations among them, tend to acknowledge that the situation is complex. Most moderates would agree with Tunisia's Foreign Minister Mongi Slim who, in apportioning blame, cited not only the Belgians who "promote hostility and sow the seeds of division" in the Congo, but also the "personal ambitions" and "regional interests" of the Congolese political leaders themselves. Insofar as "foreign interference" has contributed to Congolese disorder, it is, in the view of many moderates, a misdemeanor committed by several states and not by Belgium alone.

As to the proper definition of the Congo, the moderates, more than either the radicals or conservatives, have tended to emphasize the legal environment of the problem. Their position has been closer to the radicals than to the conservatives for they have consistently demanded a unified Congo. But this has been the case not so much for reasons of doctrine (radical doctrine concerning the threat of "neo-colonialism" dictates a strong, unitarian regime), but because the law reads that way and because confederation, under the Tananarive formula for example, would end by tearing the country apart. That is to say, when moderates have insisted that "there must be no dismemberment of the Congo," they have tended to link that requirement, not with the problems of "neo-colonialism" or "Balkanization," but with the "rule of law" and the necessity to preserve in law the entity known as the Congo. With the exception of Togo, all have refused to "deal in personalities"; the moderates have remained neutral concerning the struggle for power within the Congo.

Moderates Support UN

It is with reference to the role of the United Nations that the clearest distinction arises between the moderates on the one hand and the radicals and conservatives on the other. Unlike the two polar positions, the moderates consistently have supported the UN. More and more, the UN operation in the Congo—the UN Force, the Conciliation Commission, and principal staff members of the UN Mission—has depended upon the moderate camp. Even the Sudan, the only moderate to withdraw its troops from the UN Force, said when announcing that withdrawal was in prospect, ". . . we do not mean to imply that the United Nations, led by the Secretary General, is not doing its best."

As to the objectives of the UN, the moderates again have been closer to the radicals than to the conservatives. The UN must support Congolese legal institutions, uphold the territorial integrity of the country, maintain order, and remove foreign military and political personnel not under the UN command. At the point of procedures, however, the radicals and moderates part company. While the radicals have insisted that the UN should be made an adjunct to the legitimate Congolese Government, adding its force to that of the government in a campaign to unify the country, the moderates have maintained the propriety of an independent position for the United Nations and consistently have opposed the use of force to alter the *status quo*.

More than either the radicals or conservatives, the moderates have been exercised about the general problem of disorder, about the rebellious troops and the repeated lapse of governmental authority in the Congo. Order, or at least the avoidance of civil war, has increasingly been given a higher priority by the moderates than the establishment or the consolidation of some particular regime. To cope with the problem of disorder, the moderates have urged strengthening the UN mandate. A corollary problem has been that of relating the authority of the UN to the prerogatives of the sovereign Republic of the Congo.

Togo has suggested that the UN must become the "sole authority responsible for maintaining law and order." Other moderates have warned that the UN must under no circumstances establish a "trusteeship" over the Congo. Yet *all* the moderates have advocated an expansion of UN authority and have pressed for UN involvement in such tasks as "disarming" the army or "insulating it from politics"—tasks that surely imply certain governmental prerogatives for the UN Congo mission.

In short, the moderates have been the UN enthusiasts in the Congo. Anything less than an expanded mandate for the UN, they have argued, would perpetuate chaos and create a beachhead for great power (or small power) intervention. The terse cable of Togo's President Olympio to the Secretary General on the occasion of Lumumba's death sums up the moderate view: "Struggle for influence carried on in Congo by African and non-African States must end . . . All assistance by States Members United Nations must be channelled through United Nations only body which cannot be accused of political or other designs on Congo."

IV. GHANA'S DEVIANT POSITION

Of all the deviations from the "core" positions described above, that of Ghana is by all odds the most important and deserves a special word.

Ghana is fully in harmony with the radical position concerning the peril of neo-colonialism and the requirements of an effective response to that danger. "In my view," said President Nkrumah to the Ghanaian National Assembly on August 8, 1960, "any person who talks of a federal type of constitution for the Congo is a supporter of the imperialist cause." On September 24, 1960, shortly after the Kasavubu-Lumumba split and the Mobutu *coup d'etat*, President Nkrumah told the UN General Assembly that the point had been reached "where [UN] intervention on the side of the legitimate government of the Congo appears to be the obvious and only answer to the crisis. . . ." Indeed, Ghana's open and covert support to Lumumba was unstinting throughout the greater part of the fall.

However, as opposed to Guinea, Mali, and the UAR, Ghana frequently has exercised a restraining influence on radical attempts to terminate UN action in favor of direct intervention. In this respect, it has aligned itself with the moderates.

Ghana's Troops Remain

At the conference of independent African states in Leopoldville in August, Lumumba's call for an all-African army received support from Guinea and the UAR—but not from Ghana. At the Casablanca conference in January, Guinea, Mali, and the UAR reportedly wanted to make their UN contingents directly available to Antoine Gizenga, Lumumba's political heir. Ghana, with Morocco, resisted the idea. While all the other radicals have withdrawn their units from the UN Force, Ghana's troops still serve in the Congo. Whereas Guinea, Mali, and the UAR left the UN Conciliation Commission, Ghana, again with Morocco, remained aboard, though it refused to endorse the Commission's final report.

With the radicals, Ghana has kept one eye on the threat of neo-colonialism; but, with the moderates, it has kept the other eye on the danger of the Cold War. Direct aid to the Congo, said Ghana's Ambassador to the UN Alex Quaison-Sackey on September 16, "would definitely have the most serious repercussions."

Ghana's formula for combining these incompatibles—multilateralism to guard against East-West intervention and vigorous support of the nationalist regime to defeat the "neo-colonial plot"—has been the repeated demand for Africanization of the UN Command and Force. On September 24, President Nkrumah asked the General Assembly to delegate UN functions in the Congo to the independent African states, "especially those . . . whose contributions in men and material make the United Nations effort in the Congo possible." In his plan of February 18, Ghana's Chief of State urged that an all-African command "should take over complete responsibility for law and order in the Congo." (On March 7, he said the Command and Force should be "primarily African.") All foreign diplomatic missions, he added, ought to leave the country. (Ghana's ambassador to Leopoldville had been declared *persona non grata* the previous November.) Finally, the UN Command should disarm and retrain the Congolese Army, using force if necessary; should release political prisoners; and should convene Parliament under UN auspices.

This is tantamount to an advanced form of UN trusteeship and has obvious similarities with the moderates' advocacy of a strengthened UN mandate. But the Nkrumah plan would have Africans in full control, with the hope, no doubt, of enhancing the influence of the radicals in the conduct of UN affairs in the Congo.

How significant are these differing attitudes on the basic issues in the Congo crisis? It is easy to exaggerate. Positions are in fact being moderated as the protracted conflict drags on. In the last round of votes in the General Assembly on April 15, radicals, moderates, and conservatives found themselves in the same camp respecting many of the proposals. Hard-core radicals and many conservatives, for example, agreed that Belgian political and military personnel must leave the Congo. Conservatives, who heretofore had insisted that the UN keep "hands off" the Congo, supported a UN resolution advocating the convening of Parliament and the formation of a national government. Conservatives and moderates recently met in Monrovia and "reaffirmed faith in the United Nations as the organization best adapted to achieve a real solution of the Congo problem."

The politics of postcolonial Africa are fluid. Positions are forming but they are not fixed. Only the position of the extreme radicals has substantial ideological content. The others are flexible and subject to change—some of them, we may be sure, to violent change.

At the same time, conservative, moderate, and radical tendencies are reflections of basic suppositions concerning the very nature of postcolonial politics: how to organize the postcolonial state; how to relate that state to the former metropole; how to effect a new system of international order to take the place of the now defunct colonial order. On these issues there are cleavages—some of them serious and deep.

In a speech before the General Assembly in the middle of April, Jaja Wachuku, head of the Conciliation Commission to the Congo and leader of the Nigerian delegation to the UN, noted the existence of the three groups of African powers. "In the end," he said, "none of the three are Powers at all. A house divided against itself cannot be effective. . . . If we are going to speak effectively and act effectively in the United Nations, this is the time, because to the African states the Congo is a challenge. . . . We are responsible for whatever happens. I will not blame what you call the East or the West."

The Congo is indeed a challenge to the new states of Africa. There will be many more challenges before long. Whether the house will irrevocably divide against itself or unite in effective action, none can say for sure. But Wachuku is surely right. Primary responsibility resides now in African hands.

III

THE AFRICAN ECONOMIES AND THE OUTSIDE WORLD

Since almost the beginning of intensive contact between Africa and the outside world, it seems generally agreed, Africa has been strongly influenced politically by the impingement on her of world economic forces. What then may be the future of a politically independent Africa, still economically weak and hence also economically dependent to an unusually marked degree?

The following readings examine this question from three standpoints. First, the economic condition and status of Africa at the moment of independence. Second, the major African attitudes regarding their international economic relations. Third, the economic relationships proposed or actually being developed between the African and non-African worlds and/or within Africa itself. Each of the three is taken up in turn in the three sections of this portion of the book.

AN OVERVIEW OF AFRICAN ECONOMIES

Economic advancement is a major preoccupation of all the new African states, an imperative to which leaders feel compelled to respond. Confront this sense of an imperative with the often extreme conditions of underdevelopment found almost everywhere in Africa; the result is an intense determination to place economy, society, and government under forced draft and to begin closing the gap. Discussion of programs for doing so has given rise to a variety of viewpoints and doctrines, often associated somehow under the rather vague concept—almost a slogan—of "African Socialism."

Doctrines and viewpoints may vary widely, but they all must somehow cope with the same fundamental reality—the existing condition and situation of African economies, and the choices these tend to impose. The general nature of these problems, and of the efforts to solve them that commend themselves, are described by Professor Frankel (Selection 22). His discussion thus provides a good background against which to set the expositions by African leaders offered in the three succeeding selections.

Selection 22

Economic Aspects of Political Independence in Africa*

S. Herbert Frankel

The author of several distinguished works on African economic questions, Mr. Frankel is an economist and a Fellow of Nuffield College, Oxford.

It is somewhat astonishing to find how little attention has been given to the consideration of the economic problems which the new "independent" States of Africa will have to face. The most contradictory claims are made—often almost in the same breath—about the effects of independence. At one time facts are quoted to show that "political independence" is likely to prove detrimental to many African economies, at another it is argued that it will usher in a new era of economic well-being. . . .

It is clear that mere generalizations about these issues are not going to clarify the nature and significance of the problems which will face the newly independent territories of Africa, many of which are currently in a state of such rapid political transition or turmoil that even their boundaries are as yet not finally established.

It may prove helpful to approach the problem from a somewhat different angle in order to disentangle the basic conceptual and some of the fundamental practical problems involved. . . .

Certainly those who speak glibly of the process of transition facing the new African States forget that for most of their history their inhabitants have lived under conditions of "independence" in the most extreme form in which it can be imagined—in small tribal units

---

* From *International Affairs*, Vol. 36, No. 4 (October 1960), pp. 440–446. Reprinted by permission of the author.

separated from their neighbours by uninhabited or uninhabitable regions, and cut off from any contacts of importance with the outside world. In the vast African continent—into which it would not be difficult to pack the land areas of China, India, and the United States and still leave room to spare—the bulk of its nearly 200 million population still pursues economic activities based on subsistence production, which are for the most part conducted in isolation, cut off even from regional markets owing to the paucity of communications, and inhibited through the absence of those modern legal systems governing land and property rights without which modern productive techniques cannot be introduced.

In economic terms absolute "independence" spells absolute isolation, and the blessings of isolation—whatever they may otherwise be—are not visibly associated with greater purchasing power over the goods and chattels of this world. They involve a precarious dependence on the environment and the vagaries of nature and on its brutal control of the balance of births and deaths and the growth of population.

The extreme dependence of subsistence economy on the natural environment was brought home to me vividly when as a member of the Royal Commission on East Africa we were examining the problem of population growth and "over-population" in certain regions. Impressed by the evidence of a rate of population growth which was outstripping the subsistence economies' ability to provide for its sustenance, certain experts suggested that a new pill which was then being tested in Asia might be utilized in Africa in order to bring about a simple form of birth control. I asked an anthropologist who had spent all his life in Tanganyika among African peoples about this. He promised to make inquiries from African women as to what they thought of it. Some time later he brought me the following answer. "We do not understand the question you are asking," said most of the African women, "for us it is so difficult to keep a child alive that we cannot understand why anybody would like to stop us having children." This reply puts the dilemma of isolation in a nutshell. African societies until very recent times have been engaged in the hazardous and most difficult task of maintaining themselves in a hostile natural environment. For the most part these tribal societies have not even had the benefit of the kind of tools which Robinson Crusoe was able to wield or the skills he had at his command. The subsistence economies of Africa still dominate the economic pattern of the newly independent States of Africa. In some even shifting cultivation is still necessary—others depend on sending their "surplus" labour far afield in search of work.

As much as by lack of roads and railways and modern storage facilities, they are cut off by lack of knowledge and suitable techniques for meeting the requirements of distant markets. The real state of most of Africa is quite the reverse of that which most people unacquainted with it are apt to imagine. It is not an Africa "dependent" on Europe, but an Africa which over vast areas is cut off from the world economy: an Africa whose difficult task it is even to maintain that *status quo* in relation to the environment which only modern science and suitable forms of economic, political, and administrative organization can eventually transcend. The real enemy of the African people is social and economic stagnation—and the perpetuation of, or return to, the isolation on which it rests. Indeed, the real nature of the revolt which is taking place in the minds and activities of the African people, and which expresses itself in new economic and political demands, is a revolt against the static tradition, social organization, and economic structure of the past. Notwithstanding the fact that the majority of the African people are as yet by no means fully aware of the necessity of change, and even less of the fundamental readjustments and difficulties connected with it, the rapidity with which modern economic ideas and techniques have erupted in many parts of Africa in the last quarter of a century is astonishing; but the individual African who has been affected by these ideas is not seeking the "independence" of the past. He is reaching out for a new "dependence," i.e. participation in and links with the modern world. In so far as the new African States fail to fashion those links, political independence will prove a mirage and will throw back their emergent populations to economic misery and chaos.

It is clear, therefore, that any consideration of the economic aspects of the political changes now taking place in Africa must eschew mere wishful thinking or misplaced enthusiasm. The mere wish to attain the economic benefits of a modern way of life does not supply the means wherewith to do so. For the fact is that the extent to which the different peoples and territories of Africa have been brought into contact with the world economy not only differs tremendously over the length and breadth of the continent but also, in most of them, as yet rests on a very fragile foundation of specialized export production which is of recent growth. Fifty years ago modern economic enterprise had hardly begun north of the Zambezi, and it is but a hundred years since the first beginnings of the mineral discoveries which laid the foundations for the most advanced industrial economy of the continent—that of the Union of South Africa.

Moreover the cost of pacifying the continent and establishing the rule of law and ordered government in it was borne mainly by the colonial and metropolitan Powers, with the result that the colonial territories in Africa were in considerable measure spared the burden of maintaining peace within Africa and defence against enemies outside it. Thus the scarce resources of these territories are likely to be saddled with costs for defence which they can ill afford, and may indeed not be able to meet, without losing the apparent political "independence" so recently attained. . . .

It is in large measure due to the exploitation of valuable mineral resources (or of special agricultural export crops) and the economic activities stimulated thereby that the "sterling area" countries in Africa have reached the present stage of economic integration with the world economy. But it must not be overlooked that most of the high income-producing centres are concentrated in relatively small areas separated from each other by vast distances, and connected by only thin lines of communication and little modern activity. It is noteworthy that the chief mineral-producing territories, i.e. the Belgian Congo, the Federation of Rhodesia and Nyasaland, and the Union of South Africa (including South West Africa), alone account for 53.3 per cent of the continent's exports. Moreover, of the total exports of these four important mineral-producing areas no less than 80 per cent are contributed by the Union of South Africa, South West Africa, and the Federation of Rhodesia and Nyasaland. The farther north one travels in Africa the smaller and more sparsely distributed become the areas yielding a relatively high money income—whether from mining or agricultural activities. Special calculations were made by the East Africa Royal Commission for the years 1951 or 1952 which showed that if the net geographical money product (excluding subsistence production) was divided by the total population of selected territories in order to show the relative importance of money-producing activities, then Tanganyika reached only 8 per cent of the Union's net money income per head, Kenya 14 per cent, Uganda 15 per cent, Northern and Southern Rhodesia 47 per cent, and the Belgian Congo 24 per cent.

By and large, therefore, the newly independent territories, or those about to attain political independence, are all faced with the same basic problem: that their modern activities form a very small part of their economies. Their readily available resources for even spanning the large areas of their territories with suitable communications, not to speak here of the costs of modern government itself, are meagre.

Since capital investment and immigrant skill and enterprise from abroad have been mainly responsible for establishing the economic framework of modern economy in the advanced territories, it will be apparent what difficult tasks in economic statesmanship face territories which have suddenly attained political independence or have had it thrust upon them. They are at that very early stage of development in which political independence can hardly prove beneficial unless it is conspicuously and consistently devoted to providing a climate of political and economic security which will attract from abroad the capital, the skilled technicians, and others who can assist in developing their economies. If, however, independence were to lead to conditions of insecurity, the economic life of these territories would be most gravely threatened, and a large proportion of those of their peoples who have entered the modern economy, and particularly those working in the newly developed urban areas, would be thrown back into subsistence economic activity, an eventuality which, particularly in view of the rapid rate of population growth in recent times, would have the direst consequences. In this connection it should be borne in mind that most of the large towns in the less developed regions of Africa are either mainly administrative centres or are based, not on a prosperous integrated hinterland, but on export, import, and allied activities. Their populations are thus very vulnerable to factors which might in any way interrupt the specialized production on which their livelihood is directly or indirectly based.

Such dangers now threaten the ex-Belgian Congo. The striking economic advances in that country have been due to highly specialized financial, commercial, and technical links with Europe. They have created in the heart of Africa a complex modern mining economy as well as considerable areas of specialized agricultural production for export markets. The Congo has established also an exceptionally large urban African population directly and indirectly dependent on these economic activities. Any interruption of the world economic network on which they are based is likely to endanger the livelihood of most of the urban and the relatively skilled rural population and to force down their standards of living to those of rural subsistence economy, if indeed that economy could then still absorb those displaced from other occupations.

I have already mentioned how very recent has been the period in which modern economic development has been possible in the new or emerging independent territories. The main task with which the metropolitan Powers were faced during this period was to provide the framework of government and communications. This was difficult and expensive; and indeed most of the capital required for that purpose was provided by government or semi-government agencies. This meant that, on the whole, government had a tendency to be unduly paternalistic. This tendency was reinforced by the desire to protect the indigenous peoples against the too rapid introduction of change. From the vantage point of our subsequent experience this paternalism appears to have rested on fallacious assumptions and reasoning. It led to placing insufficient responsibility for change on to the African peoples themselves; and they were deprived of learning for themselves the arts of administration and production which they needed to cope with it.

The framework of public works required for a modern economy in these territories will now, in even greater measure, fall to be provided by liberal assistance from international sources. Moreover, great opportunities are for the first time open to the African people to press forward with changes too long frustrated by their own, and by foreign, political and social attitudes. Assuming the rule of law, order, and reliable standards of government, the newly independent States have the opportunity of sweeping away unnecessary customary and social obstacles to change which the metropolitan Powers were not in a position to remove for fear of arousing the misunderstanding and resentment of the people. Political and economic democracy in these newly developing countries can find common ground in meeting the pent-up demands for education and administrative and economic opportunity among their people. But there is more to it than the release of such energies. The African States are entering upon a stage of world economic development in which the great technical and transport developments of our time are so rapidly reducing the barriers to communication of every kind that almost any country or region which has something to contribute by way of labour or natural resources can, given even a modicum of reliability in the conduct of its affairs, attract to it those able to assist it to commence the development of potential assets.

The barriers to economic growth are far more likely to be found in the field of administration and political institutions than in the lack of resources or of individuals at home or from abroad to undertake their development. Probably at no previous time in history has there been available such a network of private and public international agencies seeking to assist in the exploitation of the natural resources of the world and experimenting in the problems of training and technique in order to do so. It is the paradox of our times that just when science and technique stand poised for major advances in easing the burden of man's labour and in multiplying his powers over the hitherto unopened, uncultivated, or under-utilized regions of the world, the forces of unbridled nationalism and outworn tribalism bar the way to that private and collective international co-operation without which these advances cannot be made.

In the last resort the future of the newly independent countries of Africa, as well as that of countries in a similar position elsewhere, will depend on the extent to which not only they, but also the more advanced countries of the world, can adapt their institutions to the new requirements and opportunities of the world economy. For in a technically shrinking world there is little room for absolute political or economic independence. If this is realized the problems of Africa will be seen as little different in kind from those elsewhere: as problems, that is, in the relative rates of change of economic and political institutions and not merely as a struggle between races, tribes, and nationalities—for, if such they should be permitted to remain, the present possibilities which Africa holds out for constructive advance will be seriously impeded.

"*AFRICAN SOCIALISM*"

"African Socialism" is a catchphrase among African leaders, the great majority of whom probably classify themselves as socialist and hence accept an "African road to socialism" as their economic objective. It is probably also true that with most of them the Leninist theory that nineteenth-century imperialism was the consequence of expanding capitalist systems strikes a sympathetic chord.

What does the term mean? Primarily, it connotes state participation in the economy and state guidance of mass efforts at developing national resources. But it may also have a secondary meaning, implying sharp limitations on foreign activity in the domestic economy, as well as perhaps a general wariness of foreign economic interests, as possible forerunners of a new imperialism. It is this secondary meaning that is of particular significance in African international relations.

Selection 23 briefly contrasts "African Socialism" in a number of West African countries, with special reference to the meaning of it for foreign economic interests. A general agreement on aims is found, but a difference on methods as between "reformers" and "revolutionaries." The article offers Senghor of Senegal and Nkrumah of Ghana, respectively, as examples of these two types.

These are good choices, for these men are outstanding examples of African socialists who have tried to resolve the dilemma between foreign economic ties and the presumed danger of renewed foreign domination. Senghor's solution (Selection 24) is significant both in ideological terms, because while novel it is arrived at within the framework of Marxist theory, and in terms of international politics, because it permits retention of close ties with Europe. Note that Senegal is a leading member of the Brazzaville group, which is closely associated with France in certain ways, and is associated as well with the European Economic Community (Common Market).

In contrast, Nkrumah's solution is rather more orthodox (Selection 25). He calls for African unity *against* the threat of "neo-colonialism" in the form of the Common Market. Note here that Ghana is a leading member of the "radical" Casablanca bloc, and has refused association with the Common Market.

Selection 23

What Is African Socialism?*

WEST AFRICA

The latest instalments of Socialist thinking contained in Ghana's new policy statement, *Programme for Work and Happiness*, have again raised the problem: what is meant by African Socialism? Most of the newly independent countries, not only in Africa but the world over, proclaim Socialism as their goal. One reason for this is that most of the leaders have been radical politicians, often operating within left-wing groups in Europe, and they carry with them into independence a European Socialist tradition.

A more profound reason is that Socialist ideas respond to much that is present in traditional African society. Again, the prevalence of Socialist thinking is partly due to the simple economic facts of life. Every government wants to achieve rapid results in economic development. Western Europe achieved its industrial revolution over a long period, largely through the amassing and investment of private savings which became capital. African hopes and plans allow no time for this. Almost all economic efforts made have to come from the State. Some form of Socialism is therefore inevitable.

These factors can all be seen in a single political speech of President Nkrumah's, made in 1959: "Our aims embrace the creation of a welfare state based on African Socialist principles, adapted to suit Gha-

* Reprinted by permission from *West Africa* (May 12, 1962), p. 507.

naian conditions, in which all citizens, regardless of class, tribe, colour or creed, shall have equal opportunities . . . we aim to create in Ghana a Socialist society in which each will give according to his ability and receive according to his needs."

These aims would, on the whole, not be questioned by any other African statesman. But there is great variation in methods. The exponents can be roughly divided into the reformers and the revolutionaries, into those who place the emphasis on drastic State action "from above" and those who favour more gradual change—"from below."

Representing the gradualists is Senegal's President, M. Senghor. On the theoretical plane, he is, if anything, more of a Socialist than President Nkrumah; he has written in books and innumerable lectures of his own concept of African Socialism. He said in the lecture he gave at Oxford recently: "We have decided to borrow from the Socialist experiments—both theoretical and practical—only certain elements, certain scientific and technical values, which we have grafted like scions on to the wild stock of Negritude. For this latter, as a complex of civilised values, is traditionally Socialist in character."

But, in the next breath, Senghor points to the practical limitations, and it is these that are most characteristic of him. As is well known, in contrast to Ghana, measures which restrict capitalist activity have been few and Senegal is still regarded as a promising, if diminishing, field for French investment. Senghor says:

"And yet we have not legally suppressed private capitalism which is foreign to our country; we have not even nationalised anything. . . . Why? Because we began by analysing our situation as an underdeveloped and colonised country. The essential task was to win back our national independence. Next we had to eliminate the flaws of colonial rule while preserving its positive contributions. . . . Where private capitalism comes into peaceful competition with Socialism, the latter must, I feel sure, emerge triumphant. . . . In the meantime, we need capital, even from private sources."

Ghanaians see this link between Socialism and decolonisation the other way round. Far from being a reason for proceeding cautiously, the European presence in commerce is a reason for applying more Socialism. As the new policy statement says: "The basic aim of our economic development is to free the country from alien control and domination. To achieve this it is necessary to participate in wholesale and retail sectors of trade throughout the country. This is the only way to protect the people from exploitation by alien monopoly interests."

Why this difference? Apart from the difference in character and temperament between Nkrumah and Senghor, the economic facts of life in the countries are different, too. Ghana is the richer country, with more varied natural resources and a more highly developed economy. Her cocoa goes as much to Europe and America as to Britain. Senegal's groundnuts, on the other hand, are still bought exclusively by France, at guaranteed prices and in guaranteed quantities. Senegal's progress depends on foreign investment, as does everybody else's, and France still makes sure her protégé does not get too much of that from undesirable quarters. This is a dilemma from which the Ghanaians have escaped. Their pacts with the East ensure that foreign capital doesn't have to be "capitalist."

Senegal's recently published Development Plan contains an instalment of Socialism: the private trader is squeezed out of the domestic produce buying trade by the setting up of new marketing boards. Lucky Ghanaians! They had their marketing boards well before independence and are able to take this aspect of socialisation for granted. But of course the big projects in both countries (the Volta in Ghana, phosphate exports and an oil refinery in Senegal) still depend on Western private enterprise. The scope for Socialist action in either country is therefore limited.

To the general statement that the new African countries' lack of private savings makes Socialism essential, Nigeria comes nearest to providing an exception. She has a comparatively high level of private saving and investment—and even a Stock Exchange in Lagos. However, if Nigeria's home resources are greater, so also are her needs; her new plan will cost over £600m. So Nigeria, too, depends on State action for economic progress, but few of her leaders have been reared in left-wing schools.

A different atmosphere pervades the Ivory Coast. Although President Houphouet-Boigny was founder-president of that very radical nationalist party, the African Democratic Rally, the Ivory Coast is now the last haven of apparently unfettered French enterprise. New industries are mushrooming, and even small trade is still in French hands. However, Houphouet-Boigny's admirers consider that he is merely being shrewd; he is letting the French lay as many "golden eggs" as possible, the better to spread the benefits later. Already the first breath of change has come to the Ivory Coast; the State has nationalised uncultivated land, higher salaries have been taxed, and a special tax has been levied on foreign firms who repatriate too much of their profits.

The social and economic policies in the different African countries are, in fact, drawing closer together as governments come to realise that the courses of action open to them are limited. Thus, conservative régimes like those of the Ivory Coast and Senegal are moving to more radical positions, and some, at least, of the radical régimes are becoming more "moderate." Ghana, with her resources and her exceptionally strong-willed régime, is an exception. She is still travelling in an Eastward and leftward direction. But both the "revolutionary" régimes in former French Guinea and Mali have made some retreats.

Selection 24

A Community of Free and Equal Peoples with the Mother Country*

LÉOPOLD SÉDAR SENGHOR

Léopold Sédar Senghor, President of the Republic of Senegal, is a poet, author, and politician who has enjoyed a long career of activity both in Senegal and France.

The peoples of Dark Africa today stand at a crossroads. Whether they want it or not, they are pushed toward *independence*, "condemned to independence." First of all they are impelled by the hurricane of nationalist feelings which was born during the revolution at the point of French bayonets and spread across Europe and from there to

* Reprinted by permission of the author and the publisher from *Western World* (October 1958), pp. 39–42. *Western World* is now incorporated in *European Review*, London.

Asia—to rebound upon Africa in the second half of the 20th Century. The arising of European nationalisms led to the conflict of nationalisms. This is a law of life, a law of history.

Here then are the peoples of Dark Africa, awakened in their turn to a *national awareness*. Here they are, "condemned to independence." It matters little whether they shrink from this, aware of their backwardness, whether they seek to cling to their mother countries, or seek to postpone matters. The course of history is irreversible; in a few decades at most, the peoples of Africa will have arrived at various stages of independence—at least a *nominal independence*.

The elite of Dark Africa, knowing that their peoples are impelled by an irreversible movement, but realizing that nominal independence does not necessarily entail real independence, wonder about the future. It is for them to prepare the future for their various peoples. It is up to them to choose between the different paths, the different political and economic systems which present themselves.

FINDING THE AFRICAN ROAD TO SOCIALISM

The *socialist path* seems to me to be incontestably the best one . . .

But there is not one socialist path; there are several. There is a Scandinavian socialism, an Israeli socialism, a Yugoslav socialism, a Mexican socialism. In the Communist bloc one may even discover several roads to socialism—the Russian, the Polish, the Chinese. In each case, it is a matter of analyzing the *concrete situation of man* to find an original solution, the only one which will be effective because it is in the service of man.

This is true because *socialism is humanism*. In almost every case, the socialist analysis presents us with the situation of men living in society as if they were foreign to it, dominated by nature, and by a minority of other men. The political task therefore is to transform an abnormal situation, and make it normal; to create order out of disorder; to restore these outsiders to their human dignity.

It is up to us to seek and find the *African road to socialism*.

Western Europe presents us with a society in which *capitalism* obstructs all harmonious development by alienating man both in relation to the product of his work and in relation to the work itself. Through this double separation, we truly demoralize and dehumanize the worker. This alienation also affects the employer. The employer, under these conditions, is a man who oppresses another man, and in so doing isolates himself and betrays his own human function. This specific situation explains the *class struggle* and the fact that the object of European socialism is to suppress social contradictions by suppressing classes.

It is quite otherwise in Dark Africa—not that the alienation is absent. On the contrary it is more serious. What is this situation in reality? It is that of men who were once free, who have now become *dependent.* It is the situation of peoples who have been deprived of the freedom to govern themselves, of their *civilization*, and more important, their *culture*, that spirit by which they adapted themselves to their environment and at the same time adapted the environment to their own character.

This political and cultural alienation is also accompanied by an economic and social alienation, which is like that of the European worker. European monopoly capitalism, reaching out over Dark Africa becomes *imperialism.* Imperialism results from an understanding between European capitalists to open up new outlets in the underdeveloped countries, notably in Dark Africa. They buy raw materials at extremely low prices and sell manufactured goods at artificially high prices. Imperialism is the *economics of slavery.*

TOWARDS INDEPENDENCE

This, then, is our situation in Dark Africa. The structure of our African Negro society is not the same as that of Western European society. The solutions for our contradictions, therefore, cannot be the same. In Europe, socialism has assigned itself the objective of suppressing classes and socializing the means of production through the "dictatorship of the proletariat." In this way man is to be liberated and become an individual. In Dark Africa, social classes are of recent formation, and *they wear the badges of color;* they are separated by the color bar. It is a remarkable fact that within African Negro society there are no clearly differentiated classes; the stratification into antagonistic classes has only begun; it can still be stopped.

It follows from this that our socialist objective in Dark Africa cannot be, as it is in Europe, the matter of suppressing inequalities resulting from the formation of antagonistic classes. Instead, the object is to suppress the inequalities which result from conquest, from the *facts of colonialism* and political domination. To suppress the inequalities resulting from political domination is to place the peoples of Europe and the peoples of Africa on an equal footing. This requires the restoration to the latter of their *self-determination*, their right to decide freely their own destinies and first of all the political regime of their own choice. In short, it means restoring their *independence*. Thus, by the same act, both the colonizers and the colonized will be liberated—for both are the captives of colonialism.

Let us have the courage to recognize the fact that independence is not in itself a solution; it is only the beginning of a solution; independence, as I have said, is nominal. Every nation today, including the United States and the Soviet Union, depends to some degree upon other nations. This is especially true of underdeveloped countries. It is not enough for such a country to resolve its *external contradictions*, expressed through its political dependence. It is still necessary to resolve its *internal contradictions*, of an economic and social character; the lack of trained leaders and capital, the imbalance between agriculture and industry; the disproportion between the respective earnings of civil servants, those in private enterprise, and of peasant masses.

These internal contradictions cannot be overcome simply by efforts at discipline and increased production, although such efforts are the prerequisites and the *sine qua non* of any national recovery. It is essential for us, in the undeveloped countries of Dark Africa to go beyond the stage of formal independence, in order eventually to achieve real independence, in a larger context. It makes little difference whether we call this context a *Commonwealth*, a confederate union or a community of free peoples. It is a matter of freely accepting limitations on sovereignty—of giving up the fictional absolute of independence—to enjoy real independence.

Yet the problem is not only political, as we can see by analyzing our internal contradictions. Since we have chosen a *Negro African road to socialism*, we are confronted with this question: what will our attitude be, or more precisely our action, in relation to capitalism?

First of all, I should note that a socialist society cannot dispense with capital any more than a capitalist society. The socialist economy takes over from the capitalist economy its techniques and notably its *capital*, by which I mean "the goods used to produce other goods." As the founders of socialism have often emphasized, socialist society cannot build itself out of nothing. It is only in highly industrialized countries that true socialism can be built but I do not say that it is only in these countries that revolution can occur. This is not the situation in Dark Africa. One cannot collectivize or even "nationalize" the "means of production" which do not exist. I may add that all economists, including the socialists, foresee the accumulation of capital as the necessary means for economic and social development.

The accumulation of capital is based on productive and private investments. Anyone who speaks of "public investments" is referring to aid from Europe, America being considered here as an extension of Europe. I shall return to this question. As for private investments we must be careful not to kill the goose which lays the golden eggs. These investments will be encouraged by long-term agreements which will exclude nationalizations and which will be scrupulously respected.

Does this mean that we must give up carrying on a socialist policy? Not at all. It simply means that we must adapt it to our own Negro African realities, to our own situation. How? By making plans for years ahead which will distinguish between a free sector, a mixed sector, and a socialized sector. Agriculture and livestock will be socialized on the basis of democratic *cooperation* which corresponds to the Negro African collectivist spirit. Trade, although regulated, will be free. As for mining and processing industries, within the plan, these will be divided into two sub-sectors. One of these will be based on a mixed economy with the participation of the Negro African state. The other sub-sector, while neither nationalized nor mixed, will nevertheless be subject to certain social obligations. There is no reason why we should not expect industrialists to agree to making certain social investments in canteens, dispensaries, workers' housing, etc. This will be achieved through suitable social legislation following bilateral discussions, between the government and employers and between the government and trade unions.

The need for European-African cooperation derives from the fact that an underdeveloped country which has achieved nominal independence cannot acquire real independence if it remains underdeveloped. It must obtain external aid. The solution can be found in its entry into a larger ensemble, in the form of a *confederacy*.

EUROPE AND AFRICA MUST COOPERATE

All the countries of Dark Africa, except for Ethiopia, have political, economic and cultural ties with a European country. This is a historic fact, and nothing is gained by denying history. There is no question of denying the fact of colonialism, but of overcoming it and going beyond it. It is therefore in the interests of these countries, once their nominal independence is achieved, not to separate them from their former mother countries, but to achieve new ties based on liberty, equality and cooperation.

I say that this is in their interest. They need technicians and capital. Long continued political and economic relations, a common language of international character, have created links which it would be catastrophic to break. Africa and Europe are genuinely *complementary*, in terms of politics, economics and culture. Is not Europe the source for the socialism which we have recognized as the most effective means for liberation? And let us note that for fifty years Negro African art has enriched European culture.

I am far from suggesting that this necessary European-African cooperation should exclude *inter-African cooperation*. The vertical solidarity mentioned does not prevent a horizontal solidarity between European states, as typified by the Common Market. It is impossible to think of uniting the states of Europe by disuniting those of Africa—the artificiality of whose frontiers is well known. Cooperation with Ghana will strengthen the roots of our Senegalese character, our Negro character, whereas cooperation with France will permit it to expand. Aspects of true culture include both *deep roots* and the *capacity for transplantation*.

How will this social structure be built, to include both the vertical and horizontal relationship? This only requires an effort of imagination. We shall certainly find a solution which will make it both flexible and strong, and able to resist the tests of time.

Readers who have followed me this far may bring up the example of Liberia and Ghana. These examples do not have the same value as evidence.

It is apparent that without the United States, Liberia could not continue to exist as an independent state. It is equally apparent that Liberia will not be genuinely independent until it has abolished discrimination between the *Americo-Liberians* and the *natives*, and enters resolutely upon the path of democratic socialism.

The example of Ghana is more convincing. If Ghana enjoys real independence, it is because it has begun to create its own cadres, to construct its own economic and social infrastructure, and to accumulate capital. It has done more than this. Having gained independence, Ghana entered freely into a *Commonwealth* which has ceased to be British, but which continues to supply British technicians. In addition to this, my friend Kwame Nkrumah, Prime Minister of Ghana, has long since chosen the African way towards socialism. I also recognize the inherent threat of *dictatorship* which is not in the Negro African tradition. I understand Nkrumah's difficulties perfectly, the more so since the opposition does not hesitate to use violence. I believe he is right in wanting a unitary state, supported by a strong and stable government. I only hope that, after overcoming present difficulties, he will be able to establish *democratic socialism.*

There is no doubt that all the peoples of Dark Africa have turned their eyes toward Ghana. Whether they are subjects of France, Belgium or Portugal, these peoples vaguely dream—and their leaders consciously think—of following Ghana's path. I speak of "Ghana's path" which means independence by stages, and the establishment with the former mother country of a community of free and equal peoples. This again does not exclude inter-African solidarity.

Europe would be wrong to disregard the realities of history. It would be wrong to remain deaf to the anguished appeals of the Negro-African elite. It would be wrong not to grasp the opportunity which has been presented to it to create a "*third world*" of fraternal cooperation with the African peoples and not only with the Negro Africans.

If Europe tries to maintain its domination, there is the risk that the whole African continent will swing heavily towards the East or towards the West, towards one of the two giant powers, both of which preach anti-colonialism. This would not be a factor for peace. . . .

Selection 25

Africa's Liberation and Unity*

Kwame Nkrumah

One of the earlier and most eminent African nationalist and Pan-African leaders, Kwame Nkrumah is now President of the Republic of Ghana.

. . . If we independent states were unified in a political and economic union, having a common foreign and defence policy, controlling a unified military command, we should be in a much stronger position to assist the territories still struggling for independence. An over-all economic plan, covering an Africa united on a continental basis, must increase our total industrial and economic power; hence, our combined strength reinforced by a common purpose would add enormously to the united front which we could turn against the enemy. So long as we remain disunited, so long as we remain balkanised, whether regionally or in separate national units, we shall be at the mercy of imperialism and neo-colonialism.

We must therefore face the issue of African Unity now; for only unity will make the artificial boundaries and regional demarcations imposed by colonialism obsolete and superfluous. African Unity will thus provide an effective remedy for border disputes and internecine troubles. In a united Africa there would be no frontier claims between Ethiopia and Somalia or between Zanzibar and Kenya, Guinea and Liberia or between Ghana, Togoland and the Ivory Coast, because we would regard ourselves as one great continental family of Nations.

Among the new states in Africa are some which, through fragmentation, have been left so weak economically, that they are unable to

---

* Reprinted by permission from *Voice of Africa*, Vol. 2, No. 6 (June 1962), pp. 7–10.

stand on their own feet. This is the result of a deliberate policy of the withdrawing colonial powers, who have created in Africa several small, feeble and unstable and unviable states, in the hope of ensuring their continued dependence upon the former colonial power for economic and technical aid. Indeed, the intention goes farther than that, and is more insidious. . . . The underlying design is to induce national jealousies and rivalries such as nourished the outbreak of the First World War. At best, it is hoped that such a policy may lead to open conflict. At worst, it must present tough obstacles to the movement for total African freedom and African unity. This is the inner plan of neo-colonialism, the latest instrument of imperialism. While relinquishing political rule it contrives to control the foreign and internal policy of the states it still dominates through the bestowal of material aid.

In effect, only the outward forms have changed, but the substance of colonialism remains. Foreign imports are still protected, local development is clamped down, social progress is retarded, and fiscal policy is controlled from the metropolitan capital. The impact of these semi-independent states on the liberation of Africa is calamitous. Bound up as they are with the policies of their sponsors, they are unable to take a determined, independent line on issues involving the colonialists and the still enslaved peoples on this continent. Some of the leaders, it must be confessed, do not see the struggle of their brother Africans as part of their own struggle. Even if they did, they would not be free to express their solidarity. Thus rifts are consciously created by the imperialists between Africans, which they can sit back and watch with sly satisfaction, as well as contempt for those who fail to see how they are being used against Africa's best interests. Regrettably, those states include some who were among the freedom fighters of yesterday and who, having won their independence, are willing to drop it for some token aid, and thereby deny to those still struggling for freedom even their moral support. Here is a phenomenon against which all African freedom fighters must be on their guard and resist to the utmost.

Even though I appreciate the difficulties facing us, I must admit I find it strange to watch some of us returning willingly to the colonialist fold. This time they don't even have the excuse of being forced to subject themselves to foreign domination. It makes one wonder why so much effort and sacrifice, and so many lives, were given up to the achievement of independence in the first place, if it can be so quickly and easily surrendered. Unhappily for us, colonialism creates in some, intellectual allegiances which are not severed at the moment of independence, but remain to condition loyalties away from Africa towards the metropolis which draws them. They are unable, it would appear, to accept the idea that Africans can get together to make a viable and going concern of a combined African continent, but rather see their salvation in coming together in associations like the Franco-African Community mooted recently at Bangui.

Although there are many here who speak English, French, Spanish or Portuguese, nevertheless we are all African—Africans fighting for Africa's independence, Africa's unity, Africa's future.

I have said that I understand the difficulties of these states which are drawing away from the African community back into that of Europe. Faced with the demands of their people for rising standards of living and better social conditions, but charged with economies that can hardly meet the recurrent expenses of administration and maintenance, they are in a dilemma. And standing at their elbows are the neo-colonialist agents, beckoning them back with a smile into the web of imperialism, though it may have a new look this time and offer the irresistible bait of immediate help. But this help will be far outweighed, as they will experience with no great loss of time, by the knots into which their economies will be tied by the Euro-African association. Imperialism does not change its nature; it only changes its front. It still needs colonial appendages, whether in name or in fact, to exploit and, at the same time, to support its cold war strategy.

In the face of the serious threat to our economy and independence in Africa, we must begin to build immediately our own continental Common Market, for it is easy for anyone who studies the Common Market Organisation* closely to realize that the Common Market is aimed at harnessing the African countries to satisfy the profit-lust of the imperialist bloc and to prevent us from following an independent neutralist policy. It is also easy to see that the imperialists and colonialists are determined to retain the African countries in the position of suppliers of cheap raw material.

---

* *Editor's Note:* Nkrumah refers here to the *European Economic Community*, established in 1957 among France, West Germany, Italy, Belgium, The Netherlands, and Luxembourg.

If we do not resist this threat, and if we throw in our lot with the Common Market, we shall doom the economy of Africa to a state of perpetual subjection to the economy of western Europe. This will of course hinder the industrialisation of our young African states. It is impossible to think of economic development and national independence without possessing an unfettered capacity for maintaining a strong industrial power. The activities of the Common Market are therefore fraught with dangerous political and economic consequences for the Independent African States. The organisation constitutes an attempt to replace the old system of colonial exploitation by a new system of collective colonialism which will be stronger and more dangerous than the old evils we are striving to liquidate from our continent.

There is an alternative to the Euro-African association, with its deadly implications for Africa's independence and progress. It is in an African Economic Community, in which we can all pool our production and our trade, to common advantage. It is not difficult to imagine that the neo-colonialists will describe this as a pooling of poverty. It is, however, too simple a distortion of fact. Africa is rich and not poor, as the great wealth that has been taken out of our continent over five centuries of despoliation and extortion very well proves. Africa has immense actual and potential wealth. Gold, diamonds, copper, manganese, bauxite, iron ore, uranium, asbestos, chrome, cobalt, a host of other minerals, our essential agricultural produce, have all been drained away by colonialist-imperialism. Africa is far from being poor. It is Africans who are poor, because of the uncounted profit that has been made out of the exploitation of their labour and their lands. If we are being baited to enter a European Community, we must have something that community needs—and needs badly, when it pretends to offer a bonus by way of aid. When Greeks come bearing gifts, should we not look them well in the mouth, if I may mix my metaphor? But I am sure you get my meaning. When we new, untried, inexperienced states are flattered into European alliances, we enter not as equals, but as suppliers of primary products at the generosity of industrial converters. How generous they can be, we have learned from our sad experience over a good long time. Who fixes prices? Who can play off one against the other by allowing the goods of associates in free of tariff and placing a tariff on others? As long as it is possible to deal with us singly, we are at the mercy of the imperialists rather than their generosity. And we shall find ourselves in the same old cleft stick of receiving the lowest possible prices for our raw materials, while those of us who are obliged to buy their manufactured goods, because of being members of their associations, will pay for them through the nose. These same states will find themselves tied up in knots which will prevent their going into an open market for their needs of goods and capital investment. And, above all, they will lose their option of non-alignment and find themselves dragged into the diplomacy of imperialist cold war politics which will operate against the independence and intrinsic interests of Africa. Those of us who cannot see through these implications can only be suffering from an intense myopia.

Within our African Community, our pooled production will place us in a position to bargain for higher prices, and so secure greater revenues, out of which we can invest in our development. At the same time, we can trade freely among ourselves and buy from overseas in the cheapest markets. We can turn for aid to those sources which will give us the most suitable terms while leaving us free to follow our own internal and external policy. But more even than this narrow co-operation, we need the wider continental economic plan which will allow us, within unity, to exploit Africa's tremendous resources for our common welfare and greater African development and progress.

If we are really sincere in our desire to see the end of imperialism in Africa, then, apart even from the considerations involved in African unity, we should turn away from any form of association with Europe which, through its neo-colonialist control of our policies, will help rather to sustain that imperialism than undermine it. It is bad enough that our economies, as a legacy of colonial rule, are imperialist-controlled, and that we have to strive by every means to rid ourselves of this economic imperialism and secure our development and progress on solid African foundations. This is another reason why we should come together in a unified African economic plan, which, operating on a continental scale, can make a solid attack on imperialist domination in Africa.

We should, without delay, aim at the creation of a joint African military command. There is little wisdom in our present separate efforts to build up and maintain defence forces which, in any case, would be ineffective in any major conflict. If we examine this problem realistically, we would ask, which single African state could protect itself against an imperialist aggressor? And how much more difficult this will be when some states are allowing the imperialists to maintain bases on their territories. I have already referred to the military force which South Africa is raising and the danger it poses for the new African states and the struggle of those still in chains. Only our unity can provide us with anything like adequate protection. If we do not unite and combine our military forces, South Africa, along with her allies, or any other colonialist-imperialist power, can pick us off one by one. Not only that: some of us, out of a sense of insecurity, may be drawn into making defence pacts with the imperialists which will endanger the security of all of us.

It follows that if we set up in Africa a common economic planning organisation and a joint military command, we shall have to work out and adopt a common foreign policy to give political direction to our continental development and our continental defence. . . .

Those problems can best be met within a unified Africa, and it should be possible, in the higher reaches of our endeavour, to devise a constitutional structure which will secure the objectives I have outlined and yet preserve the sovereignty of each of the countries joining the union. Countries within the union will naturally maintain their own constitutions and continue to use their national emblems and national anthems and other symbols and paraphernalia of sovereignty.

Regional associations and territorial groupings can only be other forms of balkanisation unless they are conceived within the framework of a continental union. There are existing models which we can modify or adapt into our pattern. The United States of America, the Soviet Union, India and China have proved the efficacy of unions embracing large stretches of land and population. When the first thirteen states of America tried to promote the idea of a United States, this was ridiculed as an empty dream and vigorously resisted by many. Today, America is the foremost industrial country in the world, and the states within her union now number fifty. And who would have thought that almost a hundred different peoples at various levels of economic, social and political development could have been welded into the mighty state which the Soviet Union has become in such a short space of time?

The example of Europe, which is left in confusion after centuries of mutually destructive economic warfare and competition, because it failed to build a sound foundation for common political action and understanding, should be a lesson for us all. But with the exigencies created by the shrinking of empires, the growing socialist world and the needs generated by the greater productive capacities inherent in present-day techniques, even Europe is now beginning to seek its common associations. It is paradoxical, therefore, that some African states should be turning away from their proper African affiliations to those of another continent. Rather we should all be working ceaselessly to bring to fruition the fond hope of African unity to which we all give lip service and to which most of us are resolutely dedicated. . . .

FREE AFRICA AND THE FREE WORLD

There are objectors in plenty to any given solution to Africa's economic dilemmas. In Selection 25, for example, Kwame Nkrumah proposed a solution (the "African Economic Community" or "African Common Market") stressing economic self-help, and rejected ties with the European Common Market. This of course fits with his emphasis on political independence and the dangers of "neo-colonialism." But a leader from former French Africa, referring to the proposed African Common Market, replies: "Our economies are, basically, entirely agricultural. They are in no way complementary. Shall we swap cocoa for coffee? That wouldn't help us catch up on the enormous development gap—a gap which we have promised ourselves to bridge with European help. For the moment, an African Common Market is a hollow formula."

As some eighteen African states, mostly former French and Belgian colonies, are now associated with the European Common Market, this economic issue is at present one of the liveliest in African international relations. In

Selection 26 Barbara Ward Jackson, the distinguished writer on economics, discusses it, showing how the European Common Market constitutes a political and economic bar to greater cooperation within Africa. She suggests a solution—parallel economic groupings in Europe and Africa, cooperating with one another.

Intra-African arrangements, or African association with the European Economic Community, do not exhaust the possibilities for economic coordination and cooperation. Such regional or interregional proposals have in fact stimulated others by complicating the lives of those left outside these arrangements. It is in part this factor, in part the general need to place the trade of the "less-developed" countries on a sounder basis, that underlie the policies formulated in Selection 27. As indicated in Blumenthal's article, the United States is now lending a hand in the effort to organize commodity price stabilization on a global basis. Africa thus will, it is hoped, be drawn into cooperative efforts to promote trade stability and expansion within a new framework transcending the African continent and "Eur-Africa" as well.

Selection 26

Free Africa and the Common Market*

Barbara Ward Jackson

Barbara Ward Jackson is a British author and journalist, trained as an economist, who has written extensively on the less-developed countries and international affairs.

It is already clear that the most serious obstacles to Britain's entry into the Common Market lie not so much in any direct clash of economic interest between Britain and Western Europe as in the difficulty of transforming and modifying the vast web of Britain's external trading commitments. A loose, worldwide, pragmatic association has to be shrunk, without too much damage, into a close, contractual relationship. For extra-European communities, the squeezing and pinching threaten economic disturbance and political resentment and nowhere perhaps do the problems seem more daunting than in independent Africa where, by a chance of history, the confrontation of Commonwealth and Common Market is physically most direct and potentially most disruptive.

A glance at the map of Africa shows the physical entanglements. Into the solid bulk of ex-French West Africa clutch the fingers of the English-speaking communities—Gambia, Sierra Leone, Ghana and Nigeria—and, one should add, Liberia. In the Cameroons, an ex-British and an ex-French territory have come together in an uneasy federal association. Down to Katanga, the French speakers prevail. But across from them, on the other side of the continental divide, in-

---

* Reprinted by permission from *Foreign Affairs* (April 1962), pp. 419–430.

dependent Tanganyika may well be the first member of a new, wide, English-speaking association in East Africa.

These intermingled territories cannot ignore each other. However inchoate and undirected, the sense of African unity is already a strong political force. The new nations, most of them desperately weak, have come to independence in an age dominated by vast federal structures—by the United States, by the Soviet Union, by the ambition if not the fact of a United Europe. And even were the idea of common markets and political associations not fashionably in the air, African leaders would still feel the gap between the frailty of their fledgling and fragmented independence and the giant communities abroad. Their post-colonial status and the continuance of Western colonial control on their southern frontiers only increase their sensitiveness. Dr. Nkrumah may not be accepted as a leader of continental scope. But few African statesmen can ignore the influence of his passionate pan-Africanism, especially among the younger men.

There are solid economic reasons, too, for transcending the new state boundaries. Apart from the Union of South Africa, the African continent is still a system of essentially colonial economies. In spite of decisive differences between the colonizing policies of the different metropolitan powers—differences which go to the heart of the Common Market-Commonwealth controversy—the results of their work bear a family resemblance. In each economy, the core of the modern sector is primary production for export, either minerals or tropical foods and fruits. In each, the main infrastructure has been built to forward that trade. All lines of communication drain down to the ports which are—save in Western Nigeria—the only really big cities. Contact between territories is so slight that in some neighboring countries roads do not meet at frontiers and telephone conversations can be conducted only through Paris or London. Inter-African trade is minimal and the earnings from exports are spent largely on the import of manufactured goods, mainly from Europe and through foreign intermediaries, and on food which a static subsistence economy in the countryside no longer produces in sufficient quantity.

This colonial pattern cannot be changed simply by intensifying economic relations with the metropolitan powers. A world surplus of coffee and cocoa is already in prospect. If all the expansion plans of the separate African economies are successful, surpluses in palm products, peanuts, sugar, citrus, bananas and pineapples lie ahead. The aim of added agricultural output appears in every plan. Yet the Western stomach cannot be stretched to consume so much. Industrialization is the alternative adopted by every government, but industrialization will hardly suceed rapidly or adequately if it has to rely on export markets already choked by the West's sophisticated products or the cheap manufactures of Asia. Africa's most urgent need—like Latin America's—is thus an *internal* market large enough to absorb the products of industrialization, and this need points toward local coöperation and integration. Economic necessity reinforces the political arguments for greater unity.

Thus the aftermath of the colonial years makes closer association essential. Equally, it makes it remarkably difficult. Although French and British colonial policy helped to produce types of local economy which are recognizably of the same type—dependent economies, *economies de traite*—the relations between these economies and their metropolitan powers diverged sharply. France saw its territories in Africa as extensions of the mother country and as, in a sense, part of the French state. Citizenship and political representation on a basis of complete equality between Frenchmen and French Africans would be the ultimate political achievement. Meanwhile, as much assimilation as possible was the rule in economic policy. This approach led to a species of economic closed circuit between France and its dependent territories. All the colonies were part of a single monetary system—the franc zone, in which the local African franc was freely convertible into French francs and had behind it the entire resources of the French Treasury. No territory had to worry with the problem either of financing imports or of balancing local expenditure against local receipts. French grants provided much of the capital and when recurrent costs rose, France covered part of the local budgetary deficits as well. In addition, tropical products had guaranteed markets in France at prices which were often well above the world price level.

As a result, those engaged in the small modernized sectors of the economy—the export trades, the cities, the administration—acquired standards of living and expenditure often much above what the local economy could really support. In return, the colonies imported their manufactures almost wholly from France at prices often above the world level, and French officials and residents sent their savings and profits back to France. So, of course, did other "expatriates" in other colonies. The French were, however, twice as numerous as the British. Thus, in a sense, the franc zone functioned independently of world markets as a species of closed economic world of its own. The circuit would have been broken only if the dependent territories had succeeded in buying extensively from other countries and thus presenting the central monetary authorities in Paris with insistent demands for foreign exchange. But strict exchange control and a quota system prevented any leaks of this kind.

Since 1948, the French Union has totally abandoned, in a rapid series of concessions, the doctrine of political assimilation. Today, all its African colonies are politically independent. But some of the economic practices which once reflected integration still continue. In some ways, they are more powerful than ever. In the last decade, the amount of public capital which France has poured into Africa, south of the Sahara, has reached the startling sum of $300,000,000 a year. At the same time, the weakening of world demand for tropical products and the steady fall in their price has made even more valuable the quotas and agreed prices available in the French market. Moreover, France's entry into the Common Market has offered to its ex-colonies—now associated with the Market under the Treaty of Rome[1]—a further real strengthening and extension of their advantages. The joint Common Market Fund for Development (FEDOM) adds another $100,000,000 a year to the sums flowing into Africa. Tariff barriers against the territories' exports to Western Europe are coming down—although internal excise taxes mitigate the advantage in some degree. Ultimately, a common external tariff will give them a competitive advantage against tropical suppliers outside the Association. It is therefore not surprising that in the talks that are now being carried on to negotiate a new form of association, based this time upon the free political choice of the African territories, the Africans are tending to demand a further consolidation of their present very real advantages, and the extension of the new agreement to cover not five but seven years. Some participants even suggest tough quota systems designed to discriminate against outside competitors.

[1] The Associated States in Africa are Cameroon, the Central African Republic, the two Republics of Congo (Congo-Brazzaville and Congo-Leopoldville), Ivory Coast, Dahomey, Gabon, Upper Volta, Madagascar, Mali, Mauritania, Niger, Senegal, Somalia, Tchad and Togo.

Meanwhile the evolution in British Africa has followed a different route. Since the ultimate aim of British colonial policy was to produce self-governing and finally independent territories, countries such as Ghana or Nigeria were not drawn into a centralized economic system directed by Britain. They had to balance their own books and cover their own expenditure. Membership in the sterling area gave no guarantee that internal overdrafts and external imbalances could be covered by London. Welfare and development funds remained small. Britain granted some imperial preference on tropical products—it varied from 2 to 10 percent—but received no preferences in return except in the two very small territories of Gambia and Sierra Leone. As a result, British Africa traded widely with the rest of the world. During the postwar boom in primary products, large capital reserves were built up by using the device of marketing boards. These boards bought the entire crop, paid the peasant producer a fixed price for his cocoa or his peanuts and then siphoned off the balance between this and soaring world prices into reserves for development. In 1957, on independence, Ghana's reserves reached $700,000,000. But these reserves were not grants from the metropolitan power. They had been truly earned and, save for some restrictions on dollar purchases, could be spent anywhere for capital imports once the local governments began—after 1955—to attempt development in earnest. The system was thus open, geared to world prices, low-cost compared with the French system and connected only loosely with British policy and control. Equally, it received nothing equivalent to France's massive outpouring of capital assistance.

II

These, then, are the two major systems[2] which confront each other in Africa—profoundly alike in basic structure and problems, profoundly different in their external relationships. And at this point in history, it is the divergence in their relations with Europe that dominates and disturbs the African scene—and, through Africa, the prospects for unity in Europe as well. Britain seeks to enter the Common

[2] The future of the former Belgian Congo is still too confused to define, but its past economic history suggests a hybrid between the British and French systems. By treaty, it was committed to non-discriminatory trade and, as a very wealthy colony, it financed its own development. But Belgian assimilation and settlement resembled the more inclusive French pattern, and since 1958 the Congo has been associated with the Common Market.

Market. Unless it can secure associate status for its African ex-colonies, they will, over the next ten years, lose their mild imperial preferences in the British market and face a rising tariff barrier excluding them not only from Europe but from Britain as well. In addition, they may find themselves more directly excluded by quota systems and price-fixing arrangements. Greater production of such export crops as cocoa and coffee may be stimulated in the associated countries by protection and by artificially high prices. The surpluses will grow and depress prices further in the world market. In political terms, the doubling of old colonial frontiers by new customs barriers will damage, perhaps fatally, any hopes of closer African union. These are the risks inherent in Britain's bid to unite with Europe. Unless they can be overcome, they may inhibit the bid itself.

For many observers, the simple and obvious solution is that Britain should secure associate status for its ex-African territories and eliminate at one stroke the difficulties and estrangements which threaten to arise between the English-speaking and French-speaking areas of Africa. But the issue is not so straightforward. Within every group concerned with the negotiations there are hesitations and objections—often opposite ones. In fact, a certain amount of schizophrenia reigns over the whole debate. Take the African associated states. Some of their leaders are pressing for even more exclusive advantages and some governments, notably the Ivory Coast, seem very reluctant to water down the very real gains they derive from trade discrimination by admitting other African competitors to the charmed circle. Nor do all relish the idea of FEDOM having more clients. Britain's record in aid-giving is not such as to suggest that it would fill the gap if the potential claimants of assistance were to increase threefold by the crowding in of the ex-British territories. Yet these same ex-French leaders go off to Monrovia and Lagos and there in solemn conference concur with the leaders of Liberia and Nigeria on the need for an African common market, an African development fund and the closest economic coöperation on a continental scale. They do not seem troubled by the fact that the policies they advocate in Brussels and Paris, on the one hand, and in West Africa, on the other, are diametrically opposed.

There are contradictions on the European side as well. The Germans are full partners in the current negotiations to revise the Treaty of Rome—negotiations which most observers expect to result in an extension and consolidation of the present preferential system. Yet Dr. Erhard has gone on record against discrimination and a quota system and the German Government is exceedingly anxious not to affront the interests of Latin American suppliers of tropical products whose markets are valuable outlets for German exports. In this concern for producers in *other* continents, the Germans share reservations that are felt by the Americans too. The United States Government is most unwilling to see Africa acquire in perpetuity preferential entry to one of the world's largest markets to the exclusion of other developing lands. Pressure from this more liberal side has influenced the Economic Commission of the Common Market to recommend that on all tropical products the eventual external tariff should be halved—a step which would bring the level down to an average of only about 4 percent. Yet in the actual negotiations, it is not yet clear whether this more liberal approach will help to modify and determine the outcome.

But even France, the fount, origin and "onlie begetter" of the whole system, seems of two minds. The traditional approach prevails but it is not unchallenged. In part, the opposition is a sheer question of expense. No one can estimate what the maintenance of the association costs the French taxpayer. Price supports, subsidies, budgetary subventions—a particularly unpopular item in the Assembly—capital aid and technical assistance must, added together, far exceed the published sum of $300,000,000 a year. True, unspecified gains accrue from high salaries to seconded French officials and from the protection granted French exporters. Even so, the amounts are formidable, and it is not only the well-known journalist Raymond Cartier who is beginning to ask whether some of the money might not be better spent in France's own underdeveloped regions—in Brittany or Dordogne.

There are political objections too. Some criticize the whole idea of the closed association as an outdated attempt to extend French *présence* and influence to what is in effect a group of client states. Others argue that once the problem of Algeria is solved, any idea of an elaborate, intensive *vocation africaine* makes little sense. And among some younger officials one even finds the conviction that the whole concept of "Eurafrica," of Africa associated by close vertical relationships with Europe, undermines precisely what it is supposed to foster—friendship with emergent Africa. "The more we recall the old colonial ties," they argue, "the more rapidly will good will towards us and towards Europe be undermined. 'Eurafrica' still suggests the subordination of Africa to Europe, of poverty-stricken primary producers to developed industrial powers, and we lay ourselves open to attacks on our 'undercover economic imperialism' and our 'neo-colonialism.' The need now is to modify or abandon the vertical approach and to encourage instead a parallel movement of unity in Africa to match the growing unity of Europe. Then, perhaps, there can be a fruitful dialogue between the two groups."

At this point we reach the fundamental reason why the straightforward solution of association for all the new African states with the Common Market is, in fact, a pipe dream. At least three politically vital and strategically situated African states reject association and largely for the reasons put forward by the young French critics. Guinea on the ex-French side, Ghana on the ex-British side, oppose association on the ideological ground that the relationship is basically dependent and neo-colonialist, perpetuating unequal relationships, making economic mockery of new-found political independence and frustrating the great pan-African dream. Nor can this simply be dismissed as an extremist view. The moderate Nigerian Government has refused, so far, to consider association and "Eurafrica" has few more forceful and eloquent critics than Mr. Jaja Wachuku, Nigeria's Foreign Minister. In the East, the Tanganyikan Government has let it be known that if Britain joins the Common Market, Tanganyika will leave the Commonwealth.

These are overt official reactions. In addition, one must reckon with a strongly dissident current of opinion emerging everywhere in Africa—even in countries whose leaders support close association. The young Senegalese with pictures of Sékou Touré on their desks, the Action Group opposition in Nigeria, the party extremists who brought about Mr. Julius Nyerere's resignation from office, the supporters—in schools and ministries, in universities and party offices—of the Nkrumah brand of pan-Africanism, all these add up to a kind of second, submerged Africa just below the level of the present leadership, but one which a political earthquake at any time or any point might bring bursting to the surface. And this Africa has in common one thing—rejection of colonialism and "neo-colonialism" in all its forms, from the Portuguese presence to the image of "Eurafrica."

Faced with this apparent *impasse*, there are those in Britain who argue that it must simply be accepted. Ghana and Nigeria, they say, have decided to stay out of the new association, in spite of all its advantages. So be it. They have chosen. Let them go. Then Britain can enter the Common Market unencumbered by either their claims or their protests. In fact, such a course would lead almost certainly to a grave political deterioration. The politics of Africa are already dangerously polarized between the Casablanca grouping of Guinea, Ghana, Mali, Morocco and Egypt and the Monrovia group which contains almost all the others. So far, it has not been entirely easy to define the difference between them. The lines are still fluid. Both support African independence and unity. Both denounce colonialism. Both speak of African economic integration. The Casablanca group includes in Mali a member of the franc zone and a state associated with the Common Market. And constant efforts are being made by one or another member of the Monrovia grouping to end what is still a gap based on emotion, ambition and rival leadership. If, however, Britain's entry into the Common Market consolidated the economic advantages of the ex-French territories leaving Ghana, Nigeria and the rest of ex-British Africa outside, it seems virtually certain that all the not negligible forces of anti-colonialism and pan-Africanism that Dr. Nkrumah and Mr. Sékou Touré between them can mobilize would be directed fiercely against the whole concept of special links with Europe and the Association would become perhaps the principal target of violent pan-African and open anti-European propaganda. All hope of lessening the Monrovia-Casabalanca split would be at an end. On the contrary, the dangerous polarization of politics between "moderates" with Western links and "extremists" with adventurous foreign policies would be fatally intensified.

Nor would the economic consequences be any more encouraging. Economic frontiers and customs barriers following the old colonial boundaries would check any genuine move towards regional integration. The states left outside the Association would be likely to sabotage any bold local schemes for better communications, more rational transport and power systems and for better coördinated planning. In addition, such small buffer states as Upper Volta or the slivers of Dahomey and Togo would come under fierce economic pressure from their neighbors. At the African end of the axis, the whole procedure looks unmistakably like a recipe for unsettled politics and economic frustration.

III

It is the bleakness of these prospects that has encouraged a growing discussion—both in Western Europe and in the United States—of possible alternatives. Underlying a wide variety of proposals and suggestions lie two principles—the first that the vertical lines of close political and economic association between Europe and Africa are not likely to last and that a sounder political aim would be to develop unity on two *parallel* lines, the absorption of Britain into Europe being matched by a steady rapprochement between the ex-British and ex-French and ex-Belgian territories in Africa. Then between the two regional groupings—European and African—there could be close and genuine ties of aid and interest but based on no more formal machinery than has proved necessary and workable in, say, the Colombo Plan.

The second principle is that a specific *general* alternative should be found for each preferential advantage now enjoyed by the associated states. Where, for instance, the robusta coffee production of Ivory Coast or the peanuts of Senegal are sustained by guaranteed French import quotas at fixed prices, agreement should be reached to tackle the world coffee surplus or the future peanut surplus in such a way that stable prices and orderly marketing become feasible. If, over the years, world prices are fixed at levels lower than those under the old system—a not unlikely outcome since French prices for robusta have on occasion risen to 50 percent above world prices—then special direct assistance would be given to tide the economy over its difficulties and to secure diversification of local output.

On the question of tariffs, the Common Market should move toward a species of "one-way free trade" in tropical products, removing all tariff barriers from tropical imports while demanding no quid pro quo in the shape of free entry for European manufactures since this would check Africa's infant industrialization at birth. In the matter of aid, general Western assistance, possibly coördinated through the Development Assistance Committee of the O.E.C.D., might supplement present contributions—and be ready against the day, perhaps not too distant, when "Cartierism" wins in France and capital aid is switched to the Dordogne. Thus the aim would be to see that no existing associated state was worse off as a result of losing its preferential position and at the same time to lay the foundations for a more integrated, yet more open, African system in the future.

What are the prospects for such a reorientation of Western policy toward Africa? The answer is as paradoxical as the problem—no prospects at all in 1962, reasonable prospects in 1967. The present generation of leaders in ex-French Africa are already signing up for a new period of preferential arrangements. Indeed, in the case of the Ivory Coast, the agreements reached with France last fall go even further than earlier undertakings. France guarantees an import quota of 100,000 tons of robusta coffee for five years—no previous agreements covered more than a year and the amounts were always smaller. In return, the Ivory Coast guarantees French industry a specific percentage of its imports of manufactures. Both countries agree to keep trade as much as possible flowing in the old channels and to mitigate the foreign exchange problem by keeping down trade with third parties. Clearly, on this analogy, the renegotiated Treaty of Rome is more likely at this stage to propose a closed association of the Ivoirien type than any retreat from the preferential system. Yet by the end of the five—or seven—years of the new Treaty, it is probable that all the political and economic pressures working against the closed system both in Africa and in the West will have gathered formidable momentum. Newer, younger African leaders will have arisen, proclaiming African unity, French taxpayers will have tired of the burden, the Germans will have refused to exclude other suppliers, steady American hostility to the arrangements will have had its effect. Meanwhile, however, it is 1962 and Britain has to reach its decision. Must one conclude that the impasse is unbreakable? Is there no way in which a sense of the likely mood of 1967 can modify the rigidities of the present stance and prevent the disaster—for disaster it would be—of Britain's inability to find its way round the African roadblock?

One possibility at least could be explored. It would be an extension of the temporary solution already reached in the Cameroons where the extreme difficulties of merging an ex-British territory with an ex-French state already associated with the Common Market were shelved by a species of standstill agreement under which, for a year, no change in existing tariff or trading arrangements was attempted. The situation was in a sense frozen to allow for fuller studies and further experience.

In this analogy, the path of wisdom might lie in accepting the next five or seven years as a period during which the economic arrangements with Africa both on the side of Britain and of the Common Market remain as they are today. The associated territories would not renounce their present preference. The ex-British territories would keep such advantages as they enjoy today. And nothing would be done on either side to increase the degree of discrimination exercised against the others. For instance, no steps would be taken to introduce a high uniform external tariff round the present associated states. This aspect of the Treaty of Rome would simply be postponed. At the same time, the Common Market powers would pledge themselves, during the five or seven years, to look for *general*, non-discriminatory solutions to Africa's particular economic problems and to put a steadily increasing emphasis on greater economic unity in Africa. In this way, Britain's immediate entry into the Common Market would not be blocked by the African obstacle, and time would be gained during which the potentially ephemeral concept of "Eurafrica" could be transcended and a more lasting pattern of coöperation evolved between two parallel movements of integration—in Europe on the one hand, in Africa on the other.

In the last analysis, the issue is one of political judgment. Is the present partially preferential solution of association with the Common Market likely to contribute to growing stability in both Europe and Africa? There are some strong reasons for doubting whether it will. The arrangements of today grew out of a particular colonial policy—the assimilationist policies of France—and conform to a type of solidarity which has been almost entirely eroded away in the political sphere. In the post-colonial phase, Africa's dominant political mood seems increasingly to be colored by pan-Africanism, by more or less explicit longings for greater unity, by an angry resentment at all forms of continued colonial control and an almost morbid ability to see them lurking under any aspect of Western policy. Given this mood, it is at least possible that policies of close "Eurafrican" economic assimilation may, for all their immediate advantage, become both the target and the irritant of a more vocal and violent nationalism in Africa and actually increase the instability of that disturbed continent. Meanwhile, they almost certainly present a daunting obstacle to Britain's entry into Europe. These are high prices to pay for discriminatory forms of economic assistance to a relatively small part of a large continent and an even larger world—especially since that assistance could, with a little patience and a little judgment, be equally well supplied by more general and less divisive means.

Selection 27

Commodity Stabilization and Economic Development in Africa*

W. Michael Blumenthal

Mr. Blumenthal is Deputy Assistant Secretary for Economic Affairs in the United States Department of State, and is the U.S. representative on the United Nations Commission for International Commodity Trade.

. . . the process of modernization requires resources: human, material, and financial. Let it be clearly understood that most of these resources must, of necessity, be local in origin, for private foreign investment, economic assistance, and other unilateral transfers of resources into the African area can form only a small though valuable part of the total required. Moreover, the resources coming in from the outside must first and foremost be directed toward speeding up the process of generating indigenous assets. They must also be employed to broaden the economic base and to help move resources out of commodities in overproduction into new lines of endeavor.

But there can be no question that, since the possibilities for local

---

* Reprinted from *The Department of State Bulletin* (October 22, 1962), pp. 616–621. Department of State Press Release 582 dated September 26, 1962. (An address by Mr. Blumenthal.)

savings are limited, the need for private investment and economic assistance from the rest of the world is great. In particular, foreign exchange resources to finance essential imports of consumer and investments goods alike are often inadequate to foster rapid economic growth.

To help meet capital and foreign exchange requirements, our European allies will this year provide aid to countries in tropical Africa to the tune of over $600 million. Our aid effort, while comparatively modest—roughly $175 million in grants and loans for tropical Africa during fiscal year 1962—will usefully supplement aid from France, the United Kingdom, the European Economic Community, and elsewhere. So too will the flow of private American risk capital into tropical Africa, which may have added net new resources of about $60 million in 1961.

Yet the fact remains that the export earnings of these countries are roughly four times as important a source of foreign exchange for them as aid and private investment.

Moreover, aid is temporary, but the development of a sound and growing volume of trade lays a more permanent and lasting foundation. The need to stimulate stable and growing income from export earnings is, therefore, of overriding importance.

FIVE SERIOUS TRADING PROBLEMS IN AFRICA

Thus the African stake in trade is crucial. Yet these countries face serious trading problems. Let me mention five:

First: There is the fact that one or two primary commodities often account for between 60 percent and 90 percent of a nation's total export earnings. For example: Nigeria earns two-thirds of its export proceeds from cocoa and oilseeds; the Ivory Coast earns about 90 percent from coffee, cocoa, and timber; Senegal 85 percent from peanuts; Ghana 75 percent from cocoa and timber; and Uganda 75 percent from coffee and cotton.

Second: The commodities on which African countries are highly dependent are subject to wide short-term price fluctuations. For example, in recent years declines in coffee and cocoa prices have been dramatic. Spot cocoa is today quoted in New York at under 20 cents a pound whereas its 1958 high was over 50 cents. Even though

Ghanaian production and exports have increased markedly in the past 2 years, cocoa earnings have merely held steady. For Nigeria, where production has grown more slowly, earnings from cocoa have declined, as they have for peanuts, where world prices are also soft. Although African coffee producers have fared relatively better than most Latin American producers in the last few years, the sharp fall in coffee prices has hurt them also. Nigeria did benefit from a 25 percent increase in tin prices from the first to the third quarter of 1961, although the price has subsequently declined again.

For agricultural commodities the major source of instability is found on the supply side. Yields fluctuate markedly as a result particularly of weather variations and crop diseases. Also, production of tree crops adjusts to changes in market conditions only with significant time lags. This fact appears frequently to work to increase price instabilities.

For the minerals the major source of short-term instability is found on the demand side, the level of economic activity in the developed countries being the leading influence on price.

Third: Not only do the prices of most primary commodities fluctuate widely, but also the long-term composite trend has been down for the past 10 years. The U.N. price index for primary products in international trade is down over 10 percent since 1953. During the same period the index for manufactured goods has risen by about 10 percent, with the consequence that African countries as well as the other predominantly primary producing areas are greatly concerned with what they refer to as the deterioration in their "terms of trade."

It is a fact that demand for primary commodities has grown less rapidly than demand for manufactured items and services. Technological change has led to economy of use of raw materials and the development of substitutes. And, even at higher incomes and lower prices, there is a limit to how much coffee Americans will drink; in technical language the elasticities of demand for primary commodities are often low.

These facts doubtless make the process of development slower and more difficult than it would be if demand for African products were growing more rapidly and if long-term price trends were not adverse.

Fourth: The pattern of trade for many African countries is directed predominantly toward the former metropoles. This is particularly true of franc area countries. For example, over 60 percent of Ivory Coast exports go to franc area countries, and over 75 percent of Ivory Coast imports in 1960 came from France. Moreover, the Ivory Coast is far from an extreme case of trade dependence.

Fifth: The efforts of African producers to industrialize are hampered by protectionism in much of the rest of the world. The pattern is all too often that they labor under artificial handicaps even in processing their own products. For example, cocoa butter is often subject to higher duties than cocoa beans, and freight rates on processed items may be disproportionately high. Unfortunately, production of light manufactured goods faces still more difficulties.

As the leading world power, dedicated to expanding peacefully the area of freedom, the United States is necessarily concerned with the trade and commodity problems of African states, committed as they are to economic progress by one means or another. Peace and prosperity are in fact indivisible, and like it or not we are inevitably concerned with the price of peanuts just as we are with the future of Berlin. Obviously, the degree of our concern differs greatly from case to case.

OBJECTIVES OF U.S. POLICY

What then would we like to do about commodity stabilization? What are the objectives of U.S. policy?

Our overriding objective is to keep commodity price fluctuations or declines from jeopardizing the development effort of producing nations—and, hopefully, to stimulate commodity trade so that it can increase its contribution to development.

We want to find solutions compatible with a growth of freedom in the world and to minimize the temptation for the nonindustrial nations to seek the illusion of an allegedly easy Communist road to rapid economic development.

More specifically our objectives are, insofar as feasible (and this is an important caveat):

1. To dampen disruptive cyclical price fluctuations.
2. To arrest the secular decline in commodity prices. This is probably the most difficult objective of all to attain, because the downward

secular price trend appears in good measure to be implicit in rapid technological progress and more efficient use of materials and primary products.

3. To mitigate problems of acute supply-demand imbalance which have arisen, for example, with respect to coffee.

4. To solve commodity problems in ways which promote the industrialization and diversification of the producing country. Indeed, industrialization and the development of trade within and among developing nations will be an important part of a solution of many of the trade problems of these nations.

5. To develop global, not regional, solutions to commodity problems or at least to find national and regional measures not incompatible with a global, multilateral, nondiscriminatory approach.

6. To avoid excessive or unworkable controls which might jeopardize the growth of free economic and political institutions. We would like to make maximum use of market forces supplemented, where necessary, by financial mechanisms and to place minimum reliance on such devices as quotas and the more direct types of price support.

7. To assure that any commodity stabilization arrangements, which necessarily will vary from commodity to commodity, operate in ways which benefit both producers and consumers.

STRATEGY IN COMMODITY STABILIZATION EFFORTS

We are under no illusions that commodity stabilization will be easy within the framework which I have outlined. But we are making a concerted effort involving both study and action. I would like to describe the major components of the strategy we are following in our commodity stabilization efforts.

To deal with the purely short-term price instabilities, we are studying a global compensatory financing scheme which might partially offset cyclical fluctuations in export earnings of producing countries by providing short-term finance to permit imports to remain fairly stable and thereby to avoid sharp stops and starts in carrying out development plans. . . .

National and regional marketing boards also can be fairly effective in smoothing out seasonal price fluctuations. These bodies also have a useful role to play in improving earnings through quality controls and distribution of better seeds, fertilizers, and technical information.

To deal with the longrun secular price declines and with problems of supply-demand imbalance, commodity agreements may provide a partial and interim answer. Thus for a few commodities with particularly serious structural problems—such as coffee and possibly cocoa—we have developed or are developing international commodity agreements with worldwide participation of producing and consuming nations. In such cases, for the agreements to be effective, producing nations must curb overproduction and shift excess resources out of primary commodities in oversupply into other areas. We believe all of the industrial nations should coordinate their aid programs to facilitate such a resource shift.

The coffee agreement which has just been negotiated here in New York is, I think, a most promising arrangement. Coffee is the second most important commodity in international trade and a crucial source of foreign exchange earnings for a large number of countries in Latin America, Africa, and Asia. We do not pretend that schemes such as the coffee agreement, which is built around a system of export quotas, are an ideal system applicable in all conditions to all commodities. Rather, we regard the coffee agreement as a pragmatic effort to make the best of a very bad situation. We are convinced that the only way to work out the structural problems of oversupply and long-term price deterioration which have plagued coffee producers is through an enforcible global agreement including both producers and consumers. I am hopeful that the agreement just negotiated will achieve our objectives.

Despite my relative optimism for the future of the coffee agreement, and for more orderly coffee trade, I would like to sound a note of caution about commodity agreements. If you will excuse my analogy, international commodity agreements are the "ultimate weapon" of commodity policy. Designed with skill and prudence, these agreements may provide an answer for our most serious commodity problems. But commodity agreements can also be a very dangerous weapon and must not be used lightly or indiscriminately.

There is particular danger that commodity agreements will lead to artificial prices involving the major risks both of stimulating primary commodity production at the expense of diversified development and of stimulating the development of synthetic or substitute products. . . .

To deal with the more general trade problems, we are working largely in GATT for the gradual elimination of preferential arrangements in commodity trade and the drastic reduction of restraints on consumption, such as tariffs and specific excise taxes on coffee, cocoa, and tea. Insofar as possible we seek free, nondiscriminatory commodity trade to increase markets for primary producers. The recently enacted Trade Expansion Act authorizes us to remove our duties on tropical products if our Atlantic partner, the European Economic Community, will do likewise; it also authorizes us otherwise to negotiate for reduction of trade restrictions, and we anticipate achievement of broad reciprocal concessions.

Then too we have already negotiated a textile agreement[1] which, while it protects American manufactures from a disrupting flood of textile imports, also provides for a gradual explansion of markets in Europe and here for the textile exports of developing countries.

GLOBAL SOLUTIONS TO COMMODITY PROBLEMS

Our efforts to obtain the gradual removal of trade restrictions and preferential marketing arrangements should be of particular interest to African countries. As you know the African states which have associated themselves with the European Common Market have duty-free access into this market for their coffee, cocoa, oilseeds, and other products while other producers of these products, including Liberia, Ethiopia, Tanganyika, and Nigeria, are faced with the EEC's common external tariff. For two key products—coffee and cocoa—the eventual common external tariff, originally scheduled to be in full effect by 1970, had been set at 16 percent and 9 percent respectively. I am pleased to say, however, that, as a result of progress made thus far in the renegotiation of the Association Convention which expires at the end of this year, the common external tariff on coffee and cocoa appears likely to be cut by 40 percent, effective in 1964. We welcome this prospective cut as a significant step toward the eventual elimination of tariffs on coffee, cocoa, and all tropical products.

The interest of the United States in pressing for the gradual phasing out of preferences rests on two convictions on our part. First, preferential arrangements give the exports of a few developing nations an

---

[1] For background, see BULLETIN of Oct. 15, 1962, p. 566.

artificial advantage over other developing countries. We cannot limit our concern to the exports of a few countries. We must strengthen or, if necessary, create institutions and mechanisms which permit the expansion of all less developed country exports on equally beneficial terms. Second, we doubt that the permanent retention of preferences is in the longrun interest of the producing country supposedly benefiting by them. Rather the industrialization and diversification of the national African economies will over time be promoted by the substitution for sheltered markets of a world competitive market.

Commodity exports are a vital source of foreign exchange for Africa, but they are also important in terms of the structure and growth potential of the various national economies. Measures designed to maximize export earnings must not jeopardize the ultimate economic growth and political stability of the producing nation. To cite a particularly painful case for the United States of undesirable commodity measures, I do not think the long-term economic and political growth of Cuba was enhanced by the sugar premiums it received in the American market even though these premiums had a substantial foreign exchange value. In retrospect it appears that this incentive for sugar production may have been one factor discouraging the growth of a more balanced and industrialized economy with better prospects of developing viable free political institutions.

Nor do I believe that the development of the Ivory Coast and various other African states will be advanced in the long run by the indefinite receipt of premium prices and other forms of preferential treatment in the French market or in the European Common Market.

In line with our conviction that special arrangements are self-defeating in the long run, the United States has pointed out to Latin American nations that in our view purely regional commodity arrangements would not be in their interests. Rather we tend to seek global solutions for trade and commodity problems. We do recognize, however, that care must be exercised in the transition from the present preferential systems to a more durable arrangement for trade in primary commodities—and especially tropical products. I therefore want to repeat here the assurance we have given those African nations now inside preferential systems.

We are not "taking sides" between developing nations; we are not interested in the development of one nation or region at the expense of another nation or region. We are equally concerned with the development of the Ivory Coast, Nigeria, and Brazil—and of Senegal, Tanganyika, Indonesia, and Colombia. The United States is aware that the gradual phasing out of duties and other preferential arrangements must generally be cushioned by adjustment measures to provide at least equivalent benefits to Africans, including acceptable safeguards. The development prospects of nations now inside preferential systems must not be jeopardized in the course of abolishing preferential arrangements. Our task is to find arrangements alternative to preferences which will help to assure all developing nations equivalent export opportunities and which will provide the maximum resources and incentives to speed the creation of diversified and industrialized economies. These alternative devices must necessarily link the flow of economic assistance from industrialized to developing countries with our efforts to stabilize commodity prices and to improve commodity trade arrangements. . . .

IV

AFRICA IN WORLD POLITICS

We have not discussed thus far in these readings the part the African nations are playing in current world politics. We have examined a past role (imperialism), and have devoted considerable attention to relations among African states and what African leaders think the role of the African states as a group should be. But the closest we have come to current world politics and the African states as actors on that scene is the section on economic relations with the "free world."

The remainder of the book is an effort to delineate some of the roles African nations are playing in the world today. Part IV is divided into five sections. The first is on neutralism, on the argument that this concept epitomizes the predominant features of the African role in world politics. The second section is a short case study of neutralism—the role of African trade unions in labor politics on the world scene. Africa and the United Nations is discussed briefly in the third section. And the fourth and fifth sections build on this foundation, taking Katanga province in the Congo as the subject for study.

NEUTRALISM

In a world riven by war, neutrality acquires enhanced status, at least in the minds of those trying to stay out of trouble. This seems to be as true in a "cold" war as in a "hot" one. Now mated with the idea of increasing security or insuring peace by some sort of collective action, neutrality has been elevated into an "ism"—neutralism. It is perhaps the main foreign-policy plank of the majority of the newly independent nations. It can be many things, since its essence lies in standing apart from either of two extremes, and there is a lot of room for intermediate positions. This makes it difficult to delineate accurately the meaning and the implications of the term.

The task is attempted in Selection 28. The author seems to accept as true neutralism the type defined by the Belgrade Conference of 1961. He then goes on to suggest the world conditions under which neutralism may flourish, and to point out that anticolonialism and "progressive social policy" are identifying characteristics of the neutralist nations. We find, however, in Selection 29 that a United Nations delegate from Senegal uses quite different criteria and feels that the Belgrade ones are inadequate.

Definition in the abstract is obviously difficult. What might then be the operating characteristics of neutralism? If we know this, then we have a definition of sorts, and one especially helpful in developing criteria for dealing with neutralists or aspirants to that title. Selection 30 is a study of neutralism as practiced by a pair of the "Casablanca" states, and suggests both operating characteristics and criteria for dealing with neutralism.

The mind returns to Hall and Lippmann (Selections 2 and 3). Their argument was that imperialism grew out of international competition over territories weakly governed. Now it is argued that neutralism is the more easily condoned the healthier and more vigorous the society of the state practicing it. Would the proper modern theory then be that neutralism is genuine (and good) if it lessens national weakness and thus makes great-power competition potentially less deadly?

Selection 28

Non-Alignment and African Problems*

N. PARAMESWARAN NAYAR

Mr. Nayar is at present a Lecturer in Political Science at the University of Kerala, Trivandrum (India). He has recently completed a thesis on *Indian Foreign Service.*

* * *

II. WHAT IS NON-ALIGNMENT?

The term non-alignment has been variously described as neutralism, positive neutrality, dynamic neutrality, uncommitted policy. It simply means keeping aloof from power blocs, and to judge each issue as it arises without prior commitment to the policy of any bloc.

1. *Cairo Conference's Definition.*—The Cairo Preparatory Conference of Non-aligned Nations, attended by foreign ministers or senior diplomats of nineteen countries attempted to define a non-aligned country. They agreed on five broad criteria for the purpose. It was on the basis of these that invitations to the Belgrade Conference were issued. According to these criteria, a non-aligned country:

(1) should follow an independent policy based on non-alignment (!) and peaceful coexistence;
(2) should support liberation movements;
(3) should not be a member of a multilateral military pact in the context of the East-West struggle;

---

* Reprinted by permission from "A Study of the Policy of Non-Alignment with Special Reference to African Problems" by N. Parameswaran Nayar, *Foreign Affairs Reports*, Vol. X, No. 12 (December 1961), pp. 132–133, 136–139, 141–142. (The title of this selection was supplied by the editor of the present volume.)

(4) should not be a member of a bilateral military pact with a Big Power in the East-West struggle;
(5) should not have granted military bases to foreign powers.

2. *More an approach than a policy.*—These criteria are no doubt very broad-based and are consequently very inadequate to precisely explain the nature of the policy of non-alignment. The difficulty of the conference to agree to more exact criteria for non-aligned nations was, however, genuine because non-alignment is more an approach than a policy and as such is difficult of precise definition. . . . A single foreign policy for all non-aligned countries goes against the very logic of this approach, which sets its claim for an independence of judgement from prior commitments to bloc alignments.

3. *Factors of non-alignment.*—The foreign policy of the non-aligned nations are determined by the same general factors as that of other countries like national traditions and experiences, internal and international conditions and the various kinds of national interests. The changes among nations in these various respects lead to changes in foreign policy also. The broad similarity in approach to aspects of international relations by the non-aligned nations arises from the existence of a certain amount of similarity in these factors that generate their foreign policies, but beyond a certain level these similarities vanish and lead to differences in policy.

These common features in the foreign policies of these nations are related mainly to three general facts:

(1) Subjection to foreign rule or control and racial discrimination in the recent past. All the non-aligned nations come under this group. The consequences of this has been a powerful and emotional resentment against imperialism and the imperialist powers, distrust of their policies, an extreme self-consciousness and sensitivity about their newly won independence and the equality of status with other nations.

(2) The emergence of a strong and triumphant nationalism with an anti-colonial tradition, but also with social objectives of a very general character, often bordering on socialism. The importance of this factor is seen when one compares the nature of the nationalist movements in aligned countries like Pakistan, Philippines, Thailand, Iran, etc. (where they were either weak, less anti-colonial or thwarted) and those of non-aligned countries like India, Indonesia, Burma, etc. Ceylon came

to independence more on the impelling drive of extraneous factors than of a nationalist movement within the country. Till 1956 when there developed a powerful Ceylonese nationalism her policy was aligned to that of the West. But with the accession to political power by the nationalist movement in the elections of 1956, Ceylonese foreign policy has sharply turned towards non-alignment.

(3) Underdeveloped society and economy and a strong urge for modernisation and social and economic development. In foreign relations the country therefore seeks to create such attachments and conditions as would help it in the pursuit of its objective of development. . . .

. . . *Non-alignment in Africa.*—Out of the twenty-five governments that were represented at the Belgrade conference in September 1961 ten were from Africa.* Of these, nine represented established states (excluding Algeria), of the twenty-five independent African nations at the time.** Since then Tanganyika has become independent (on 9 December 1961) and has declared herself for a policy of non-alignment. The present trends in Algeria, Angola, Kenya, Mozambique, South West Africa, Uganda, etc., show that after independence they are also likely to become non-aligned. . . .

. . . the trends of thinking in a number of African states should show divergence of emphasis from that of the more advanced nations in Asia. For example, it has been demonstrated very often in recent times that India's outlook on a number of problems is much more cautious and moderate than that of many African states like Ghana or Guinea. Other nations of Asia, similarly conditioned by circumstances, stand at various levels of agreement or difference with them.

---

* Algeria, Congo (Leopoldville), Ethiopia, Ghana, Guinea, Mali, Morocco, Somalia, Sudan and Tunisia (UAR is treated as an Asian nation).

** This total is on the basis of the membership of the United Nations. Mauritania has not therefore been counted. The Republic (Union) of South Africa is also not counted here for obvious reasons.

Of the remaining countries 6 are in the *French African Community* (Central African Republic, Chad, the Congo (Brazzaville), Gabon, Malagasy and Senegal); 4 are of the *Conseil de l'Entente* (Dahomey, Ivory Coast, Niger and Upper Volta); the remaining 6 are Libya, Liberia, Sierra Leone, Cameroun, Nigeria and Togo.

(a) *Assessment of the world situation.*—These differences are noticed even in a basic assessment of the world situation today. This was for example demonstrated in a very obvious way at the recent Belgrade Conference. Statesmen from African countries like Ghana, Guinea, Mali, etc., tended to regard colonialism as the most urgent, the most pressing problem in the world today. The Prime Minister of India said, however, that the problems of imperialism, colonialism, racialism, etc.—though they were in themselves important and evil enough—were overshadowed by the more pressing question of war and peace. The Indonesian stand on this question seemed to have been closer to the more militant attitude of the African states than of India's, which seemed cautious and reluctant to be drawn into making an open condemnation of Western imperialism. This would explain why when leaders from India and Egypt hastened to deplore the resumption of nuclear testing by the USSR, the African countries were more or less indifferent about it. The Indian view was openly challenged at the conference by Guinea. Nehru stated that the general attitude of the African states at Belgrade as being due to the fact that the newly independent states of Africa were "full of their own problems." "And the rest of the world does not seem to exist for them except vaguely as an imperialist, colonialist world against which they are striving to free themselves."

(b) *Communism* versus *capitalism.*—A similar difference in emphasis in the approach to the problems of cold war or bloc alignments can be detected in the foreign policies of the more developed nations like India and the younger nations of Africa. Asian non-aligned nations had previously criticised Western policies in Asia as being too much obsessed with the question of communism which, according to them, was not of direct and immediate relevance to the Asian situation. But yet the Asian policies themselves had always been with a definite consciousness of the question of communism, either due to the presence of powerful Communist Parties within their countries or due to the existence of powerful communist neighbours. Africa has still lesser reason than Asia, to be persuaded to view world problems in terms of communism and capitalism, both of which seem so remote from the context of most African states. Moreover, the nationalist movements and their leadership in many African countries have a less definite social base than in the economically more advanced nations of Asia. African states have consequently shown little inhibitions about ideology in foreign affairs. In general they have maintained their relations with Soviet Union and other countries of the Communist bloc more spontaneously and naturally than Asian countries. This is evident, for example, from the nature of the increasing ties of relationship between certain African countries like Guinea, Mali and Ghana and the Communist countries.

When one enters the area of specific issues the respective scope for agreement and disagreement in the foreign policies of these Asian and African countries becomes clearer.

(c) *Events in the Congo.*—The policies of these various governments towards the tragic events in the (Belgian) Congo brought out the areas of agreement and disagreement among them in their foreign policies. The recent events in the Congo have intensely shown all the tragedies of a new nation which has suffered from a very crude colonialism, foreign economic exploitation, social backwardness and political under-development. Various forces were at work to undermine this independence—the old imperialism and other foreign economic interests trying to keep the country under a covert colonialism, the policies of certain big powers concerned primarily with considerations of cold war, regional, tribal and other loyalties clashing with a national loyalty and concept, struggle for political power between rival political groups violating all principles of constitutionalism, etc. The African non-aligned nations like Ghana, Guinea, etc., saw in these events primarily the struggle between imperialism and colonialism. The more sophisticated policies of India were drawn from nearly the same analysis, but with further considerations of international connections and attachments. While all non-aligned nations of Asia and Africa stood therefore for the liquidation of overt or covert colonialism in the Congo, the unification of the country and the setting up of a democratic system, the methods they had advocated varied considerably. India was less outspoken of her support to Lumumba than Ghana, Guinea and UAR were when the Congolese President and Prime Minister had fallen out with each other, but voted with these countries to seat the Lumumba delegation at the United Nations. India was at first hesitant to send her armed forces to the Congo, while

Ghana, UAR, Guinea and Morocco did so, but when these countries had decided to withdraw their contingents in dissatisfaction with the UN policies India decided to send her forces to the Congo. . . .

VII. PROSPECTS:

The policy suffers from certain obvious limitations of scope and action. It came into being as a result of the interplay of a variety of circumstances relating to the international situation as well as the national conditions within the countries themselves. It continued to grow as an important force in modern international relations as a result of the persistence of these same circumstances.

The most important of the international situations relating to the emergence of the policy of non-alignment was the division of the world into two blocs threatening to engulf the world in a mighty conflagration. The new and weak nations of Asia, Africa and other parts of the world that turned to non-alignment were seeking refuge from the dangers to their own freedom and existence from this bloc antagonism. The practical successes of the policy were registered only when the balance of power between the two blocs had reached an even keel, as from 1950 onwards. The policy has operated in international affairs within the scope of this balance of power.

In this, the non-aligned nations were aided by certain new trends in international relations. The possession of adequate power by both the blocs to destroy each other completely has made it necessary for them to place an increasing emphasis on factors other than that of superior military power in their diplomatic practices. The growth of the democratic practice of counting votes in world politics through the functioning of international organisations has given the smaller nations an importance beyond their limited military power. As uncommitted nations, the position of the non-aligned countries has become particularly important in this respect. The growth of an independent public opinion, as different from the opinions of various governments, has also helped this process of international relations. In consequence of these developments, the non-aligned nations are today in a position to negotiate and mediate between the bigger nations and to assume a really independent position for themselves. This means that a major shift in the present balance of power position would make the operation of the policy difficult, if not impossible. The ending of bloc divisions and antagonisms would also remove the scope and need for the continued operation of the policy.

It has often been pointed out that the basic elements of the policy are negative—keeping aloof from power blocs, opposition to racialism and colonialism, etc., and that the unifying forces of the policy are derived from this common opposition to them. It is, therefore, pointed out that with the natural death of colonialism, racialism and the like these elements of unity are liable to vanish. The increasing expressions of disagreement among major non-aligned countries are pointed out in justification of this view.

There is apparently a large element of truth in these views. At the same time, a further factor of major importance has also to be considered in this context. It is not by simple accident that the governments of those countries that pursue an active non-alignment policy—countries) like Ghana, India, Indonesia, United Arab Republic, etc., which form the real centres of the non-alignment policy in the under-developed world—are seen to be more stable and more popular (though not always realised through parliamentary democratic institutions, but this is largely due to the special circumstances in these countries) and to be more conscious of and responsive to the needs of their people and country than the governments of countries aligned to the Western bloc. In other words, the policy of non-alignment in world affairs is linked up with the general policy of these governments of progressive social and economic action within their own countries. This interrelationship between foreign and domestic policies may not be equally evident in certain non-aligned countries like Saudi Arabia or Nepal, but so far as the non-alignment policy is concerned these countries are only peripheral. Further the very fact that these countries have claimed to pursue a non-aligned policy indicates the pressure exercised by the operation of progressive social forces on these governments, even though this has not expressed itself in more visible forms in their political and social organisation.

Non-alignment as a policy in international relations might tend to become irrelevant under a different set of international relations. But the real political content of the policy, *viz.*, the emergence of a long-delayed social revolution in these under-developed countries, might continue to be expressed in their external policies in other forms.

Selection 29

Another View of non-Alignment*

DOUDOU THIAM

M. Thiam was Minister of Foreign Affairs of Senegal and chairman of the Senegalese delegation to the United Nations at the time this statement was made.

* * *

28. Our desire to be independent of the two blocs is expressed by the different countries in formulas which must be carefully scrutinized. Some speak of "positive neutralism," others of "non-commitment" and still others of "non-alignment." What is important, of course, is not the formula but the reality of our independence; we must therefore avoid using ambiguous terms which are open to criticism. When we speak of positive neutralism, we must first remember that it is impossible to be neutral. The course which we have chosen is not a neutral one; it is a political attitude, a specific and positive action, in regard to the problem of peace. We must define our policies not in terms of blocs, for that would be superficial, but in terms of the fundamental problem of peace. We say that we are fierce and stubborn champions of peace and we decide to take action on its behalf. By that very fact we are committed, and that is why the term "non-commitment" is not appropriate either. We are just as committed as the East or the West, but we are committed to objective action for peace, in the universal meaning of that term. Some countries have laid themselves open to criticism because they have not made the meaning of that policy perfectly clear in correct terms. They are told, if you are neutral and

* Reprinted from the *Official Records*, Sixteenth United Nations General Assembly, 16th Session, Plenary Meetings, Meeting No. 1012 (September 22, 1961), pp. 43–44. (The title of this selection was supplied by the editor of the present volume.)

uncommitted, why have you taken a position in such and such a matter? Why have you voted in such and such a way?

29. In reality, the policy which is described by the terms "neutralism" or "non-commitment" is a policy of non-alignment, or rather a policy of non-dependence, since independence is never a final achievement but something that has to be won daily. Before it can become a political reality, independence must first of all be a state of mind.

30. What does this policy of non-alignment or non-dependence amount to in practice? It is a matter of considering each problem that arises independently of the blocs and of adopting an attitude which is consistent with our chosen political system and our commitment to peace. In practice, it may happen that, for this or that problem, our attitude may be the same as that taken by the East or by the West. This is only natural. But in any case, there can be no question of being systematically for one or the other. To take the particular case of Senegal, for example, we voted in favour of including the question of the representation of China in the agenda and we are in favour of admitting mainland China because we still think its admission to the United Nations is a necessity. We shall continue to support the admission of China, which, incidentally, we recognized a few months after we attained independence. On this problem we find ourselves in disagreement with the majority of the Western countries, but on other problems our vote has been completely different from that of the communist bloc, on the problem of Mauritania, for example; we consider that there can be no discrimination in the application of the principle of independence and self-determination.

31. That is what true non-alignment is. By not keeping in close touch with reality, some countries, even among those for which we have the highest esteem, made the mistake during a recent conference of defining what they call "non-commitment" in what we think is a very unobjective way. After laborious discussions, they apparently decided to consider a country "uncommitted" if it had no military bases and was not a member of a pact or a military alliance with either of the two blocs. The weakness of such an argument is obvious. I do not wish to mention any country in particular, for this international rostrum should be the rostrum of peace, but I cannot help thinking that some so-called uncommitted countries which are members of the Balkan Pact,[2] for example, have military links with other countries

[2] Balkan Pact, signed at Bled on 9 August 1954.

which are members of the North Atlantic Treaty.[3] But, as I said, I do not wish to raise any inflammatory questions here. If we want our policy of peace to be a true policy we must avoid indulging in baseless recriminations. We must cast off resentments and consider nothing but our objectives, which must be resolutely directed towards peace. We must also, of course, ensure that the policy of so-called non-commitment is not simply a mask behind which satellites may hide. The road to peace is a difficult one and requires great courage and loyalty, especially loyalty to oneself. . . .

Selection 30

The Uses of Neutralism*

PAUL E. SIGMUND, JR.

A university teacher in both Africa and the United States, Paul E. Sigmund, Jr., is the author of a recent book titled *The Ideologies of the Developing Nations* (1963).

The recent Casablanca conference of Ghana, Guinea, Mali, Morocco, and the U.A.R. has solidified the division of Africa into two blocs of opinion. For all the rhetoric about African unity, the events in the Congo and the United Nations have produced a split between pro-Western Africans, principally those associated with the French Community, and a more radical group of African states which met at Casablanca. The policy followed by the Casablanca conferees also exerts a strong attraction on other African countries, such as Nigeria, Togo, Libya, and Ethiopia, who are usually identified as pro-Western but who have, in fact, at various times voted with the neutralist group on a number of issues in the U.N.

---

[3] North Atlantic Treaty, signed at Washington on 4 April 1949.

* Reprinted by permission from *The Commonweal* (February 17, 1961), pp. 523–526.

The fact that the Casablanca group has voted consistently in the U.N. with the Soviet Union and against the West has led to descriptions of their policy as "left-wing," "neutral against the West," or even "pro-Soviet." In September Secretary of State Herter described Ghana as "very definitely leaning toward the Soviet bloc." Then three weeks later, in the third T.V. debate with Nixon, Senator Kennedy blamed the Eisenhower Administration for the fact that Ghana and Guinea had moved "within the Soviet sphere of influence." On election eve, Kennedy repeated this charge and added the Congo to the list of African states in the Communist orbit. This was followed by a series of press articles about Communist influence in Africa, singling out Ghana and Guinea as particularly disturbing examples.

At first appearance, the Soviet presence in these two countries *is* disturbing. Guinea's capital city of Conakry is swarming with advisers from the Soviet bloc and China. Czech doctors staff the hospital and Hungarian sports instructors assist the youth section of Sekou Touré's political party. Soviet aid is being used to build a powerful radio station and printing press (Conakry has no newspaper, only a mimeographed news bulletin of limited circulation). Several hundred students are on scholarships in the Soviet Union, and Eastern goods outnumber Western products in Guinean shops.

While the situation in Ghana is quite different from Guinea, there are indications that it is rapidly expanding its economic relations with the Soviet Union. Last August, a Soviet trade delegation arrived with banner headlines and Nkrumah's *Ghana Evening News* headlined a Tass interview with the Ghana minister of labor, "The Soviet people are our real friends." Moreover, at the same time that the Ghana government was concluding an agreement with the World Bank, the U. S. and Great Britain for an $84 million loan to finance Nkrumah's cherished Volta River project, a Ghana delegation without World Bank or Western knowledge was in Moscow negotiating Soviet involvement in the proposal.

Nkrumah has described himself in his autobiography as a "non-denominational Christian and a Marxist Socialist," but those who listened to his denunciations of the West in the United Nations this fall heard more Marxism than Christianity in his vocabulary and attitudes. Touré's Marxism is no secret, and characteristically it is much more doctrinaire and consistently worked out than the curious conglomeration of attitudes and theories which is Nkrumah's political and economic philosophy. Both Nkrumah's Convention People's Party and Touré's *Parti Dêmocratique de la Guinea* use Marxist terminology ("comrade," "imperialism," "the class struggle," and in the case of Guinea, "politbureau" and "Young Pioneers").

In Guinea, there is only one political party and a single youth organization. Opposition has no way to express itself except through the party, and it is rumored that among those arrested in an alleged revolutionary plot last spring were Guineans who had proposed the establishment of an opposition party. While Ghana still retains many of the forms of British parliamentary democracy, there have been a series of moves in recent months in the direction of authoritarianism. An opposition party still exists, but thirteen members of the United Party have been arrested under the Preventive Detention Act, bringing to nearly a hundred the number imprisoned without trial. Last August, after fifteen minutes of debate, a censorship law was passed by the Ghana parliament forbidding statements "prejudicial to public order or the national economy." Strikes have been outlawed in Ghana and membership made compulsory in the Nkrumah-sponsored Trade Union Congress. There have been press reports, vigorously denied by the government, that Ghana plans to nationalize its largely European-owned private enterprises.

But what really seems to have convinced American opinion of the leftist orientation of Ghana and Guinea is the continuing support which they have given to Patrice Lumumba in the Congo. In American eyes Lumumba committed the unpardonable offense of asking for Soviet assistance in dealing with the problem of Katangan separatism. The U.S.S.R. responded with fourteen Ilyushin planes, a shipload of trucks, and large numbers of advisers and technical aides. Yet Nkrumah and Touré did not seem disturbed at this development. Their concern was that Lumumba have the resources to prevent the dismemberment of the Congo and, ultimately, that the Congo federate with Ghana and Guinea, since, as Nkrumah wrote to Lumumba, "The Congo and Ghana are one" and "Brother, we know how to deal with the imperialists."

Marxist anti-colonial rhetoric, authoritarianism in domestic politics, acceptance of Soviet aid, and support for Lumumba—this is the case against Ghana and Guinea, and (with some minor qualifications regarding Morocco) against the other Casablanca conferees as well. Taken together they add up to something new and important on the African scene—an orientation which may be in opposition to various aspects of American policy, but which is essentially African, rather than Soviet, in inspiration.

Take the case of support for Lumumba. The Casablanca powers are not the only Africans who favor the return to power of Patrice Lumumba. Only those Africans support him who are closely tied for economic reasons to French policy. Ghana and Guinea have reasons of their own (for instance, their Pan-African plan) for the strong backing which they have given Lumumba, but even others who may have strong reservations about his personal capacities find it politically and psychologically impossible to do other than endorse him. Pro-Western nationalist leaders in East Africa, such as Mboya and Nyerere, have publicly demanded Lumumba's return to power, not necessarily because they sympathize with his policies, but because they see him as the legally elected Prime Minister of the Congo, who has twice received the confidence of the Congolese Parliament, and who would receive it again if Parliament were reconvened. Moreover, Lumumba stands for the same principles for which they stand, the unity of his country against centrifugal tendencies of tribalism and its political and economic liberation from colonialism. . . .

African desire for rapid economic development, not ideological sympathy, also explains the expansion of Soviet trade and aid programs to Africa. While aware, and in a few cases a little frightened, of the risks involved in taking aid (e.g., the massive incursion of Eastern advisers which accompanies it), the African leaders have the example of the U.A.R., India, Iraq, Indonesia and other states that have taken Soviet assistance without, it appears, ill effects. "Aid without strings" from both sides is at once a declaration of neutrality in the cold war and an effective way to extract concessions from one side or the other. Peter Ustinov's portrayal in "Romanoff and Juliet" of the prime minister of a tiny central European state shuttling back and forth between the American and Soviet embassies bears a close resemblance to the reality in an increasing number of African states. As in the play, this signifies no special sympathy for the Soviet Union; only a desire to extract a maximum of assistance from both the U.S. and the U.S.S.R., without in any way being committed to either side.

This tactic is known as "playing the game"—playing off one side against the other for one's own benefit. India has been playing it for a decade; Nasser for five years; and Guinea and Ghana have taken the lead in playing it in Africa. While U. S. policy-makers and organs of public opinion seem to have adjusted to Egyptian or Indian neutralism (largely because Nasser and Nehru have demonstrated that it is possible to pursue a neutralist policy and still not become a Soviet satellite), the possibility that Lumumba would play the same game led to his downfall. Yet other Africans are likely to play it as well, since it gives promise of rapid economic assistance on a competitive basis and appears to offer the flexibility and freedom of choice which Africans associate with economic independence.

Economic independence is now a slogan and rallying cry for the Casablanca group, and it is being used effectively against other African states which have retained close economic relations with the West. Behind the charge is a kind of modernized Leninist theory about the relations between the newly independent states and the former colonial powers. Ignoring the substantial sums expended in recent years by Britain and France on the development of their African colonies, they see the class struggle in terms of exploiting imperialist powers, and exploited present or former colonial areas. In order to attain real independence, economic relations must be developed with other countries than the former colonizing power, and in particular with the Eastern bloc. In a way, it has become a kind of demonstration of national independence to open up formerly forbidden economic and diplomatic contacts with the East as a gesture to indicate that the colonial prohibitions are no longer operative. While to the West, this may look like an ideological smokescreen for economic blackmail, for the African, contacts with the East have become an assertion of national freedom, and Mr. Kennedy's references to the dangers of "riding the tiger's back" are not likely to deter them from the acceptance of Soviet aid.

The largest amounts of Soviet and Eastern bloc assistance now go to Guinea. When Guinea voted "no" in the referendum on the de Gaulle constitution, it found itself rudely cut off from all French assistance in what was a calculated (and ultimately unsuccessful) move by de Gaulle to demonstrate to the other colonies the disadvantages of opting out of the close association and partial dependence of the French Community. French administrators and technical personnel were withdrawn with the threat of denial of pension rights to those who stayed. Scholarships for Guinean students studying in France were cut off. Everything from typewriters to telephones was removed by the departing French.

Moreover, apparently under pressure from France, the United States did not recognize Guinea until fifty other countries had done so, and Guinean requests for assistance, forwarded to Washington immediately after independence, were unanswered. By contrast, the Soviet Union and most of the satellites hastened to sign trade agreements with Guinea. Soon after independence a shipment of Czech arms arrived in Conakry harbor and Hungarian buses and Czech trucks appeared on the streets. Subsequently, a $35 million loan at 2½ percent interest was signed with the U.S.S.R. and, recently, Communist China has agreed to lend Guinea $25 million, interest free.

If American assistance was slow in coming at the start, however, by 1960 the situation had changed. First came surplus food, one million dollars worth of wheat, rice, flour and milk, paid for in local currency which can be re-used in economic development. This was followed by lengthy negotiations for an I.C.A. agreement, which was signed in November, but even before its signature I.C.A. was sponsoring an English language instruction program for Guinean teachers in Conakry. In the field of education, only eight Guineans were studying in the United States last year, but an accord has now been signed for one hundred and fifty to come to this country in 1961, and thirty-five of this number arrived in New York early in November. If this number is added to the hundreds of Guineans studying in Eastern Europe and the Soviet Union, Guinea's population of two and a half million is not doing badly from "playing the game."

Even before these agreements, Guinea was not completely tied economically to the Soviet bloc. It signed a trade agreement with Great Britain a year ago, and with West Germany this year, and although Guinea left the franc zone last March, there is still considerable trade with France. In the area of private investment, for all the Marxist oratory of some of the P.D.G. leaders, the huge Fria aluminum plant, financed by a private consortium of U.S., British, German and Swiss companies, continues to expand and to receive strong Guinean governmental support.

By playing the game, Touré has thus succeeded in achieving economic independence from France and in extracting substantial concessions from both East and West. Moreover, economic assistance from the U.S.S.R. has not prevented him from criticizing Khrushchev in his U.N. speech last fall. It also has not discouraged private companies from investing in Guinea, a lesson that is not lost on other African countries contemplating a similar policy.

"Playing the game" means adopting a neutralist nationalist policy, and when a country formerly under Western control begins to pursue a neutralist policy, by definition it is going to move away from the West and toward the Soviet Union. However, this does not mean that the neutralists are pro-Communist or under Soviet influence, and the difference is a significant one, if at times hard to detect in a U.N. vote.

One of these differences, as the case of Guinea illustrates, is the African attitude to Western investment, both public and private. Communist ideology brands this as in all cases exploitative, while it labels Soviet assistance as enlightened and altruistic. The ideology of the new African states insists on aid from both sides, "without strings." An understanding of this difference is important in avoiding the kind of moralistic withdrawal by the West which had such disastrous consequences in the case of Dulles and the Aswan Dam. Soviet policy does not seem to regard the creation of African satellites as either feasible or desirable at this time, but the wrong kind of Western reaction might enable the U.S.S.R. to move in this direction faster than it had anticipated.

If there is anything that a review of the last decade should demonstrate it is the impossibility of preventing the rising nationalist leadership from "playing the game" and dealing with the Soviet Union. When India, Egypt, and Iraq began to take Soviet aid, the same fears of Communist influence were voiced as are heard now regarding Ghana and Guinea. Today it is recognized that a strong internal regime can avoid the dangers of infiltration and even, as in the case of India, use Soviet aid to help in the development of a free society.

This should also be the principal objective in Africa, to assist in the establishment of strong and, let us hope, free societies, which can resist efforts at subversion and infiltration from whatever source. This was the real problem in the Congo—not the taking of Soviet aid by Lumumba, but the inability of a weak and divided government to control the influences which accompany it.

In this context, authoritarian government may be to our advantage in strengthening nationalist governments against Soviet-controlled ideologies and movements. This does not mean that we must condone violation of basic human rights and governmental repression by nationalist leaders. It is difficult to see, for instance, why the one hundred opposition members imprisoned in Ghana under the Preventive Detention Act could not be tried under normal conspiracy statutes if they were really plotting Nkrumah's overthrow, or why the leading plotters arrested last spring in Guinea were all "shot while trying to escape." However, our distaste for the methods and criticism of the policies of certain African states should not be a determinant of our foreign policy any more than it is in the case of other states such as Yugoslavia or Spain whose internal politics we may criticize.

If we do stand for basic human values and believe that democratic methods and not violence should be the method of social change, American and Western programs of economic and technical assistance can demonstrate that the underdeveloped nations do not have to choose the methods of the Soviet bloc and China in order to achieve economic development. But although we believe that freedom and economic progress are not mutually incompatible, many newly-independent nations are not yet convinced. This is the real competition, not for domination, but between economic development by compulsion or by methods which respect freedom and human dignity.

There is no reason to underestimate the difficulties which are created by emergence of a large number of newly-independent nations with a policy of active neutralism of the Casablanca variety. Certainly the extension of their ideology to Latin America will create enormous problems for the U.S., accustomed to thinking of the Western hemisphere as closed to outside powers. Already the United Nations is an area where the neutralists are creating difficulties for the West.

Yet, in our relations with Africa and with the other uncommitted areas, we have cultural, economic, and linguistic ties, as well as an enormous reservoir of good will which some of the vagaries of recent policy have not yet dispelled. However difficult "playing the game" on our part may be, when others play we must join in. If we can by our efforts assure that the newly independent countries can develop themselves in freedom, and can maintain basic human values, however different their institutional structure may be—then the game will be worth playing.

NEUTRALISM: THE CASE OF THE AFRICAN TRADE UNIONS

What might be the African attitude toward neutralism? There are rival interpretations, as demonstrated by the differing alignments of states within Africa. One instance in which distinctions have been clearly made is found within the African trade-union movement. Briefly, the issue between rival interpretations of neutralism in this area developed in the following way.

At the end of World War II, the World Federation of Trade Unions (WFTU) was organized, with extensive participation on both sides of the Iron Curtain. As the cold war grew, however, Western trade unions withdrew to form the International Confederation of Free Trade Unions (ICFTU), leaving the WFTU under Communist control. These rival organizations have encouraged the African trade-union movement, each in their own way, and have developed ties with African trade unionism.

For Africans, the coming of independence and the adoption of neutralism as an attitude toward the cold war posed the issue quite simply. Should African unions make and maintain connections with international trade-union organizations? Some leaders maintain that neutralism demands cutting of ties, others reject this viewpoint.

Selection 31 is a journalist's account of the formation of

the African Trade Union Confederation (ATUC) by unions from various African countries. The ATUC accepts affiliation of its members with the ICFTU and other non-African labor internationals.

The article makes it clear that the issue is not one simply of defining neutralism. Ideology is involved, and the question of government domination of trade-union movements. This is made even clearer in Selection 32, which is essentially a rejoinder by adherents of the rival African international trade-union organization, the All-African Trade Union Federation (AATUF), to the formation of the ATUC. The excerpt is from the official publication of the Ghanaian Trade Union Confederation, a major supporter of the AATUF.

This "case study" on neutralism and the African trade unions is rounded off with an article (Selection 33) describing in somewhat greater detail some of the activities of the ICFTU and WFTU in Africa, and discussing some implications, for African society, of this activity.

Selection 31

African Free Unionism Builds Solid Foundations*

ARNOLD BEICHMAN

Arnold Beichman is a journalist specializing in the area of foreign relations and the international labor movement.

When the labor history of modern Africa is written, January 14, 1962 will be a date with a chapter all its own. For it was on that day that 84 delegates from African trade unions, meeting in Dakar, Senegal—the capital city of this one-time French colony—did what a year ago seemed impossible.

Representing 41 national labor centers in 30 independent states and dependent territories, the African delegates created the African Trade Union Confederation (ATUC) comprising 22 affiliates of the International Confederation of Free Trade Unions, 12 affiliates of the International Federation of Christian Trade Unions and 7 independent of any affiliation.

By doing so, they defied the government-dominated labor organizations of Ghana, Guinea, Mali and the United Arab Republic and the government-threatened Moroccan center. These in May 1961 fabricated a rump All-African Trade Union Federation (AATUF) at Casablanca.

Despite numerous objections, the Ghana-led group at that time rammed through a resolution demanding that African unions withdraw from ICFTU within 10 months—or else, said John K. Tettegah, Ghana Trades Union Congress labor secretary and cabinet member, it would be "total war" against violators of the edict.

African labor leaders, particularly from Tunisia, Kenya, Nigeria

* Reprinted by permission from *AFL-CIO Free Trade Union News*, Vol. 17, No. 2 (February 1962), p. 2.

and Senegal, were neither amused nor cowed by Tettegah's threat. Instead they issued a continent-wide appeal for a pan-African labor conference to which they invited all bona fide trade union groups as well as the AATUF members in a bid for what was called "African unity."

The conference ran from January 9 to 14.

From a political standpoint, the congress was a triumph for the free world. This is not to say that ATUC intends to become an appendage to Western political or military alliances. It means that African free trade unionism has no intention of withdrawing into neo-isolationism and anti-foreignism, but that it intends to maintain its relationship with the free trade unions in other parts of the world.

It became apparent during the six-day conference that the delegates intended ATUC to be genuinely neutral and uncommitted. . . . While condemning colonialism, repudiating capitalism and imperialism, ATUC specifically singled out and rejected "Communism and other dictatorships" for Africa.

A key speech of Lawrence L. Borha, secretary of the Trades Union Congress of Nigeria, was punctuated by applause, particularly when he said:

"Is it not more honorable to affirm Africa's brotherhood with the ICFTU and the IFCTU who can hold up their heads as proud and brave men, free to differ with their governments or with those who are chattels and slaves of dictators? These men who call themselves neutralists and condemn only one side are not neutralists but tools in the service of an ideological machine which feeds them not bread and butter, not social justice, but empty slogans.

NOT 'NEUTRAL' ON LIBERTY

"If we are to be honest and avoid hypocrisy, let us acknowledge the simple truth of the modern world—there are no neutral men when the choice is between liberty and servitude. Dictatorship robs men of dignity and it destroys the institutions such as trade unionism—which protect man's dignity.

"Even here in Africa we have seen what bitter suffering dictatorship has caused workers. We have seen and sorrowed at how dictatorship has turned trade unions in certain countries in Africa into fawning prostitutes."

Alphonse Kithima, general secretary of the Confederation of Free Trade Unions of Congo (Leopoldville) received as warm an ovation as Borha when he said:

"A new imperialist wave is preparing to fall on Africa. This new imperialism speaks of freedom and the brotherhood of nations, but behind it lies the workers massacred in the streets of East Berlin for demanding bread and justice; the Korean peasants dead in the fields over which a ruthless war of conquest has just passed; the workmen and students of Budapest, crushed by foreign tanks for having dared to proclaim their country's right to independence and the government of its choice.

"The AATUF leadership regards it as undesirable for the young African trade unions to get to know that other unionism which keeps itself free from all governmental pressure and which has made it possible for workers even in certain Western countries with a heavy record of imperialism to support us, the colonized, as against their own governments, the colonizers."

If there was an underlying theme it was a dedicated effort to find some common, genuine basis for the slogan, "African unity," the merest mention of which is guaranteed to evoke as many cheers and as much applause as an oratorical citation of the Declaration of Independence at a 4th of July picnic. It was a desire by Africans to find something distinctive in themselves without necessarily separating themselves from the rest of the world. . . .

Selection 32

The Illusions of the AFL-CIO*

AFRICAN WORKER

In an article in the AFL-CIO Free Trade Union News of December, 1961, headed "Role of Free Unions in Africa," there appeared some statements which explain the frantic attempts being made by the Unions affiliated to the ICFTU to discredit the AATUF in general, and the Ghana TUC in particular, by labelling them as Communist directed organizations. This accusation is an old-technique adopted by the Imperialist countries to divert the attention of world opinion from the

* Reprinted by permission from the *African Worker* (April 1962), pp. 8–9.

realities of the situation. Such a technique can no longer delude anybody except its users themselves.

While we do not wish to enter into any controversy regarding all of the illusions of the AFL-CIO, there is however, one important basic fact which we hope that organization will recognise in time, before they add more to the great damage already inflicted to US/African labour relations by their stubborn refusal to face the realities of the African situation in their role as obstructionists, via the ICFTU, to the cause of African labour unity. Under a sub-title "Basic Characteristics," it is stated in the article:

> "There is no contradiction between the development of a genuine All-African Trade Union Federation and the continuation by African free trade unions of their relations with a free and independent international labour movement, such as the ICFTU in whose ranks are found millions of workers from Asia, Latin America, Europe, Australia and North America. In this light, it is most deplorable that certain hostile and totalitarian forces wish to exploit Pan-Africanism and AATUF as a front for their anti-democratic designs and objectives."

We challenge this statement because the realities are that there is another rival international organization, the WFTU, which also claims to represent many more millions than the ICFTU can claim, of workers, who are as equally independent, democratic, free (and all other adjectives you can think of) as the ICFTU, in Asia, Latin America, Europe and other parts of the world. These two rival international bodies—the ICFTU and the WFTU represent two different social systems which are at present engaged in a "cold war" in almost all spheres of activity.

The ICFTU by its constitution, does not permit any of its affiliates to have contact with the WFTU. Why this is so, has nothing to do with African Labour. It is a quarrel between the ICFTU and the WFTU, and it is precisely because of the need to avoid being drawn into such conflict that African Labour has taken a stand to remain in its own international, the All-African Trade Union Federation.

Those of us in the AATUF are the first to recognise that we cannot live in isolation, that we must maintain friendly relations (but on our own terms, and not through any compulsion, constitutional or otherwise), with other international labour groupings whether christians, democrats, republicans, conservatives or socialists.

If a national trade union centre in Africa is therefore, affiliated to the ICFTU, it could not maintain any relation with the WFTU (Free Trade Unionism indeed). That national trade union centre therefore, joins the others in the ICFTU to sing the song of "Freedom" while the negroes in the membership of the AFL-CIO are still being discriminated against in some public places in the United States.

Automatically, resolutions condemning communism are subscribed to by thousands or millions of African affiliates of the ICFTU, who in actual fact do not even know where Moscow is situated except with the help of an Atlas. That is how African Trade Unions become wagons or trailers in the ICFTU.

This is the insult to all that Pan-Africanism represents which the AATUF is determined to halt. This is the role of second-fiddle which African Trade Unionism rejects. This is what all those who wish African Labour well, whether enemies or friends, past or present must recognise.

Africa, and for that matter, African Labour, rejects domination, humiliation and oppression. Africa has arrived and African Labour has taken her rightful place in the world. It is left to those who have hitherto usurped her rights to abdicate. If they don't they will be forced to capitulate.

Those who are still in doubt will sooner or later realise their folly and discover that their rightful place is not within an international which is less fit to translate their asperations and objectives no matter how voluble they might express their sympathy, but within the ranks of the All-African Trade Union Federation, the only instrument at the disposal of African Labour to achieve total freedom and complete unity of our continent.

Selection 33

African Nations Band Together*

BUSINESS WEEK

A new pan-African labor federation—one promising continued ties between African unions and world labor—was formed in the Senegalese city of Dakar last week. Approximately 50 unions from 30 nations and territories agreed to cooperate in a loose organization called the African Trade Union Confederation (ATUC).

From the Western point of view, the ATUC's most important action was something it didn't do: it didn't forbid member unions to belong to existing world labor bodies, such as the anti-Communist International Confederation of Free Trade Unions (ICFTU). . . .

This is a decision that affects more than unions, or even the eventual course of African labor-management relations. It affects Africa's political future in the most direct way.

Actual or potential union members are almost the only Africans who count politically. There is no one else except a sprinkling of merchants and professionals, too few to carry weight, and a mass of tribesmen, in most areas politically blank except when manipulated occasionally by tribal chiefs. Africa's industrial work force and political electorate are all but identical.

Leadership training. In the same way, union leadership means national leadership. Many of Africa's top officials—from the Congo's Premier Cyrille Adoula to Upper Volta's Ambassador to the United States, Frederic Guirma—are trade union alumni. In a society essentially without organizations—no lodges, no PTAs, no political parties on the ward-and-precinct model—unions provide almost the only op-

---

portunity for a man to show leadership qualities or learn how to use them.

An awareness of this situation lies behind the tug-of-war being conducted by the ICFTU and labor organizations of the Eastern bloc. Most African unions have links with ICFTU. Others—including some that helped form ATUC—belong to the International Federation of Christian Trade Unions, a Catholic organization. Comparatively few belong to the leftist World Federation of Trade Unions.

The Stake. The stake is some degree of influence over an estimated 14-million workers (including sugar and other plantation workers). Most of the 14-million are not even union members in the technical sense of signing union cards or paying dues. They are members, however, in the effective sense of following union leadership. They will answer a strike call even if they never paid dues to the union.

This mode of operation is the problem that faces African labor leaders: They must convert followings into organizations. To do so, they must train local leaders in the most basic techniques of union administration—how to run a meeting, how to keep books, how to write a letter. It's a huge job and they cannot do it without help from the outside.

ICFTU program. The ICFTU plans to raise $10-million—$2-million of it pledged by AFL-CIO—for the next three years' operation of its International Solidarity Fund, the fund that finances work in underdeveloped countries. How much of this will go to Africa will depend on ad hoc decisions made during the next three years.

The ICFTU doesn't know, of course, how much money Communist labor groups will have for African work, but past experience indicates that it will be many times the ICFTU's budget. ICFTU has a simple standard of comparison.

"We were able to offer two scholarships for our Kampala (Uganda) Labor College to an Ivory Coast union with 4,000 members," an ICFTU spokesman said. "The same union got 96 offers from Communist sources." Among these were scholarships to a rival labor college at Conakry in Guinea, whose students generally return "full of notions about an elite manipulating the masses for their own good."

Curriculum. Kampala courses emphasize the values of discussion, debate, loyal opposition. Officials concede that these values are often brushed aside by Africans impatient to get things done quickly. But they believe there is no other way to lay the groundwork for future democratic unionism.

Kampala and the scattered classes that preceded its opening in June have 150 graduates. Many of these served as teachers while they were students, holding one- and two-week seminars for local leaders in the field. A similar college for French-speaking unionists is in the works.

The ICFTU also assigns representatives to assist African unions in organizing, negotiating, or other activities. So far most representatives have been Europeans or Americans.

ICFTU plans to assign Africans to these tasks on a permanent basis, instead of sending in "outsiders" on a temporary one, as soon as trained personnel is available.

ATUC's role. ICFTU will have no direct links with the new federation. Although ATUC will permit its members to join world groups, it will join none. It sees its own role as purely African—all-African if possible. An attempt to persuade the Casablanca unions to join will probably be made. . . .

AFRICA AND THE UNITED NATIONS

One of the more notable features in the evolution of the United Nations since 1946 has been the enormous increase in membership. Newly independent Africa has contributed the largest share of such new members. Total membership has jumped from 51 in 1946 to more than 110 at present. Members from the African continent have increased in the same period from four to more than thirty, with a number of other African states to follow as they enter into independence.

The effects of this increase have been reciprocal. The United Nations has acted as a magnet to the new nations, which were eager to set the seal of approval to independence through acceptance into the world formum, and has affected their subsequent conduct of foreign relations. In turn, the new states, by virtue of their numbers and their characteristic preoccupations, certainly very much influenced the business of the United Nations.

By almost any criterion other than physical size, the great majority of the new nations in Africa fall into the category of "dwarf" states. In West and Equatorial Africa together, for example, sixteen of the nineteen independent states have under five million each in population. A similarly high proportion have very weak, underdeveloped economies, at least by modern standards. Fragmented as it is into an increasing number of such countries, Africa might well be called the continent of the "dwarf" state.

It is not difficult to perceive the dangers of this situation. At worst, such states are easy targets of aggression. Even if not subjected to such extreme treatment, they may become pawns in the great game of power politics, or clients of larger powers which offer them protection and assistance. On the other hand, they could find themselves living an isolated, relatively stagnated existence, neither knowing much of the world about them well, nor contributing much to it. The best of these possibilities could not be considered attractive by Africans eager to modernize and to assert their right to equal voice and consideration in the public affairs of the world.

Because most of the African nations are "dwarf" states, membership in the United Nations seems for them particularly advantageous. A poor nation cannot afford a large foreign service. Tanganyika, for example, upon becoming independent announced that for economy reasons she would assign diplomatic personnel only to London, Washington, and one other post. Furthermore, it is reported that almost none of the new African nations are attempting to establish diplomatic representation in the capitals of *all* of the other African nations. Under such circumstances, the United Nations offers the most direct access, through contact with the delegations of the 110-plus member states and with the activities of the organization itself, to knowledge and understanding of current international affairs. In the opinion of one diplomat, the United Nations "is probably the best place in the world to pick up information on other governments."* The student of the organization who reported this comment went on to remark that United Nations reports and records "provide voluminous documentation that covers virtually all international problems. . . . This documentation is, of course, more important to some nations than it is to others. For smaller nations and nations not directly involved in some issues, United Nations information sources may provide virtually all of the data on which national positions are based."†

As the African nations are all represented at the United Nations, and (as a group) at few other spots in the world, the United Nations offers the most convenient place to coordinate their policies. This fact was specifically recognized and acted upon by the (First) Conference of Independent African States meeting at Accra, Ghana, in April 1958. This conference adopted a resolution instructing representatives of African nations at the United Nations to organize themselves on a permanent basis, for

---

* Chadwick F. Alger, "Non-resolution Consequences of the United Nations and Their Effect on International Conflict," pamphlet issued by the Program of Graduate Training and Research in International Relations, Northwestern University (March 1960), p. 18.

† *Ibid.*, pp. 18–19.

purposes of consultation and cooperation. They did so, and the grouping which resulted still flourishes, growing larger with each entry of a new African nation into the United Nations. The United Nations thus serves as a clearing house among the African nations. It has been suggested, further, that by preventing isolation of "dwarf" nations and by placing the mantle of responsibility upon them, the United Nations lessens the instability which the sudden addition of so many "dwarf" states might otherwise bring to the international system.

Beyond this, the United Nations affords opportunity for "dwarf" states to put forward for consideration policies and points of view they otherwise might not be able to place effectively before the world public. For evidence of this, we have but to look at the space on the United Nations agenda occupied nowadays by questions of self-determination ("colonialism"), human rights (apartheid), and economic and social advancement. These are matters of great concern to the African nations, a concern which has demonstrably helped make such questions bulk larger on the United Nations scene in recent years.

These considerations carry us to the other side of the reciprocal relationships between African nations and the United Nations—the effect of the new nations upon the United Nations. In Selection 34 a close observer of the United Nations analyzes patterns of politics in the United Nations in relation to the interests of the United States in particular and of the whole Western alliance in general.

Voting patterns are of special interest and importance because the increase in number of "uncommitted" states shifts control of the United Nations more and more out of the hands of the strong original members. Some see this shift in dark colors, others see at least a silver lining to the cloud. We find an example tending toward the first viewpoint in Selection 35, in which Lord Home, Foreign Minister of the United Kingdom at the time the speech was delivered, deplores the "crisis of confidence" in the United Nations created by the influx of new nations. But in Selection 36, it is suggested that if we "ride with the punch," and accommodate with neutralism in the United Nations, benefits may accrue.

In Selection 37 an individual with extensive experience in the United Nations adds his observations to the others—he is in general optimistic about the political consequences for the West of the vast expansion in African membership. In the latter part of his article, however, he adds another dimension to the discussion, that of the United Nations programs for economic and technical assistance and specifically of United Nations aid to Africa.

Selection 34

New Diplomacy in the United Nations*

LINCOLN P. BLOOMFIELD

Dr. Bloomfield is a senior staff member and director of the United Nations Project at the Center for International Studies at the Massachusetts Institute of Technology.

THE IMPACT OF THE NEW MEMBERSHIP

It has always been true that the United Nations diplomatic scene makes sense only when it is explicitly related to events and forces external to the organization itself. This is the familiar argument, immortalized by Sir Gladwyn Jebb, that the United Nations is a mirror of the world around it and that if the reflection is ugly the organization should not be blamed. I profoundly believe this to be true. But against it there has always been the complaint by some of Sir Gladwyn's fellow Europeans that the ratio between the United Nations and the outside world is by no means a simple one-to-one correlation. This view, in its most critical form, has always castigated the United Nations as an inciter to riot. According to its doctrine the United Nations, because of its composition and because of its inherent ideological bias, distorts and magnifies to intolerable proportions certain matters of crucial interest, particularly in the colonial area. This arsonist argument has by no means prevailed in the United States or Scandinavia or in many other areas. It is far more commonly held that United Nations attention and pressure, particularly in colonial relationships, is not

---

* Reprinted by permission from *The United States and the United Nations* edited by Francis O. Wilcox and H. Field Haviland, Jr. (Baltimore: The Johns Hopkins Press, 1961), pp. 51–60.

only right but can actually improve situations which, if uncontrolled, would produce even less acceptable results.

This issue is by no means a purely theoretical one. If it is true that the Afro-Asian group is using its near-majority position in the United Nations simply to stir up racial and political trouble in the Portuguese colonies, and if one were confident Portugal would act with farsighted and enlightened preparations for self-government, then we should re-examine our own premises. The evidence is all to the contrary, and we can only conclude that while United Nations debates may encourage unrest, the conditions for unrest were there first. It may be that without the United Nations the colonial powers might have hung on a little longer in certain areas. But it is unlikely that the basic contours of the problem would be very different.

The revolutionary process that has taken place in the once-imperial world to the south has left a legacy of colossal problems about how the new nations are to be brought into a durable and mutually satisfying relationship with the established order as we know it. The categories of problems involved in the transition to nationhood are familiar ones and many of them are covered elsewhere in this book. But the political and diplomatic effects of the process are intimately tied to the substance of the problems. Most of all, the diplomatic task is bound up with the priorities assigned by the countries directly concerned, as they—not we—view those priorities.

The countries we are speaking of all share in varying degree the qualities of being non-European, non-white, politically neutralist, and anti-colonial. I have cited the colonial problem. Many people give equal weight to the problem of gross economic disparity between rich and poor nations. Until the gap begins to close, no enduring stability is possible between the nations involved, or in any diplomatic forum in which they interact. Unquestionably this issue is paramount, and American diplomacy in the United Nations has labored for many years to offset our negative attitudes toward multilateral financing of economic development, toward more predictable international commodity prices, and toward the problems of foreign and absentee ownership of resources. American policies in some of these areas are, I believe, loosening up.

I myself give equally high rank to the racial issue. If the behavioral sciences have anything to say about contemporary diplomacy it is undoubtedly in this realm of misunderstandings, attitudes and images, hostilities and frustrations. At root, George Kennan is right about the domestic basis for successful diplomacy. For so long as the United States tolerates racism at home, that long will all our bridges to the black, brown, and yellow nations be shaky and poorly supported against stress.

The north-south revolution by its very nature poses the problems of statehood itself—of evolving political forms, of relating the central governments to regions and integrating these nations in other ways. Perhaps most importantly, there are problems of dignity and of the pride which representatives of new nations have displayed abroad since the first American diplomatic agents refused to bend the knee to foreign potentates.

Clearly, if there were no United Nations these issues of both substance and diplomatic style would still be the vital stuff of international politics in much of the world. Because there is a United Nations, they come together there and in their totality add up to a new political force which by its numbers and by its pivotal role in the East-West competition confronts the Western powers with perhaps its central diplomatic challenge. . . .

THE NEW ARITHMETIC

The new arithmetic now comes into focus. The facts about it have become commonplace. From 10 at the San Francisco Conference, the Afro-Asian membership has grown to 46 and will soon increase again. Where there were two African states south of the Sahara, there are now suddenly 20. Add Cuba, and, sometimes, Mexico, and it comes very close to a numerical majority. Add the Soviet bloc, grown from 5 to 9, plus Yugoslavia, and only 9 more are needed to make up the crucial and decisive two-thirds in the General Assembly. Another popular way to arrange the numbers is to add together all the underdeveloped countries, i.e. the Afro-Asian group plus, more or less, Latin America. Without the Soviet bloc this hypothetical majority already commands a two-thirds vote, and, with the Soviet bloc added, it has a clearly commanding position.

There have been no such exact combinations—yet. But these possible combinations of voting strength furnish the concrete basis for much of the concern about the future of the Western position in the United

Nations. Actually, the numbers can be used to support any side of the argument. In the last General Assembly some votes tended to show that the worst had finally happened—if the worst is a minority position for the United States. The neutralist call for a summit meeting carried over United States opposition, 41 to 37. The American proposal on Arab refugee relief received only 31 votes to 30 against and 15 abstaining, the first time in memory that the United States had not carried its way on that issue to which we contribute the lion's share financially. Then we lost, 10 to 47, in the final refugee resolution with the unacceptable reference to property rights. The United States was in the minority in the vote on the Mexican proposal to discourage states from using their territories or resources to interfere in the Cuban civil war. It was in a tiny minority in a committee vote on a crucial paragraph on the Cuban resolution. And we could not carry a proposal to finance the Congo operation even though it cut the share of the poorest countries up to 75 per cent. The measure carried only after the reduction was made 80 per cent.

The same Assembly session, however, can demonstrate the opposite case. Who in a pluralistic world could legitimately ask for more decisive support than the United States received in such votes as these: 62 to 12 to reject Soviet disarmament propaganda moves in the plenary session; 54 to 10 to require orderly rather than spectacular debates on the RB-47 incident; 53 to 24 to seat the Kasavubu delegation from the Congo; 81 to 9 to approve the 1961 budget to which the communist bloc objected so vigorously; 61 to 27 for a proposal on Cuba that we could live with—far more, incidentally, than we had much right to expect under the circumstances; and 83 to 11 on a Congo resolution calling for effective measures by the Secretary General, in the midst of the Soviet attack upon him and on the office as presently constituted?

A third set of votes is interesting because of its ambiguity. Here one comes closer to the truth about the divergent interests within the Afro-Asian bloc and the growing fluidity in alignments in general, particularly the present distinction between "British" and "French" Africans, reinforcing the impression that the present may be a poor time for confident political prediction whether optimistic or pessimistic.

One of the interesting phenomena of the United Nations has been the superimposition of the political process upon that of diplomacy. The substance, that is to say, is diplomacy; but the milieu is that of politics, with qualities common to both Ward 6 and the Congress of Vienna. The growth of bloc politics in the United Nations was in this sense inevitable. What is now happening is a shift within the blocs themselves, a fluidity of voting alignment reflecting the dynamic shifts within regions such as Africa and Latin America. The Afro-Asian bloc, for example, has become four discernible sub-blocs: the five Casablanca powers, the French community nations, the pro-Western, and the middle of the road group.

Given this fissiparous trend, the Afro-Asians alone still do not hold the parliamentary whip-hand, even though East and West seek their support. In the 41 to 37 vote on their summit proposal the Communists were among the 17 abstainers. The Afro-Asian call for a United Nations referendum in Algeria received 40 votes in favor, 40 against—a striking example of the close balance between the forces involved. Time and again the bloc failed to get two-thirds or even a simple majority on such proposals as breaking relations with the Union of South Africa, giving priority to the Angola question, or adjourning debate on the Congo.

Of course the numbers tell only part of the story. The case for pessimism is incomplete without the slap administered to the United States by the Africans, through the Nigerian delegate, in the matter of the proposed American aid program for Africa. Opinions differ about this: was the American gesture insufficiently followed up by concrete proposals? Was the Nigerian delegate being excessively unkind to us for his own purposes? Or are all American initiatives, however sincere, to be unavailing until the storm has spent itself a good deal more? Here the armchair strategist can only fall into the traps of insufficient knowledge and Monday morning quarter-backing.

But once again the coin has two faces. It is widely believed that in the crucially important Security Council vote in the early hours of February 21 supporting the United Nations operation in the Congo and authorizing the use of force, if necessary, to prevent the occurrence of civil war, the Soviet Union shifted at virtually the last minute from expected opposition to abstention. The resolution was sponsored by three Afro-Asian states, the episode dramatized the dilemma facing both the Soviets and ourselves. For both powers must constantly reappraise their diplomatic priorities, and each periodically has to balance its books in just such haste. . . .

THE PROBLEM FOR THE WESTERN ALLIANCE

One of the grounds for the Western pessimism about the future of the United Nations stems from growing European irritation with the "irresponsible" majorities that ride roughshod in areas that are traditionally no one else's business. General de Gaulle's extraordinarily virulent attack on the United Nations seemed to put an exclamation point to increasing European disaffection. Some students of Western unity are saying that the United States must again face a choice between the Western alliance and the will-o'the-wisp of African and Asian nationalism. There are many today who will argue that the United Nations can only worsen Western relationships while holding no promise whatever of winning the ephemeral, unprofitable—even hopeless—popularity contest with the Soviets in—or out—of the United Nations.

This line of reasoning involves several dangerous fallacies. First of all, there is nothing new about the European problem in the United Nations. Some of our Western European allies distrusted and feared United Nations action, particularly on colonial matters, long before the newer nations developed their present political strength. Both before and after Suez, United Nations majorities have run against what some European nations conceived to be their vital interests as well as their right to privacy in colonial affairs. Without documenting the analysis (which I have made elsewhere), I believe that the final passing of the colonial issue in its present form will profoundly transform the European-United Nations relationship, just as it will transform European-African relations over-all. The truth of this is demonstrated by the shadings among Western Europeans on this issue discernible for some years past. The spectrum began with those having least sympathy with the United Nations and allegedly most to lose from its intervention in colonial matters—France, Portugal and Belgium, with the added French nostalgia for lost hegemony in League days. Mid-point was Britain, where the parties were sharply divided on the United Nations-colonial issue, and Mr. Macmillan's winds of change had rather long since been measured and quietly but irrevocably yielded to. At the far end were countries such as the Netherlands—which but for the West New Guinea issue would have been planning and acting even more positively in the United Nations in such fields as economic development—and Italy, which looked across the Mediterranean in a frame of mind geared to an entirely new and clearly noncolonial era.

The end of the colonial era in Africa will not end the problems for Western diplomacy. It is predictable that they will still be numerous and thorny. But the sooner that day comes, the sooner the West, the United States, and the United Nations will be relieved of what has been a truly crippling incubus. . . .

Selection 35

The United Nations: The Crisis of Confidence*

Lord Home

Lord Home was Secretary of State for Foreign Affairs in the British government at the time he delivered the speech reprinted here. He later became the Prime Minister of the United Kingdom as Sir Alec Douglas-Home on October 18, 1963, succeeding Harold Macmillan.

Delivered to the Berwick-on-Tweed branch of the United Nations Association, December 28, 1961.

PURPOSES OF THE UNITED NATIONS

In order that none of us may have any doubts as to the purposes for which the United Nations was founded I will remind you of the obligations which were assumed by the member countries which signed the Charter. They resolved to "save succeeding generations from the scourge of war which twice in our lifetime has brought untold sorrow to mankind," and they pledged themselves never to use force for the resolution of conflicts "save in the common interest" but to be a "centre for harmonising the actions of nations." The United Nations was

* Reprinted by permission from *Vital Speeches of the Day* (February 1, 1962). pp. 237–239.

founded to provide security as the basis of peace and that is the purpose for which it exists today. . . .

THE CRISIS

Why then, if there is such a universal urge for peace and the machinery to achieve it is ready to hand, is there a crisis of confidence in the United Nations? . . .

Many of us had foreseen this crisis of confidence. For years the Russians had been frustrating the proper working of the United Nations, but lately a new and dangerous practice had begun to prevail.

Resolutions have been persistently passed by the Assembly, in particular on colonialism, which could only be described as reckless and careless of peace and security. Everyone has seen the chaos in the Congo and everyone knows that it derives from a premature grant of independence to a country whose people were totally unprepared for their new responsibilities. Yet many Delegates were instructed by their Governments to sponsor and vote for resolutions which could only multiply and magnify that chaos in other places.

I will quote Resolution 1514 of December 14, 1960 which says:

> "Immediate steps shall be taken in Trust and Non-Self-Governing Territories, or in all other Territories which have not yet attained independence, to transfer all powers to the peoples of these Territories without any conditions whatever."

and the Resolution goes on:

> "Inadequacy of political, economic, social or educational preparedness should never serve as a pretext for delaying Independence."

Such a resolution and others like it reveal an almost total lack of responsibility, and certainly pay no heed to the main purpose of the United Nations which is to ensure order and security of peace.

FAILURE OF SOME COUNTRIES TO PAY COSTS

Then again, although countries are free enough with their votes, they are not nearly so ready to pay their legally assessed subscriptions without which the organization cannot be solvent or efficient.

Eighty-two out of one hundred and four are in serious arrears with their payments. The Soviet and their satellites do not pay anything towards the operations in the Congo or on the Israel-Egypt border, and France does not pay towards the Congo expenses.

When, therefore, we have reached a stage when a large part of the organization which is dedicated to peace openly condones aggression; when an organization which was founded to sustain law and order encourages policies which must endanger it, or when a refusal by many to carry their share of the cost brings a prospect of power without responsibility, it is an understatement to say that there is cause for anxiety.

CAUSES OF THE PRESENT DISCONTENT

Tonight, therefore, I would like to analyse some of the causes of the present discontent, and discuss with you what we can and should do to save an organization in which so many of the hopes of men reside.

One of the main causes of the present troubles is an apparent difference of aim and purpose between the fifty-one founder members and many of the fifty-three newly independent countries which were elected to membership subsequently to the United Nations' foundation.

. . . the founder members laid the whole emphasis on the organization of peace through collective security. They united for maintaining the peace. They named the great powers as permanent members in the expectation that they would agree on how to keep international order, and would deal together with any breach of the peace by the smaller powers by united decision and coordinated action.

In the event of disagreement between the great powers each was armed with a veto on action by the others.

The best there could be was collective security collectively imposed—the worst (so it was supposed) stalemate and the status quo.

The supposition was wrong, for almost immediately the Russians showed themselves determined to use their veto to further the international objectives of communism. Russia's decision to subordinate the main purposes of the Charter to her own national ends was the first breach in the spirit of the Charter and the first threat to the life of the United Nations.

For years the Russians have used the platform of the United Nations to prosecute the Cold War using racialism, nationalism, and the exuberant individualism of newly independent countries to further their ends. All this put the United Nations under serious stress and strain.

Now another breach is beginning to appear and the origin of it is somewhat similar. A large number of new countries are putting their campaign for acceleration of independence for colonial territories before the main purpose of the Charter which is to provide peace and security. They are more concerned to impose their views on "colonialism" on others than to fulfill their primary duty which is to "harmonize the actions of nations."

I would not equate their motives with those of the communists, although far too often they find themselves bedfellows, but the effect of their actions is to weaken the Charter and to call in question the good faith of the United Nations. Unwittingly they play the communists' game.

DOUBLE STANDARD OF BEHAVIOUR

This leads me to illustrate how this concentration on colonialism leads to the adoption of a double standard of behaviour by many of the newly elected countries.

Russia's empire is occupied by military force and ruled by fear. No one who has witnessed what has happened in Hungary and East Germany can have any doubt that Russia's colonialism is the most cruel and ruthless in history. In the United Nations her technique is undisguised—it is that of the bully.

By contrast, the British record is one which has freed six hundred million people in fifteen years, and transferred them from colonial dependence to complete independence within the Commonwealth, where they are equal partners and in no way subordinate. We are moving fast—perhaps faster than in prudence we ought—in the direction in which the new countries want to go. The United Nations members know that to be true, but they seldom condemn the Russians and constantly harass us. It seems as if pushing at an open door is not good enough for them. To cooperate with the metropolitan power in completing the process of independence in an orderly way—to ensure that new nations get a good start in international life—is apparently emotionally unsatisfying and politically unrewarding.

Since we in Britain are agreed on independence anyway, the only way to pick a quarrel is over timing. Self-government today, regardless of whether there is anyone capable of governing—independence tomorrow, even though it would mean other Congos.

The double standard as applied to Europeans and Russians, and Europeans and Afro-Asians became so blatant that I felt bound to draw attention to it in the U. N. Assembly. I said:

> "The United Nations, and in particular this Assembly, must show itself to be impartial, must be seen to be impartial. I am only going to ask this question: I am not sure of the answer. Is there growing up, almost imperceptibly, a code of behaviour where there is one rule for the Communist countries and another for the Democracies? One rule for the bully, who deals in fear, and another for the Democracies because their stock in trade is reason and compromise?"

But if the United Nations is to be the body which we wish to see, which guards the weak and is jealous of the independence of small nations, then they must not yield to the temptation to put public pressure always upon the reasonable nations because they feel that in the last resort those nations will be decent and therefore will give way. That would be to deny justice to others which they themselves wish to enjoy. . . .

Selection 36

Can Neutralism Create a New Balance?*

VERA MICHELES DEAN

Mrs. Dean has been research director and editor of research publications with the Foreign Policy Association, and director of the Non-Western Civilization Program at the University of Rochester.

The defeat suffered by Moscow in the United Nations on February 21 when the Congo resolution introduced by the United Arab Republic, Ceylon and Liberia was supported by 9 out of the 11 members of the Security Council—with the U.S.S.R. and France abstaining—may prove to have been a turning point in the history of the world organization. For this defeat was inflicted, not by one great power on another, but by three small nations acting in the international forum and determined to end intervention in the Congo by any non-African nation, whether Communist or anti-Communist, by strengthening the role of the UN.

This unprecedented action introduced a new factor into the traditional struggle between great powers—whether armed with ideologies or weapons, or both. The new factor is neutralism, which had hitherto been considered by both sides in the East-West struggle as inimical to their respective interests. Today, however, neutralism may act as a weight in maintaining a balance, however precarious it may be, between the two great-power blocs which have seemed to polarize the world since World War II.

* Reprinted by permission from *Foreign Policy Bulletin* (March 15, 1961), pp. 103–104. *Foreign Policy Bulletin* is published by the Foreign Policy Association, New York City.

U.S. ACCEPTS NEUTRALISM

The success of the Congo resolution was due not only to the decision of the UAR, Ceylon and Liberia (the first two, advocates of nonalignment; the third, traditionally friendly to the United States) to take the initiative in breaking a mortally dangerous deadlock. Most important, it was also due to Washington's acceptance of neutralism as a positive, not merely negative, factor. This acceptance, implicit for some time in United States policy, had been made explicit by Secretary of State Dean Rusk when on January 12, in answer to questions by the Senate Foreign Relations Committee about his views on neutralism, he replied:

"Well, I do not believe that we ourselves should be unduly concerned about what might be called the genuine neutralism because if a new nation is internally vigorous, viable, strong, progressive, its orientation in foreign policy is not so important as its health and strength, its orientation as a neutral. . . . I do not believe we ought to ask commitments of a sort that would make it difficult for them to lead their own peoples in development, or difficult for them to draw together in regional associations of their own, as the opportunity might arise, or difficult for them to take their proper place in such an organization as the UN." Mr. Rusk went on to say that we can work together with other countries on common practical problems in many fields, "without having political pledges which may in many cases be beyond the competence of the governments concerned to make good on."

In the case of the Congo some of the African countries (notably Ghana, Guinea and Mali), as well as the UAR in the Middle East and some of the Asian nations, had regarded Patrice Lumumba as the Congo's legitimate leader, and had been critical of what they claimed to be the UN's failure to protect him from his political enemies. They had also sharply criticized the continued presence of Belgian armed forces in the province of Katanga, with its rich copper resources owned by the Belgian concern, Union Minière du Haut Katanga, and had demanded their immediate withdrawal. But while criticizing the UN for its alleged weakness in dealing with Joseph Kasavubu, Colonel Mobutu and Moise Tshombe, they also attacked it for what they asserted was undue intervention in the affairs of an African country.

In spite of their criticisms of the Belgian "colonialists" and of Western powers which tolerated the continued presence of Belgian military personnel in Katanga, the African nations did not support the Soviet bloc, although their policies—like the policy of Yugoslavia—were in important respects similar to that of the U.S.S.R. and its Eastern European satellites.

In the Congo crisis, as had happened on previous occasions, the United States might have decided to identify the policies of some of the non-Western nations, which proclaim their nonalignment, with those of the Communist countries. Had the United States followed this course, it might have left most of the Afro-Asian-Arab countries no choice but to be aligned, in their UN votes if not in their actual sympathies, with the Soviet bloc. This the United States refrained from doing—and it thereby gave the nonaligned nations an opportunity to exercise their initiative in the UN—with the result that, contrary to the expectations of pessimists, the U.S.S.R. was isolated when it came to a showdown and, fearing to antagonize the African nations by rejection of their resolution, had no choice but to abstain. . . .

In the Congo and in Laos the United States has made it clear that henceforth it does not regard neutralism as equivalent to or inspired by communism. This development in American foreign policy has two important results. First, the neutralist countries are now in a better position to make moves in world affairs which could, at best, ease tensions between the great-power blocs or, at the very least, could create buffer zones between them. And, second, the United States, as well as our Western allies, will have far greater flexibility in negotiating with the neutralist countries instead of leaving them stiffly to their own devices—with no choice, as had happened in the past, except to turn for military and economic aid to the Communist bloc.

This new policy should greatly strengthen the UN in a critical period when the U.S.S.R. is making vicious attacks on the world organization and on Secretary General Dag Hammarskjold. As Ambassador Adlai E. Stevenson pointed out in his testimony before the Senate Foreign Relations Committee on January 18, the essential characteristic of the UN is that it is based on democratic principles. He then said, "the UN—as an idea and as an institution—is an extension of Western ideas; of Western belief in the worth and dignity of the individual; of Western ideology. It is based on a Western parliamentary tradition. Its roots are in the Western ideal of representative government." The great powers which observe these principles in their relations with small and weak countries thereby demonstrate their belief in democracy not only at home, but in the world forum. If the Communist nations refuse to abide by these principles, they will face the choice of either leaving the UN (and UN observers believe Moscow would hesitate to do this), or else of abiding by democratic principles in the world forum, even if they oppose them at home.

Selection 37

The New Africa and the United Nations*

Sir Andrew Cohen

Now director of the Department of Technical Co-operation in London, Sir Andrew Cohen was formerly British representative on the United Nations Trusteeship Council.

... A few years ago the only member States from Africa, apart from the Union of South Africa, were Egypt, Ethiopia, and Liberia—three countries of widely differing background and traditions, which at that time formed no African grouping in the United Nations. African issues from the start dominated the debates of the Trusteeship Council and the Fourth Committee of the General Assembly, and petitioners from the African Trust Territories have long been a familiar sight at the United Nations. But at that time the lead on the anti-colonial side was taken by Asian and Latin American countries and, although to many of the members the debates on trusteeship and non-self-governing territories have been specially important, until recently African problems in general have not emerged as one of the major features affecting the work of the United Nations.

---

* Reprinted by permission of the author and the publisher from *International Affairs* (October 1960), pp. 477–488.

Now, with the rapid emergence of new independent countries, Africa has come into its own. Recently the African group has consisted of nine States, the three original African members together with the Sudan, two members from West Africa, and three from North Africa. As a result of the formation of the Organization of Independent African States in 1958, the African group works closely together—more closely than any other group except the monolithic Soviet bloc. Because of its organized work as a group and of the wide sympathy for African aspirations felt in all sections of the United Nations, the African members are able to exercise a considerable influence; this is enhanced by their membership of the looser Afro-Asian group, which sometimes, but by no means always, adopts a common position on important issues, at any rate for the majority of its members. At the last session of the General Assembly in 1959 the African members played a major part in the discussions in the Fourth Committee on South West Africa and the Cameroons and in the First Committee in the debate on the Sahara bomb test—the first African issue in the field of security which has come up in the Assembly. Earlier in the year a resumed session of the previous year's General Assembly, lasting for three weeks, was devoted exclusively to the future of the Cameroons. . . .

VOTING STRENGTH AT THE UNITED NATIONS

Taking Africa down to the southern borders of the Congo and Tanganyika, there are likely to be well over twenty members of the United Nations by the 1961 Assembly and nearly thirty at some later date. The total membership is likely at that time to be just over a hundred; and since resolutions of the General Assembly on important questions require a two-thirds majority, the African States, if they voted together, could almost muster a blocking third by themselves. As a group they will be the largest of any, nearly equal in numbers to the Western European and pre-war Commonwealth countries and the Soviet bloc combined. The Afro-Asian group would at the same time cover not far short of half the membership, since there are twenty Asian States. In these circumstances it is quite certain that the African members will be able to make their influence felt more strongly than ever before.

There are some people who think that the accession of this large number of new members will change the whole character of the organization, and change it to the detriment of the West. Any opinion at the present stage must be purely speculative; but there are a number of reasons for thinking that this represents altogether too gloomy an attitude. The organization will admittedly have some technical troubles at first in digesting its new membership; for example, the conventions governing the elections to the Security Council and the Economic and Social Council (which already cause considerable difficulty) can hardly remain unaffected. The increase in membership will inevitably also have the effect of adding to the weight of small-Power opinion in the United Nations. In the end this may strengthen rather than weaken the organization, which has increasingly become a sounding-board for the opinions of the middle and smaller Powers and the place where many of the new countries conduct much of their foreign policy. The new members from Africa are gaining their independence through joint action between themselves and the European administering Powers, and the granting of independence is unquestionably a source of strength to the free world generally; in the United Nations this may not make itself felt immediately, but seems likely to do so in due course. There is no reason to suppose that on the great issues of peace and disarmament, or in the economic relations between countries, the new members will be opposed to the West; the attitude of the smaller countries to the Soviet accusations in the Security Council after the Summit Conference showed how they can contribute to stability and the lowering of tension.

It should not be assumed automatically that the African group as a whole will necessarily be completely monolithic in its voting, except on certain issues; as groups become larger in numbers they tend to become less rather than more so. There will admittedly be strong forces operating in the direction of cohesion: Africa's geographic unity; the recent emergence of most of the African countries from colonial status; the common need to promote economic and social development; the passionate desire of Africans to assert their complete equality with the rest of the world as individuals, as countries, and as a race; the determination to help the political advance of those people in Africa who have not yet attained independence; the organization of independent African countries for joint international action.

All these factors will certainly have a powerful effect in encouraging uniform voting, and on a number of issues the group will no doubt vote together. But we should not overlook the variations in conditions between the different African States, between the North African countries and those south of the Sahara, between those with conservative traditions and those with a more radical outlook, between those with French culture and those which have been under British administration. All the African members will of course be completely independent in their voting. The extent to which they vote together may be much affected by the attitude towards them of the United Nations as a whole and the Western countries in particular. If the African members feel that the African point of view is being taken into full account by others, particularly on racial issues, they may tend to operate less solidly as a block on other issues. If they feel frustrated, they are likely to be more monolithic.

It must be remembered also that, important as votes and numbers are in the United Nations, they are not the only thing which is of importance. Strength of principle and sound policies are much respected; a great Power which is regarded as pursuing such policies increases its influence. Skill and experience in the affairs of the United Nations and expert knowledge of the problems under discussion count for much in the preparation of proposals, in their discussion in the lobbies, and in the public debates. In determining the final results these things may indeed be decisive. In this respect the larger delegations are at a considerable advantage, which does much to counterbalance the advantage of numbers increasingly enjoyed by some of the regional groups mainly composed of smaller and newer countries.

There are three issues on which African attitudes can be predicted with some degree of assurance. First, in the field of peace and security, the African States in general will wish to stay out of the cold war; and they will not want military alliances. This should not of course be put down to unfriendliness towards the West. On the contrary, their ties with the West are very strong. The majority of their leaders—and increasing numbers of their people—have enjoyed a Western type education. Many have attended universities in Western countries. Although they naturally attach great importance to African culture and traditions, they have embraced Western ideas and ideals. Even bitter political opponents of this or that Western country during the period of colonial rule often retain a deep love of that country and respect for its culture and institutions. This attachment to the West is endangered only when the West falters in its policy. When the policy is sound the ties of friendship are enhanced and made closer by the granting of independence. But Africa wants to stay out of the disputes and antagonisms between the West and the Communist world, and for that reason the free world is likely to be strengthened by keeping military and political strings out of its relations with the countries of Africa.

Secondly, on racial issues which come up in the United Nations the attitude of the African States can be foreseen with certainty; on the principles involved they are bound to be unanimous. Opposition to any form of racial discrimination based on a superior position for the white race is already general in the United Nations. The accession of a number of new African States will not change the position, but will strengthen the feeling which is already widespread and add force to its expression. There seems little doubt that racial issues will become even more prominent in the future than they have been in the recent past. It seems clear also that, so long as they remain unresolved, they will be a source of increasing embarrassment to the West and weakness to the free world as a whole.

The third field in which the attitude of the African States can be clearly foreseen is that of aid to under-developed countries. It is certain—and perfectly natural—that they will seek to use their numerical strength in the General Assembly to press for constantly increasing aid through the United Nations and Specialized Agencies. They will be in a good position to do so. Of the hundred or so members of the United Nations, between sixty and seventy—all the Africans, nearly all the Asians and Latin Americans, and one or two of the Europeans—will be anxious to get increased aid from international sources; this is what is sometimes known in United Nations circles as the south-north axis. Such pressures cannot of course succeed unless the richer countries are prepared to provide more finance; but the voting strength of the Africans, combined with the urgency of African needs, will reinforce the natural desire of these countries to do all they can to help. Even those like the Soviet Union, which for political reasons greatly prefer bilateral aid to assistance through the United Nations, will hesitate to oppose publicly the general tendency to do more for the African countries—as indeed was shown on a recent occasion when this subject was under discussion in the Economic and Social Council.

NEEDS AND AID

What are the practical needs in terms of the African countries themselves, taking only those countries south of the Sahara and down to the borders of the Congo and Tanganyika? As is to be expected, they vary widely from country to country. Some like Ghana, the Ivory Coast, Senegal, and Western Nigeria are relatively well off. They have achieved a considerable degree of development, their systems of administration are well established, their steadily expanding education services are producing more and more well educated men and women, thus reducing their reliance on outside personnel. Others like Northern Nigeria and Tanganyika, with well established and stable systems of government, are very backward in secondary, technical, and higher education and must rely heavily on staff from overseas for the running of their administrative and technical services. The Congo is well developed in mining and agriculture, and has more industries than most tropical African countries and good urban social services; but it is desperately short of highly educated men and women. This, combined with its complete lack of experience before independence of the running of central political institutions, may inhibit development, and place a serious strain on the working of government institutions; much outside aid is bound to be needed for these purposes. Finally there are those countries, such as the Somali Republic, Niger, and Chad, which are largely without economic resources, developed services, or trained local personnel; such countries cannot hope to make any progress without aid from overseas on a large scale.

In spite of these variations, the African countries have much in common. Every one of them, in greater or less degree, has insufficient basic utilities, inadequate scientific knowledge, insufficiently developed natural resources, and a shortage of highly educated people. All of them need access to capital from public sources overseas, outside private investment, technical assistance from abroad, help from outside for education and the training of skilled personnel. Some are desperately short in all these things. None has reached the stage of "economic take-off" when it can finance its development from the proceeds of its own economic growth. Sometimes the very speed of the political development which internal and external pressures have forced on these countries has itself created an acute need for outside aid in new forms.

Thus the world faces a new situation in Africa today. A largely colonial continent has been transformed in the short space of fifteen years, over nearly the whole region we are discussing, into a collection of independent States or countries moving rapidly towards that status. The achievement of independence has not solved the problems of social and economic development, nor could the granting of independence have been delayed until they were solved. The power of decision in these countries has passed into the hands of the elected leaders. Where the political units are so small as to impair economic viability, it is the elected leaders who will decide whether to work closely with their neighbours, and if so under what constitutional or other arrangements. It is they who will decide for what purpose and from what sources they will seek outside assistance for their economic and social development. The decision *whether* to seek outside aid has been taken from them by the pressing needs of their countries. Every political leader recognizes this, and all are anxious to secure aid on as large a scale as possible.

The needs of the new independent countries of Africa are a challenge to the whole Western world and present us with a great opportunity. It is very much in our own interests to give material assistance to these countries, to maintain their political stability, and, by helping to advance their economic growth, to increase the volume of their trade with us and the world at large. Without aid, at best their economic and general progress would be slowed down or stopped; at worst some of them might suffer a partial or complete breakdown of government, with all the internal and external dangers which that would involve. But the aid which we are ready to give must be offered on terms acceptable to them; their public opinion will be suspicious of anything which appears in any way to threaten or impair their newly won independence.

The year 1960 may well be taken by future commentators as the end of an era in Africa in the historical sense, although the process of political advance in the continent is by no means complete. We may look back with pride to the transformation which we have helped the Africans to achieve during the last two generations, not only in converting collections of tribes into nations, but also in economic, social, and educational growth. But it would be unrealistic not to recognize how much remains to be done. It is clear that we in Britain have an important part to play in the future in meeting their requests for material aid, because of our position as one of the richer countries of the world, because of our past experience in helping countries to develop, and because of the evident desire of many of the new countries to seek our help.

AID THROUGH THE UNITED NATIONS

The most important part of the aid we give is likely in the foreseeable future to be direct; but I will deal first with aid through the United Nations and Specialized Agencies, for which, as we have seen, there is likely to be steadily increasing pressure from the African members, supported by the Asians and Latin Americans. Under the arrangements in force at present, the United Nations can supply aid only on a relatively limited scale, and the aim is to inject it at key points in the economy and administrative systems of the receiving countries. Through the regular and expanded technical assistance programmes the United Nations can provide personnel for technical and specialized surveys, can make available scientific, technical, and economic advisers, and can help with the training of local personnel. Through the International Bank loans can be made for self-supporting economic projects, and through the International Development Association, now being established although with relatively limited resources, loans will be available on somewhat easier terms.

Earlier in the year the Secretary-General of the United Nations, following his African tour, put forward proposals designed to help the African countries to adjust themselves to the transition from colonial rule to independent status. Under the Secretary-General's suggestions, more money would be made available for aid from the United Nations to African countries and others particularly in need of such aid, and the machinery for using this money would become more flexible. He also has it in mind to appoint resident representatives of the United Nations in those countries which want them, to advise on the best ways of securing aid from international sources and on development planning and programmes. These ideas of the Secretary-General have been generally well received by member States and have since been under study in the Economic and Social Council. They represent a valuable and important initiative. Because of the general feeling in new countries that United Nations aid is least likely to impair their independence, there is a general tendency in Africa to look to the United Nations. Even those countries which are content to rely almost entirely on bilateral assistance will want some aid from international sources. In countries which are threatened with political or economic instability or which almost entirely lack expert personnel of their own at present, the United Nations may have a vital stabilizing role to play, particularly in the early stages of independence. In some countries there may be definite political limits beyond which the local leaders are not prepared to look to the former administering Power or to the bigger individual countries, such as the United States. In such cases the United Nations itself may be able to supply expert personnel and advice which is indispensable to the orderly working of the government and to keeping up the momentum of development.

It is here that the recently established U.N. organization known as OPEX (Operational and Executive Personnel) may be particularly useful. Its task is to supply skilled and specialized officials to occupy positions in the government machine of countries which ask for them, for such purposes as development planning, financial or general administration, the organization of a civil service, or the working out of a training programme. For these purposes, or for example for financial negotiations with a former administering Power or with other governments, a new country may prefer to use the services of an international official rather than to rely on a man, however expert, supplied direct by a particular government. It seems therefore that there may be a great and growing need for an international service of this kind. At present OPEX is on an experimental basis, with limited funds and no assurance of continuity. Partly as a result, it had only succeeded in recruiting twenty-four officials in its sixteen months of life up to May 1960. The demand for OPEX officials now far exceeds the authorized supply and the Secretary-General has accordingly asked for the scheme to be considerably expanded and placed on a permanent basis. It is much to be hoped that this will be agreed to. If a service of this kind is to be successful, it must have continuity and be able to attract experienced people of the first calibre in the early stages and, later on, highly qualified young men who can be trained.

The United Nations Special Fund, with its task of breaking the bottlenecks inhibiting economic development and organizing investigations designed to lead to investment in new projects, is likely to assume increasing importance—an importance which was recognized by the United Kingdom Government when it quintupled its contribution last year. The Special Fund is now interpreting its terms of reference with considerable flexibility, and has recently indicated its readiness to make grants in suitable cases to promote secondary education as an essential prerequisite of economic development. The whole field of secondary, technical, and higher education, as well as training in public administration, economics, and commerce, is gaining increasing recognition in the United Nations as the first priority in promoting development. It is now generally felt that a steadily increasing supply of educated local personnel to man the civil service and managerial and professional positions is even more important than capital investment from outside; for without it capital investment, and indeed all forms of outside aid, will be wasteful and ineffective, and only with an adequate local staff of efficient administrators and managers can a country hope to reach the stage of being able to finance its development from its own resources. It therefore seems likely that the United Nations will be increasingly involved in assistance schemes designed to promote education and training programmes. New methods of handling and financing such programmes internationally may have to be worked out.

It may also be found during the next few years that the international arrangements for helping to improve the infrastructure of new countries need to be supplemented, particularly to deal with cases where a full economic return from such improvements can only be expected after a period of thirty or forty years, as is frequently the case under African conditions. In such cases aid from the International Bank would not be likely to be available; and, unless the International Development Association can supply this need, there may be further pressure in the General Assembly and the Economic and Social Council for the establishment of direct United Nations machinery for this purpose on the lines of SUNFED (the proposed Special U.N. Fund for Economic Development). Such pressure, however, may come up against the views of those countries, particularly the United States, which for obvious reasons may prefer to see the supply of capital from international sources under the control of an organization where voting is weighted according to the financial contributions of the member States concerned.

AID FROM INDIVIDUAL COUNTRIES

Whatever new proposals for the supply of capital from international sources may be considered in the future, the position at present is that, even with the increased provision for technical assistance contemplated under the Secretary-General's proposals, even with the expansion of OPEX and the Special Fund, if these things should be agreed to, the United Nations and other international agencies can supply only a limited part of the needs of the new African countries. By far the greater part of the outside aid must come direct from individual countries. The States in the French Community, together with the former Trust Territories of Cameroun and Togo, have made or are engaged in negotiating agreements with France, under which, by their wish, her massive assistance in loans for development, grants for the expansion of services, and the supply of administrative and technical personnel will continue. The United States Government is increasing its aid to the African territories, both through the Development Loan Fund and through technical co-operation; for 1960/61 it has sought Congressional approval for about $24 million for technical co-operation for Africa and $20 million for special assistance.

In former British dependent territories Colonial Development and Welfare assistance and Colonial Development Corporation investment in new projects cease on independence. But Commonwealth Assistance Loans become available: technical assistance schemes have already been negotiated with Nigeria and Sierra Leone, and one is in force in Ghana; similar schemes will be available for other independent Commonwealth countries. Help is also likely to be available in the field of research, and in education scholarships are to be provided in Britain for the training of teachers and for graduate study in other fields, while teachers will be made available from the United Kingdom to those independent countries which want them. In the case of Somaliland direct aid in the form of financial grants has been promised, amounting to £1½ million in the first year, and, although this figure may be expected to decrease in future years, direct aid may well continue for some time. It may well be that similar schemes will be needed by other new countries in the first years of independence. A recent Visiting Mission of the United Nations to Tanganyika has laid great emphasis on the need for substantial United Kingdom aid both before and immediately after independence to help expand secondary and technical education and to provide for the training of increased numbers of local people to man the government service. Tanganyika herself lacks the financial resources at present to undertake the rapid expansion which is needed, and it is difficult to see how her essential requirements can be met unless, in the early years after independence, substantial assistance is forthcoming, both in finance and the supply of teachers, either from the United Kingdom or from some other source.

AID ON A MULTILATERAL BASIS

With most aid likely to come from outside the United Nations, probable African attitudes to this form of aid must be considered. Sections of public opinion will tend to be suspicious of too much reliance on bilateral aid, attributing neo-colonial motives to former administering countries and economic imperialism to the United States. It is therefore worth looking at the possibility of multilateral arrangements, in which giving and receiving countries would participate on a fully equal basis.

The African States may well work out arrangements among themselves for a common approach to outside aid; the possibility of setting up an organization of African States for economic and development purposes has been discussed at African governmental conferences, including the meeting at Addis Ababa last June. The United Nations Economic Commission for Africa, of which both African States and administering Powers with responsibilities in Africa are members, is not a direct channel for the supply of aid, but deals with many problems affecting both aid and development generally. The Commission for Technical Co-operation in Africa South of the Sahara (C.C.T.A.) originally a clearing house set up by the colonial Powers for the discussion of technical and scientific problems, now has Ghana, Liberia, Guinea, and the Cameroun Republic among its members and headquarters at Lagos; most of the new African States are likely to become members as they achieve independence. It and its technical assistance body (F.A.M.A., the Foundation for Inter-African Mutual Assistance), small though that is, might develop into a co-operative aid organization on a multilateral basis. It seems more likely however that, if such an organization is to be established, this will be a new body, set up in response to a collective act of statesmanship by African leaders as part of the joint action which appeals so much to African public opinion.

It is significant that Dr. Nkrumah proposed a Colombo plan for Africa at this year's conference of Commonwealth Prime Ministers—an encouraging suggestion which is now being studied by the Commonwealth Governments. A Colombo-type organization, suitably modified, seems particularly suitable to African requirements. Like the Colombo Plan itself, it could be established on whatever basis the African States preferred, with the donor countries outside Africa adapting their arrangements to these African preferences. It could be flexible both in organization, in geographical scope, and in the types of aid it covered, providing, if desired, both for bilateral aid under a multilateral umbrella or in appropriate cases for multilateral projects covering a wider area than a single country.

It is to be hoped that, if a Colombo-type organization is set up for the West African region, this will not be confined to the Commonwealth countries only, but will be extended also to the states in the French Community, if the Governments concerned agree. There are many common economic and technical problems cutting across frontiers, and much would be gained by co-operation on a regional basis. It is notable that the Guinea Government recently proposed to C.C.T.A. a joint scheme to study the water resources of the Niger. It seems worth encouraging anything which can be done to mitigate the consequences in Africa of the European problem of the Six and the Seven and to iron out the disadvantages which African countries not participating in the European Economic Community fear that they may suffer. President Tubman of Liberia has proposed an Organization for West African Economic Co-operation, and M. Sylvanus Olympio, of Togo, an African version of the O.E.E.C.

Any scheme for establishing a multilateral aid organization, bringing together African States and outside countries willing to give aid, should not be regarded as in any sense competitive with United Nations assistance. The two channels of aid would be complementary; the volume of the needs of the African countries should ensure that there is no conflict. In fact there should be no difficulty in securing full co-operation by associating the United Nations bodies concerned, including the Economic Commission for Africa, in such a multilateral organization; there are precedents for this both in Asia and Latin America, and President Tubman's proposal provides for such a link.

To sum up, with the rapidly increasing number of independent African States, there is likely to be growing pressure for increased economic, social, and educational aid to Africa, both through the United Nations and outside it. The needs of the African countries are great and urgent. In most cases outside aid is necessary to keep up the momentum of development; in some cases it will be found indispensable to the preservation of orderly government. It is in the interests of the Western world to give aid, both to preserve political stability and to increase the volume of trade with the African countries. We should encourage the extension of the United Nations' aid activities in Africa as a stabilizing factor particularly well suited to the needs of newly independent countries. We should be prepared to increase the volume and perhaps widen the scope of our own bilateral aid to such countries, and should be willing to participate in multilateral aid arrangements, outside the United Nations but in close co-operation with it, if, as seems likely, African countries so wish.

With nearly all the African countries down to the southern borders of the Congo and Tanganyika having achieved or approaching independence, we face an entirely new situation in Africa. Independence has not solved their social and economic problems, and they are in urgent need of many more educated men and women. They want us, among others, to help them: if our help is to be effective, if the resources which we can afford to make available are to be deployed to the best advantage, we need a new, carefully thought out, and comprehensive policy towards Africa, fitted to the needs of the new situation and the aspirations of the new countries. This decisive year of 1960 is a good opportunity to start working out such a policy.

One thing which may have to be considered in the process is the governmental machinery through which we operate at present. The three salient points of view in Africa today—at any rate throughout the region discussed in this article—are the anxiety of African countries to promote independence where it does not already exist, their wish to work together in international affairs, and their determination to push ahead in economic, social, and educational development. These views are held equally in independent countries inside and outside the Commonwealth and in countries still dependent. Our relationship with the three classes of country is of course different and for that reason receives different handling. But, since throughout this very large part of the African continent the problems and attitudes are so similar, it seems that there might be considerable advantage in devising machinery, in whatever form was thought most suitable, to promote a comprehensive and as complete as possible a view of the whole African position, and to ensure that policy towards Africa is not only co-ordinated, as of course it is at present, but is conducted, in the sphere of aid at any rate, through a single agency.

THE KATANGA CRISIS

The secession of Moise Tshombe's Katanga province from the Congo created a crisis which dragged on for over two and one-half years. In the tangled web of that crisis we find ample examples of many of the things discussed in the various readings in this book. Tribalism, neo-colonialism, the issue of African unity, the appropriate role of the United Nations; all these were involved. A case study of the Katanga crisis thus seems a suitable device for closing this book.

Selection 38 offers a history and analysis of the crisis, together with some summary conclusions concerning its effects on the United Nations. With this as background, we turn to the political situation within Katanga which produced Tshombe and secession from the Congo (Selection 39). This emphasizes the role of tribalism, but one must not be misled into overstressing this factor in the rise and temporary success of Tshombe.

Succeeding selections, to be introduced at a later point, describe Mr. Tshombe in his role as international politician, sustaining his power by cooperation with other states inside and outside of Africa, and by extending cooperation across tribal and racial lines. The book concludes with a description of conditions in the Congo as of the summer of 1964, after Tshombe's return as Prime Minister of the central government.

Selection 38

Katanga: U.N. Crucible*

PETER V. BISHOP

Peter V. Bishop teaches in the Department of Political Economy at the University of Toronto.

. . . The U.N. operation in the Congo has illustrated two principles which will be discussed here. These are: the independence of executive action by the Secretary-General of the U.N.; and the impartiality of the U.N. in the case of internal political struggles. First, however, it will be necessary to sketch a rudimentary account of developments in the Congo during the initial twenty months of its independence.

I

There are four broad divisions for the entire period. The first ot these begins on June 30, 1960, and ends with the firing of the Congo's premier—Patrice Lumumba—on Sept. 5, 1960. In this stage the first two weeks were the seedbed for the future.

June 30, 1960 was independence day for the Belgian Congo. Six days later, the new government almost collapsed when its national army rioted in Thysville near the capital of Leopoldville. Within two days Belgian paratroops arrived in the country to protect Belgian civilians from the mad mob violence. After a further three days, Moise Tshombe, provincial premier of Katanga, declared his secession from the central government. The reason he gave publicly was his intention to prevent the spread of violence into Katanga. It appeared that the central government had not only lost control over its troops, it was also fast losing control over the country's richest territory. Under these

* Reprinted by permission of the author and the publisher from *Queen's Quarterly*, Vol. LXIX, No. 1 (Spring 1962), pp. 113–120, 123–127.

chaotic conditions Lumumba sent an urgent S.O.S. to the U.N. on July 12 for help in restoring order to his country. All further developments in the Congo have their roots in the army riots and in the secession of Katanga.

Just before dawn of July 14,[1] the Security Council authorized Hammarskjold to give "all the military assistance which may be necessary" to create order in the country in cooperation with the Congo government. The same resolution asked Belgium to "withdraw her troops" from the Congo. During the next day the first 600 U.N. soldiers landed at Leopoldville, and on July 18 Tshombe prohibited U.N. troops from entering Katanga. Discussions between Ralph Bunche—personal representative of the Secretary-General in the Congo—and Tshombe on the question of U.N. admission to Katanga ended in failure on Aug. 4. Another eight days of frustration passed before Hammarskjold personally led a U.N. advance party into the provincial capital of Elizabethville. It had taken nearly one month to crack even slightly the stubborn resistance of Katanga's government.

Lumumba's impatience with the U.N. over the delayed dispatch of troops to Katanga had two consequences. Almost immediately it caused the withdrawal by the U.N. of Ralph Bunche owing to the loss of confidence in him by the Congo government. Rajeshwar Dayal was sent in his stead to be the personal representative of the Secretary-General on Aug. 20. The second effect was more ominous, for it threatened to bring the Cold War to the Congo's jungles. Lumumba appealed to the U.S. and to the U.S.S.R. for military aid to launch a campaign to conquer Katanga. The U.S. refused, as the U.N. had done, to lend arms and planes for this purpose, but the Soviet Union complied. Still, Lumumba failed in his attempt to subdue Katanga militarily toward the end of August, and Kasavubu, the president of the Congo, dismissed his premier on Sept. 5 in accordance with the constitutional procedure. Joseph Ileo became the new premier.

The second stage extends approximately from the middle of September until the official announcement of Lumumba's death in February. This period was characterized by further fragmentation and a confused interregnum. On Sept. 14 Col. Mobutu announced that the army was taking complete control until the end of the year. He sus-

---

[1] Pertinent parts of the four most important resolutions are quoted in Section III of this article.

pended parliament with the approval of Kasavubu and installed a college of commissioners as a caretaker administration under his direction. This *de facto* government remained in power until Feb. 9, 1961, when a provisional government—again under Ileo—was formed.

The breakdown of constitutional government in Leopoldville was reflected in a wide reduction of the territory over which the central government could exercise any authority.

Although Kasai province declared its independence from Leopoldville in the middle of August 1960, this proved to be a move resting on little real political power in the hands of the provincial leader Kalonji. Of much more lasting importance was the announcement on Nov. 13 that Antoine Gizenga, a deputy premier of the Congo's first independent government, had assumed power in Stanleyville, capital of Orientale province. When Lumumba was finally captured by Col. Mobutu on Dec. 1, 1960, Lumumbist supporters in Stanleyville consolidated their forces and declared on Dec. 13 that they represented the only legitimate government for the entire Congo. The Soviet Union immediately recognized this new breakway régime. At the same time the U.N.'s position in the Congo was weakened seriously through the recall of about 5,500 troops by six of the nations contributing to the international peace force of nearly 18,000 men. Thus, the second stage of developments in the Congo included the crystallization of at least three strong political contenders in the country, and a dangerous depletion of U.N. strength in the field. The combined negative effect of these events marked the period as the low point in the Congo's history since independence. At the grisly end of these months lies Lumumba's bullet-riddled corpse. The Katanga government announced his death on Feb. 13, 1961, nearly three weeks after he had been murdered, according to a U.N. report issued on Nov. 14, 1961.

The third sequence of this story begins with a firm U.N. resolution—passed by the Security Council on Feb. 21, 1961—aimed at ending the Congo chaos with "the use of force, if necessary, in the last resort." Moreover, the Council demanded the "immediate withdrawal" of all Belgian military personnel and political advisers. In fact, the period ends with a determined attempt by the U.N. on Aug. 28, 1961 to expel the white soldiers of fortune from Katanga.

Relations between the Leopoldville government and the U.N. were beset with frictions. Still, the U.N. offered some careful advice which was eventually accepted in part by the Congo government. A U.N. Conciliation Commission, composed of eleven Afro-Asian countries, went to the Congo early in the new year and issued two thoughtful reports. The preliminary report was issued on Feb. 16, the day the commission left the Congo, and its final report was published on March 21. Both documents found the *Loi Fondamentale* of May 19, 1960 one source of the constitutional difficulties. The commission recommended alteration of the constitution in the direction of a flexible federalism, and urged the reopening of the Congo Parliament.

Between the release of the preliminary and the final report, Congo troops and U.N. soldiers came to blows over the touchy issue of sovereignty. Mobutu's forces drove the U.N. out of the port of Banana on March 2, and three days later out of the more important port of Matadi. The delicate situation was finally patched up on June 13, but not without some loss to U.N. prestige. Dayal had angered the Leopoldville régime during the Lumumba-Kasavubu quarrel, as well as by his insistence on the U.N.'s rights at Matadi. Finally, on May 25, 1961, Hammarskjold announced Dayal's resignation. This was the second time the personal representative of the Secretary-General was withdrawn during the Congo operation, and no further personal representative was appointed. Instead, Dr. Sture Linner became the administrative chief of the complete U.N. undertaking—civilian and military—in the country.

Internally, Kasavubu tried three times to revise the constitutional framework of the Congo so as to accommodate to some extent the real political power inherent in the Katanga and Stanleyville régimes. First, he called a round-table conference in Leopoldville. This group met from Jan. 27 to Feb. 16 without any representation from Stanleyville. It adjourned with an announcement for another constitutional conference, this time on the neutral territory of Tananarive, capital of the Malagasy Republic. Again, Gizenga was absent when the conference finally opened on March 8, after waiting three days for the Stanleyville leader. In the four days of debate a framework was approved for a very loose confederation, and a resolution was passed rejecting the U.N. mandate of Feb. 21. Katanga's government had attended both conferences. Still, its influence on Kasavubu was shown to be less than had been assumed, when Leopoldville and the U.N. signed an agreement on April 18, accepting in full the U.N. mandate of Feb. 21.

Furthermore, Kasavubu admitted on April 24 that the conference at Tananarive had failed to compose "existing confusions and ambiguities." This was a second repudiation of Tshombe's pressure, and it opened the third constitutional conference in three months. It was convened at Coquilhatville, inside the Congo. Tshombe again attended, and Gizenga again refused to come. Tshombe, however, was very critical of Kasavubu's recent cooperation with the U.N., and tried to walk out of the meeting. Instead, he was arrested by the Leopoldville authorities just before boarding his plane on April 26. One month after the conference began, on May 24, a proposed constitution for a federal republic of the Congo was approved. The agreement granted the central government the necessary powers of a modern state, which had been denied to it at Tananarive.

After the conference ended on May 28 Kasavubu opened talks with the imprisoned Tshombe and with Gizenga in Stanleyville, in order to obtain their concurrence in the new proposed constitution. The Stanleyville régime went part of the way in meeting Kasavubu's conciliation move. Gizenga's cooperation extended at least to an agreement on June 19 to participate in a reconvened Congo parliament under U.N. protection. Tshombe was released three days later, after he, too, promised to send delegates for the opening of parliament. However, once he was back at Elizabethville he repudiated his undertaking in a statement on July 12. Thus, the situation of the previous months was reversed when parliament met on July 17; this time delegates from Stanleyville were present, but those from Elizabethville were not. Despite this partial failure of Kasavubu's mediation efforts, a new Congo government was formed and approved by parliament on Aug. 2, 1961. Cyrille Adoula was named premier, and Gizenga became one of the two vice-premiers. As evidence of his good faith Gizenga formally dissolved his "legal" government of the Congo, and asked the Soviets to move their embassy back to Leopoldville. They did.

The new government was the Congo's first potentially viable administration since Lumumba's dismissal in the previous September. In his presentation address to parliament Adoula affirmed the territorial integrity of the entire former Belgian Congo, and pledged his government to ending Katanga's secession. By letter of August 15 Hammarskjold recognized Adoula's government.

In this third period, therefore, the Congo government at Leopoldville had strengthened its position internally and internationally. Stanleyville was prepared to cooperate in a settlement of the internal crisis, and the U.N. gave full backing to the new central authorities. It remained to achieve a similar degree of cooperation from Katanga. In order to ease this task, the U.N. prepared to eliminate finally all foreign military and political supporters from Katanga's régime. As a preliminary step U.N. troops occupied Elizabethville's radio station and post office on Aug. 28. This action ended the third stage, and opened the fourth, and probably last, period in the Congo's debut as an independent state.

These last months brought tragedy and increased crisis to the U.N.; they brought fighting and perhaps final conciliation to the Congo. What sets them apart as a distinct chapter of the story is the U.N.'s determination to end Katanga's secession.

Soon after the August action by the U.N. in Elizabethville the Katanga government formally released from service most of the foreign personnel ordered out of the whole Congo by the Security Council one year earlier. However, according to U.N. reports, more than 100 foreign personnel remained in Katanga on Sept. 9, the date set for their departure. After four tense days, fighting erupted between Katanga troops and U.N. soldiers, who had been ordered to occupy strategic points in the provincial capital. Two bombastic statements were made on the following day. Tshombe called for "total warfare" to secure Katanga's independence; O'Brien, the U.N. representative in Elizabethville, declared Katanga's secession at an end. He was completely mistaken. Heavy fighting continued until Sept. 20, and during that week the U.N. suffered its most humiliating military reverse at the hands of a single Katanga jet. The U.N. lost control of Elizabethville airport, and an Irish contingent at Jadotville. Tragedy followed defeat. On Sept. 18, Hammarskjold was killed in a plane crash on his way to Northern Rhodesia to sign a cease-fire agreement with Katanga.

A provisional cease-fire was arranged at Ndola on Sept. 20, and further strengthened by a protocol of agreement signed on Oct. 13 between the U.N. and Katanga. Reaction by Leopoldville was swift and negative. On Oct. 16 Adoula spoke of his "deep apprehension" over the documents, claiming they were a U.N. surrender to the Katanga government. None the less, the U.N. Secretariat ratified the protocol on Oct. 24, and Tshombe began to release U.N. prisoners the next day. With a passionate charge about Anglo-French complicity in Katanga's secession, Dr. O'Brien resigned his post in a dramatic gesture on Dec. 1.

In the meantime, the U.N. had reinforced its presence in Katanga by two means. The first was an announcement on Sept. 23 that its lack of fighter aircraft was being made good by the delivery of fourteen jets from Ethiopia, Sweden and India. The second was the severe Security Council resolution of Nov. 24 authorizing U.N. forces to eliminate foreigners from positions of influence in Katanga, whose secession was declared illegal. Both were instrumental in gaining undisputed military victory for the U.N. when once more cruel fighting broke out in Katanga on Dec. 5. The immediate cause had been the refusal of Katanga forces to remove roadblocks which barred U.N. troops from Elizabethville airport. After twelve days of grimly successful street fighting by the U.N., a truce was announced on Dec. 18. Tshombe left Elizabethville the same afternoon for a meeting with Adoula at Kitona, arranged through the good offices of the U.S. At 3 a.m. of Dec. 21 the two Congo leaders signed an eight-point agreement. It included Tshombe's acceptance of the country's constitution, and of the "indivisible unity" of the Congo.

The worst of the fighting appeared to be over, and U.N. superiority in Katanga seemed established. To bring this period to a close, it now remained for the central government to convert the U.N. military victory into substantial diplomatic gains at home and abroad.

Domestically, the Leopoldville government cleared the way for a final reunification of the state by destroying the political base of the other two two separatists—Kalonji and Gizenga. The legislature at Leopoldville first withdrew parliamentary immunity from both, and then impeached them. This made it possible for the central government to put these former secessionists in jail; and a government spokesman announced the imprisonment of Kalonji on Jan. 3, 1962, and that of Gizenga twenty days later. Speedy exploitation of the Katanga battle had won the central government important results.

While Adoula's government eliminated Gizenga and Kalonji as contenders for power in the country, Tshombe continued his Fabian tactics. On the same day on which the Kitona agreement was signed by Tshombe and Adoula—Dec. 21, 1961—Tshombe declared on his return to Elizabethville that the accord had to be ratified by the Katanga provincial assembly. This sounded suspiciously like the same old excuse. However, this time it appeared Tshombe simply tried to save face during the involuntary political retreat. He manoeuvred for a surrender by installment.

On Dec. 28, 1961 the first six Katanga legislators joined other Congo parliamentarians near Leopoldville. One week later—on Jan. 3, 1962—the Katanga assembly met to begin debate on the ratification of the Kitona agreement. Finally, after some melodramatic delays, a resolution was passed by the assembly on Feb. 16, 1962, declaring an end to Katanga's secession from the Congo. After twenty months and five days it seemed the terrible labour pains had ceased, and the Congo was born—weakened but perhaps not crippled for life.

Internationally, the central government was similarly skilful. Diplomatic relations were resumed with the U.S.S.R. on Dec. 2, and with Belgium on Dec. 27, 1961. To underline the new vitality of the central government, Premier Adoula travelled to the United States on Feb. 2 for one week of talks with U.N. officials and President Kennedy. At the same time that the U.S. government reiterated its unqualified support for the Congo central authorities, it emphasized its opposition to Tshombe. He had been invited by an American right-wing political group to come to New York on March 7. Instead of the expected ovation he received the diplomatic snub which the U.S. government reserves for unsuccessful political upstarts: on Feb. 15, 1962 Tshombe's request for a visitor's visa was refused by the U.S. State Department.

In this way the four sequels of the Congo's struggle for survival ended early this year—in Katanga—where they began. A new historical period may well have started on March 15, 1962, when Tshombe arrived at Leopoldville for detailed constitutional negotiations with Premier Adoula on the reincorporation of Katanga into the Congo state. Thus, this spring, two facts stand out in the Congo story: a strong and confident government at Leopoldville, for the first time since the summer of 1960, included a legislature representing the entire Congo; the U.N. had secured its unambiguous presence in the entire country. Chaos had preceded the interregnum, which was followed in turn by internal consolidation ending with the battle to finish Katanga's secession. These important achievements, however, were bought at an immense cost to both the world organization and to the people of the Congo. . . .

III

Accusations of U.N. partisanship in the Congo came almost immediately after the first contingent landed at Leopoldville. Yet, by its very nature, involvement by a national or international power in a situation such as the Congo presented in July 1960, could not be impartial, in practice or in law. In fact, complaints of U.N. partiality have almost always been made by the party against whom certain U.N. operations were directed, and never by those in whose support the U.N. acted at the time. Still, the demand that the U.N. demonstrate an impartial position was raised by nearly all internal and international *dramatis personae* in the Congo.

It is true that the first official request by the Congo government for U.N. support was made on the day *after* Tshombe declared Katanga an independent state. Despite this chronological sequence, however, it cannot be argued convincingly that the province of Katanga was not included in the spirit of the Security Council resolution of July 14, 1960. Such an interpretation would be all the more contrary to the meaning of the U.N. operation in the Congo, inasmuch as the explicit purpose of interposing U.N. troops between Belgian soldiers and the Congo government was subsidiary, and supplementary, to the implicit goal of assisting the Congo government in its struggle for survival. Therefore, sustaining the birth of a viable Congo could not contemplate the amputation of an area responsible for nearly two-thirds of the country's economy. It was, thus, clear from the outset that the U.N. would have to act on the assumption that Katanga was constitutionally a part of the Congo. This reasoning was certainly also in line with the consistent refusal of any U.N. member to recognize diplomatically Katanga as an independent state.

The problem was not whether the U.N. should abide by any abstract principle of impartiality, but rather how it could pragmatically extend its physical presence over the entire Congo. Furthermore, the range of action available to the Secretary-General is at all times dependent upon a consensus among U.N. members concerning the direction and force such action should take. The United Nations is, after all, a political institution, reflecting the political interests and pressures of its members. Consequently, the first U.N. resolution on the Congo represented the best compromise on rapid action which could be arranged by a harassed Security Council.

This first resolution had the support of all members of the Council except Britain, France, and Nationalist China, who abstained from the vote. In its substantive portions the resolution called on Belgium to "withdraw her troops from the territory of the Congolese Republic." Equally important, it authorized the Secretary-General to "take the necessary measures, in consultation with the Government of the Congo Republic, to furnish that Government with all the military assistance which may be necessary until, by the efforts of the Congolese Government with the technical assistance of the United Nations, the national security forces are, in the opinion of the Government, in a position to deal fully with their tasks."

Difficulties arose immediately over the attempt to implement this mandate. The Belgians could not be made to leave Katanga, because Tshombe refused to permit U.N. troops in his province until Aug. 12. Hammarskjold tried from the outset to execute the Council's instructions without the application of force in the explosive climate of the Congo. Yet, Bunche's failure to negotiate for the peaceful entry of U.N. soldiers into Katanga on Aug. 4, gave the appearance of U.N. leniency—if not partiality—toward Katanga. This position was taken publicly by Lumumba and the Soviet Union on Aug. 5.

The Security Council debated the Congo on Aug. 8 and 9, 1960. A new resolution passed on the second day by nine votes to none, with France and Italy abstaining. In a much sharper tone than before, the Council demanded that Belgium "withdraw immediately its troops from . . . Katanga," and declared that U.N. entry into that province was essential to the implementation of the resolution. None the less, the Council affirmed that the U.N. force would "not be a party to or in any way interfere in or be used to influence the outcome of any conflict, constitutional or otherwise." On the face of it, the instructions and the statement were clear. Their translation into concrete action, however, produced ambiguities.

The U.N.'s entry into Katanga was welcomed by Lumumba for the obvious reason that it effected a U.N. involvement in the constitutional conflict between the central government and Katanga on the side of Leopoldville. Still, on Aug. 15, he wrote to Hammarskjold, accusing him of failure to comply with the resolution of Aug. 9, by withholding the use of U.N. troops for the purpose of conquering Katanga. The intemperate language of Lumumba contributed to Bunche's recall a few days later. Hammarskjold was charged with not being partial enough. Yet, his judgment was vindicated nearly fifteen months later, when it was shown that the political consensus among U.N. members would not extend to a U.N. war for a conquest of Katanga. At all times, Hammarskjold acted within the limits of the possible as it was expressed by the realities of political relations between U.N. members.

The seriousness of dissension among U.N. members became so great in the middle of December, 1960 that the inability to make any decision whatever was the only common ground among member nations. This stultification was part of a response to Lumumba's arrest on Dec. 1. Within one alarming week the Security Council as well as the General Assembly cancelled rival resolutions in both chambers by voting against all proposals presented. The stalemate in the Security Council occurred on Dec. 14; that in the General Assembly on Dec. 20, 1960. Hammarskjold's comment on this paralysis of the decision making bodies was that it robbed the Congo operation of the moral and political support necessary to its success. Owing to the inability of the U.N. members to issue further instructions to the Secretary-General he continued his efforts quietly against the growing violence in the Congo. Then, the shock over the ruthless murder of Lumumba in Katanga electrified the member nations into a resolute decision.

A meeting of the Security Council on Feb. 21 approved the well-known resolution, authorizing the use of force by nine votes. France and the U.S.S.R. abstained. In essence, the resolution urged "all appropriate measures to prevent the occurrence of civil war in the Congo, including . . . the use of force, if necessary, in the last resort." The first substantial Congolese reaction was a rejection of this mandate on the grounds that it insulted the country's sovereignty. However, after some considerable resistance to the U.N. at Matadi was ended, the government at Leopoldville signed an agreement with the U.N. accepting the resolution of Feb. 21.

At about this time Hammarskjold privately expressed his opinion that the solution of the Congo's internal difficulties would have to recognize the existence of three effective political centers: Leopoldville, Stanleyville, and Elizabethville. He remarked that all three must be contained in a broad administrative framework extending over the entire Congo, but that a completely unitary state appeared unlikely as a final settlement. His intention was to keep a "wet blanket" over the country to prevent the smoldering passions from igniting a catastrophe comparable to the Spanish or Korean wars. There can, thus, be no question that he admitted frankly the incompatibility between impartiality and meaningful support in the weaning of a new nation. Characteristically, he chose to support, while keeping violence under the maximum control his forces could exert.

In Dr. O'Brien, Hammerskjold had a capable—and headstrong—representative in Elizabethville. O'Brien became convinced toward the end of last August that Western commerical interests were the only really powerful props of Katanga's continued independence. There had, in fact, never been much doubt about this assumption, although the U.N. did not publicly support this contention until Dec. 11, 1961. In order to smash the foundation of Tshombe's real power, O'Brien, therefore, hoped to strip Katanga of its foreign supporters. The action of Aug. 28 was only partially successful and left enough foreigners in Katanga to enable it to repel the U.N.'s military operation in September. Despite the signing of a truce between the U.N. and the Katanga government in late September, Katanga continued to violate the agreement, and to obstruct the free movement of U.N. troops in the province. Furthermore, approximately 100 Belgian and other foreign advisers remained at Elizabethville.

Amid increasing friction between the U.N. and Katanga forces, the Security Council approved its resolution of Nov. 24 by nine votes, with France and Britain abstaining. It was the most forceful resolution yet passed by U.N. members. After expressly deploring "the secessionist activities illegally carried out by the provincial administration of Katanga," it gave the Secretary-General the following authority. He was instructed "to take vigorous action, including the use of requisite measure of force, if necessary, for the immediate apprehension, detention . . . or deportation of all foreign military and paramilitary personnel and political advisers not under the United Nations command, and mercenaries as laid down in . . . the Security Council

Resolution of 21 February 1961." Armed with new jets and this unambiguous mandate, the U.N. forces won their military victory in Elizabethville less than one month later.

A comparison of the four important resolutions on the Congo reveals two characteristics, both bearing directly on the question of U.N. impartiality. In the first place, one or more of the major powers abstained from voting on all four resolutions, although France is the only power which voted on none of them. This record underlines the difficulty which Hammarskjold experienced in conducting the operation in the field. The U.N. simply cannot act decisively on the executive level if its members cannot agree substantially on the course of an action. Impartiality, under such circumstances, is, indeed, easier because indecision on the part of U.N. members is reflected in a tendency toward eventual inactivity of U.N. field forces.

Secondly, the language of the consecutive resolutions sounds in sharp staccato the members' mounting exasperation with the wily Tshombe. Although it may be contended that the latest resolution of Nov. 24, 1961 amounts almost to a bill of attainder in its spirit, it can never be said that it endorsed U.N. impartiality in the Congo. On the contrary, the resolution is at the opposite position to that taken by members on Aug. 9, 1960. That resolution pledged the U.N. force not to intervene in the constitutional struggle. Nearly sixteen months later the U.N. forces were made a deliberate instrument for the solution of the constitutional struggle in favour of the central government.

IV

Any conclusions about events in the Congo must be tentative at this time. None the less, four observations suggest themselves. The U.N. operation has been surprisingly successful for the period as a whole. Its intervention has required a force three times larger and six times more expensive than the U.N.'s only previous experience with a peace force during the Suez crisis. It further has required negotiations between four successive central Congo governments and four[2] separate U.N. Congo chiefs under two Secretaries-General. These gargantuan tasks helped to establish a central government more promising than

[2] The U.N. announced on Jan. 26, 1962 that Robert Gardiner of Ghana would relieve Dr. Linner who had been on continuous duty in the Congo since July 1960.

any the country has had since independence. This is an achievement of undeniable political and diplomatic merit.

Secondly, the U.N. has withstood for the moment—and simultaneously with its Congo operation—a vicious attack upon the very executive structure that made the support in the Congo possible. There is little doubt that in the battle over the Secretariat the war has not been won by any means. At most, it would seem, a successful holding action was fought to give a reprieve until April 1963.

Thirdly, the members of the U.N. changed from a position of implied neutrality to one of admitted and purposeful partiality in the constitutional battle in the Congo. The result of this increasing firmness was that the field forces were given the instructions, as well as the means, to break the resistance of Katanga. The U.N. has, in fact, finally fought the war over which Lumumba lost his post and his life. Providing that the battle in Elizabethville during December 1961 was the last to be fought on the issue of Katanga's secession, it is reasonable to assume that the U.N. has helped to bring about the proper conditions for an eventual, peaceful settlement of the Congo's constitution.

Finally, the U.N. has been exposed to the greatest danger in its history by the action in the Congo. The cost of the undertaking threatens to drain the organization of the financial support without which it must accept non-involvement by necessity. Furthermore, the war with Katanga may have an effect on future U.N. operations not unlike that produced by the Korean war—rather than becoming a precedent, it might turn out to be the last and only such experience. Western European reaction to the fighting in Katanga strongly points in this direction. Although the cancer called Katanga appears to have been exorcized—we must now hope that no further surgery is needed, for the patient's advisers are nearly hysterical after watching the operation.

Selection 39

Politics in Katanga*

Smith Hempstone

Smith Hempstone is an American journalist who has published several books on African affairs.

In 1956, [Tshombe] founded the Lunda Tribal Association. The Belgians gave it their approval: after all, Tshombe was known to be "safe" and the association was a nonpolitical debating club and welfare organization. By 1959, this inevitably grew into Katanga's first political party, the *Confédération des Associations du Katanga*, popularly called CONAKAT.

The hard core of CONAKAT, although seventeen tribes are grouped under its banner, was and is Tshombe's own Lunda tribe. The fact that he is not only a Lunda but a member of the royal house and the son-in-law of the Lunda paramount chief assures Tshombe of the total support of one of the largest tribes in Central Africa, one that remembers its great days under Tshombe's royal ancestors. But CONAKAT also drew to it the majority of Katanga's smaller tribes. The word "confederation" in CONAKAT's name is significant. Tshombe, like other African nationalists—such as Chief Obafemi Awolowo, the Nigerian Yoruba leader—believes that the tribe should be the firm foundation of the nationalist movement. The majority of African nationalists, however, look on the tribe as a rival focal center of political power and wish to sweep it away. Because he is a tribal nationalist, Tshombe had no desire to submerge Katanga's other tribes. By adopting a confederal form of organization for CONAKAT, he imitated the structure of the old Lunda empire, which was no more

---

* Reprinted by permission from *Rebels, Mercenaries and Dividends* by Smith Hempstone (New York: Frederick A. Praeger, Inc., 1962), pp. 71–77, 95–97. (The title of this selection was supplied by the editor of the present book.)

than a confederation of tribes that accepted the Lunda paramount chief as the first among equals. Consequently, it was logical and inevitable that Tshombe should resist the centralist drive of Patrice Lumumba, aiming instead for a confederal Congo, solidly based on tribal pillars.

That this tribalism is not exclusive to the point of denying authority to members of other tribes is demonstrated by Tshombe's selection of his top CONAKAT lieutenant. Rather than naming one of his own Lundas, Tshombe turned to Godefroid Munongo. Munongo, born at Bunkeya in 1925, occupies relatively the same position in the Bayeke tribe that Tshombe does among the Lundas: His grandfather was M'Siri, the great Bayeke Chief who conquered most of southern Katanga in the nineteenth century, and his brother Antoine Mwenda, is paramount chief of the Bayekes. . . .

Not all of Katanga's tribes, of course, share the enthusiasm of the Lundas, Bayekes, and Batabwas for Tshombe's government. We have seen how, in the middle years of its operations, *Union Miniere* brought Balubas from the Lomami Plains to work in the mines. The Balubas, like Kenya's Kikuyus and the Bassas of Cameroun, are an intelligent and industrious people. Also like these two tribes—perhaps to some degree because of this intelligence and industry—they are generally detested by the other tribes with whom they come in contact. We have seen also that the Balubas once had a great empire and have been, for five hundred years, the bitter rivals and implacable enemies of the Lundas. Over the course of the years, more than 100,000 Balubas moved south into the country of their enemies to work in the white man's mines, in commerce, and in the administration. Because of their brains and perseverance, they gradually secured for themselves the most important and best-paying jobs in these fields. It is estimated that before independence the Balubas outnumbered all other tribes in Katanga's three major cities of Elisabethville, Jadotville, and Kolwezi. Such a situation never makes for harmonious relations. The lid was kept on by two factors: the Belgian security forces and prosperity, which meant that there were jobs for everybody.

The situation began to worsen in December, 1957, when municipal elections were held in Elisabethville. CONAKAT had not yet been formed, and consequently, the voting of the local people was fractionalized among the competing tribes. The Kasai Balubas and other "alien" Africans, however, voted as a bloc. As a result, three of the capital of Katanga's four burgomasters were Kasai Balubas and the fourth was a Bakisu from Kivu. This situation became exacerbated in 1958 and 1959, as falling copper prices and failing confidence on the part of local Belgians produced a serious recession in Katanga. As more and more Africans found themselves out of work, they turned in their misery, anger, and frustration against the Balubas, who now were not only competing with them but depriving them of their bread. CONAKAT's principal plank became the repatriation of 160,000 "alien" Balubas to Kasai (there are 600,000 Katangan Balubas in addition to these, the Balubas being Katanga's largest tribe, followed closely by the Lundas). Here began Tshombe's first active cooperation with the *Union Katangaise*, the association of Katanga's whites, and the forty-three-year-old leader's first thoughts of secession. The whites, of course, wanted secession—or at least federation—for entirely different reasons than Tshombe: The whites were fearful of their future under the radical African leaders of the northern Congo and felt they could best preserve their way of life (their privileged status, if you will) if Katanga were autonomous and under the control of a man they knew, a man obviously moderate in racial matters and favorably disposed toward private enterprise. On Tshombe's part, the idea of secession arose almost completely out of the recession and tribal hatred for the Balubas. Only an independent or autonomous Katanga, Tshombe reasoned, could keep the majority of its mineral revenues for its own development; only a state in charge of its own immigration affairs could halt the flow of Kasai Balubas into the southern heartland of Katanga and repatriate those who not only threatened to become the dominant political force in the country and the most prosperous community, but to lead the rest of the tribes to the brink of starvation in the competition for jobs during hard times.

At any rate, CONAKAT adopted "Baluba, go home!" as its principal article of political faith. As in physics, any political action produces an equal reaction. In this case, the reaction to CONAKAT's belligerent action was the formation of the BALUBAKAT CARTEL (sometimes called the *Parti Progressiste Katangais*) under the leadership of Jason Sendwe. The CARTEL was an amalgamation of three tribal organizations. The first of these (and the most important) was Sendwe's BALUBAKAT, composed of those Balubas indigenous to Katanga. The second was FEDEKA, an organization representing the "alien" Balubas from Kasai. The third was ATCAR, the political spearhead of 100,000 Chokwe tribesmen whose ancestors broke the Lunda empire in 1887. . . .

Sendwe's policies were more or less dictated by the posture assumed by Tshombe. If CONAKAT stood for the expulsion of "alien" Africans and a loose confederal relationship with Leopoldville, it was inevitable that the BALUBAKAT CARTEL should espouse the cause of the "aliens" and demand a unitary form of government for the Congo. Thus Sendwe lined up with Lumumba. . . .

The provincial elections in May, 1960, did not come off as smoothly as Tshombe had expected, nor were the results as favorable as he had predicted. The voting took place in an atmosphere of rising tension. In recent weeks, at least thirteen had been killed in clashes between the Lundas (CONAKAT) and warriors from the Baluba and Chokwe (BALUBAKAT CARTEL) tribes. A three-day strike affecting twenty-four local firms had shaken the whites, many of whom were purchasing firearms. SABENA reported its international flights out of Katanga fully booked through August. Partisans of the two parties kept strictly to their own home areas, visited only their own bars, even drinking their own beer exclusively ("Simba" for CONAKAT members, "Kasai" for BALUBAKAT CARTEL supporters). Sendwe, chugging around the country in his battered blue Opel, was campaigning hard. Tshombe, still debonair and confident, secure in the knowledge that he could count on winning a majority of the rural votes, confined his campaign largely to the cities, where BALUBAKAT was strong. When votes were counted for the sixty-member Provincial Assembly, the result was almost a draw: CONAKAT had won twenty-five seats, BALUBAKAT twenty-two, while thirteen seats went to splinter parties or independents. At this crucial moment in Katanga's history, Tshombe showed his skill as a politician by quickly bringing all thirteen independents into line, thus gaining control of the government. In elections held two weeks later, during which the Provincial Assembly selected the delegates to the Senate in Leopoldville, CONAKAT won eight seats and BALUBAKAT settled for six. Among the latter's six delegates was Sendwe. Tshombe, however, decided to remain in the Provincial Assembly. BALUBAKAT did not take its defeat with good grace. It turned down Tshombe's offer of a coalition government, and the Baluba delegates walked out of the assembly three times, paralyzing its proceedings, because a two-thirds attendance was required by law if business was to be transacted. In desperation, the province's Belgian governor declared a state of emergency when Tshombe threatened to secede unless the quorum law were amended to allow him to govern effectively. Faced with a breakdown in the administration of all the Congolese provinces, in only one of which a party had won an absolute majority, the Belgian Parliament quickly amended the quorum law to permit the provincial assemblies to operate with a 50 percent attendance.

How much influence had whites wielded in the Katanga elections? In 1944, the white settlers in Katanga formed an association essentially professional in character called UCOL (*Union pour la Colonisation*). UCOL devoted itself to such matters as trying to get a reduction in the bond ($1,000 for a man, $500 for his wife and children) demanded of intending settlers in Katanga. As the wind of change began to blow through the Congo, UCOL sprouted a political arm, called the *Union Katangaise* (UKAT), under the leadership of handsome, greying Elisabethville attorney Jean Humble, a veteran of thirty years in Katanga. From the beginning, UKAT was opposed to the excessive centralization of the colonial government, favoring a federal organization for the six Congolese provinces with Belgium as the seventh member of the federation. In the last resort, UKAT favored the secession of Katanga and *Anschluss* with the Federation of Rhodesia and Nyasaland. Despite its protestations the organization was designed to perpetuate white privilege, if not white supremacy. Tshombe and CONAKAT immediately attacked UKAT and it soon backed away from this position. But UKAT had more success in convincing Tshombe of the desirability of federalism. Although UKAT itself was never openly associated with CONAKAT (UKAT was officially dissolved in 1960), many of its prominent members either joined CONAKAT or openly acted as advisors to Tshombe's party. CONAKAT also unquestionably received funds from local whites. This is true, too, although to a lesser extent, of BALUBAKAT. . . .

THE RESOLUTION OF THE KATANGA CRISIS

In Selection 38, Peter V. Bishop carried the Katanga story to the point of apparent success in ending the crisis.

Mr. Tshombe had agreed at Kitona to end the secession, and in early 1962 was taking steps seemingly directed at fulfilling the agreement. But commitment on his part turned out to be more apparent than real—as the months passed, it seemed more and more obvious that the old stalling tactics were still the order of the day. Katanga continued to retain the revenues from the mining industry in Katanga, Tshombe still conducted his own foreign relations, the Katanga armed forces remained separate from those of the rest of the Congo and received equipment from abroad as well as training and leadership from foreign officers (the famous "mercenaries"). Such trappings of sovereignty as Katanga currency and postage stamps continued to be highly visible.

Tshombe was presumably encouraged to continue in his reluctance to end secession by a political situation containing many factors favorable to him. He controlled the richest part of the Congo, but also had many foreign sympathizers (including the "American Committee for Aid to Katanga Freedom Fighters"). These foreign interests are sensitively discussed in Selection 40. As the author, Mr. Weiss, also points out, Mr. Tshombe was in a position to exploit political situations within the Congo as well. The central government under Cyrille Adoula was barely able to stay afloat in a sea of troubles—even though the United Nations was there to pour great quantities of oil on the waters. For example, opposition was aroused by efforts to accommodate "localism" or "tribalism" within a federal constitution by increasing the number of provinces. The Bakongo, resenting the separation of the capital, Leopoldville, from their own province under this measure, instituted a blockade on farm produce that seriously reduced food supplies to the city. Various dissident elements, including at some points Tshombe's representatives, joined together in Parliament in attempts, which came very close to success, to obtain a vote of no-confidence in the Adoula government

As negotiations with Tshombe dragged on through 1962, the urgency of a settlement ending secession increased. Adoula's government, as well as his foreign supporters and the United Nations itself, needed this success to discourage Congolese opponents of the government. The United Nations, faced by a crisis over the financing of operations in the Congo, needed a settlement stabilizing the country, thus enabling the United Nations to reduce its military and other commitments. Accordingly, in August 1962 U Thant, the Secretary-General of the United Nations, produced a "Plan of National Reconciliation," calling for integration of Katanga with the rest of the Congo under a federal constitution. The Plan had almost the force of an ultimatum, for it included a phased program for applying pressure to Katanga; first, merely diplomatic, then if necessary economic (for example, an international boycott of Katanga copper), and as a last resort, more direct measures of unspecified nature.

Even with this threat, Tshombe's regime was not inclined to settle, and negotiations continued through the fall of 1962. The Chinese attack on India brought the prospect of withdrawal of the Indian Army contingent in the Congo—well over a quarter of the much too small United Nations force. Spurred by these difficulties, U Thant in early December 1962 called for economic sanctions against Katanga. Coincidentally, and rather providentially from the United Nations standpoint, the Katanganese gendarmerie engaged in a series of minor assaults on United Nations positions in the region of Elisabethville. In retaliation, the United Nations units went over to the attack, and in the course of brief operations ended Katanga's resistance to reintegration into the Congo.

Tshombe remained as provincial president, but after central-government officials took over effective control, and his personal company of bodyguards was disarmed, he went into exile. Apparently to lessen still further Tshombe's influence, the Congolese government divided into two provinces the portion of Katanga which he had controlled (this was also part of a program whereby the six original provinces of the Congo were remade into twenty-three "provincettes").

By June 1963, partially as a consequence of the events related above, the United Nations forces in the Congo had been cut by one-half, and at the end of June 1964, the last units were withdrawn. United Nations intervention had presumably resolved the Katanga-Congo crisis.

The problems encountered in trying to deal with that crisis, however, remain for contemplation by the student of international relations. One very obvious point is that the limits of United Nations power to police conflicts of this type are soon reached, and easily exceeded. In Selection 41, Stanley Hoffmann is at pains to point this out. His extension of the argument should especially be noted, for it relates directly to the program of the independent African countries to develop pressure upon the white-dominated areas of southern Africa. United Nations intervention in the Congo-Katanga conflict was undertaken in the name of anticolonialism. Some future United Nations venture for the same reason is, Hoffmann seems to think, both highly possible, because of Afro-Asian voting strength in the United Nations, and full of dangers similar to those encountered and barely evaded in the Congo.

The independent African states are encouraging or actually participating in activities directed at the white regimes of southern Africa (for example, support for exile operations out of Dar es Salaam, or for the Angolan revolt from Congolese territory). The prestige and interests of African states and the emotions of Africans in general are becoming heavily engaged. If the African states (most of them "dwarfs" as regards strength in international affairs) are unable directly to move events in a direction favorable to their "anticolonial" views, the result might be another call to the United Nations similar to that made in the Katanga case. The United Nations would then face the familiar dilemma—whether to chance its feeble strength, or to allow the situation to fall by default to individual states which, unable to obtain, or agree upon and support, United Nations action, might feel in a position to intervene. This would, at best, divide the African states as in the Congo crisis; at worst, might simply transplant the cold war to the African continent.

The situation just described is still hypothetical, but in the Congo itself we have in a sense again come full circle to 1960. The writ of the central government is defied in wide areas; Moise Tshombe (made Prime Minister in July 1964) is a key political figure; the United Nations no longer keeps the peace in the Congo. Conditions thus seem ripe for intervention. The question is merely, who intervenes, and under what conditions?

We close this book with an analysis (Selection 42, by William R. Frye), of the international potentialities of the topsy-turvy Congolese situation. He perceives a cold-war contest, an African split over support for Tshombe in particular, and (apparently, as he does not even mention the possibility) no further United Nations intervention, as present prospects. We leave the reader with Frye's suggestions, to contemplate according to his lights and learning the lessons of the Katanga experience.

Selection 40

The Tshombe Riddle*

HERBERT F. WEISS

Herbert F. Weiss is with the Center for International Studies at the Massachusetts Institute of Technology, and recently spent a year in the Congo.

Moise Tshombe's acceptance of the latest United Nations plan for Congo reunification once again raises the hope that the Katanga crisis is approaching an end. But, judging from past experience, excessive optimism would be unwise. Until now two factors have encouraged Tshombe to refuse to end his Province's secession: (1) foreign interests have supported him, and (2) he has found it advantageous in terms of his own position in internal Congolese politics. Today both these factors are still very much in existence.

The first foreign interests to support Katanga's secession in the summer of 1960 were, of course, the Belgian Army and the Union Minière mining company. Before long, however, Katanga came to be seen as a kind of *cordon sanitaire* between the independent, nationalist African states north of the Congo and the colonial and settler states to the south. It clearly suits the latter's interests to keep it that way.

Perhaps no country is more directly concerned with keeping Tshombe's secessionist venture alive than Portugal. The independence of the Congo in June 1960 was a crucial event for the Angolan nationalist movement, and this naturally made it crucial for Portugal—fighting

---

* Reprinted by permission of *The New Leader* (September 17, 1962), pp. 3–6.

for its entire colonial empire in Angola. In fact, almost immediately after Congolese independence one of the most important ethnic groups in Angola, the Bakongo, who straddle the border between the two countries, began a revolution that has successfully used the frontier to evacuate civilian refugees from Salazar's repressive measures and to refurbish its military contingents.

Two other important ethnic groups, the Tshokwe and the Lunda, live on the Katanga-Angola border. Yet, despite ample geographic opportunity, they have not attempted any rebellious activity largely because Tshombe has turned Angolan escapees over to Portuguese authorities. He has pursued this anti-nationalist policy, even when it has involved his own ethnic brethren, because most of Katanga's copper and other minerals are exported through Angola. Especially after the breakdown of transportation facilities between his Province and Leopoldville, Tshombe has every reason to support Portugal.

At the same time, Portugal has every reason to support Tshombe. If the Angolan revolution were to extend along the entire border with the Congo, the Portuguese forces would probably be unable to contain it. In short, for Portugal a reconciliation between Katanga and the Central Government would be close to catastrophic.

A similar situation exists in the case of the Rhodesias. Hard pressed by the radical nationalism of Kenneth Kaunda in Northern Rhodesia and Hastings Banda in Nyasaland, Sir Roy Welensky, the Rhodesian Federation's Prime Minister, has staunchly supported Katanga's secession. In return, Tshombe has used his influence in Northern Rhodesia to back Harry Nkumbula, Kaunda's more "moderate" opponent. In addition to financial subsidies, Tshombe is reported to have provided military training for Nkumbula's supporters in Katanga.

There are other elements in the Welensky-Tshombe bargain, too: Welensky currently controls one of Katanga's export routes. He also has given Tshombe invaluable aid in his two fights with the UN. True, the racial discrimination practiced in the Rhodesias has already resulted in embarrassing incidents between the Katanga government and the Rhodesian authorities. But Tshombe can be expected to overlook the discriminatory treatment of Africans—which in the past has involved his own Lunda brethren and, on one or two occasions, even his own ministers—as long as he needs Welensky's backing.

Britain's position in the Katanga affair is closely tied to internal politics in the Rhodesias and to British commercial interests. It is no secret that the Macmillan Government has been reluctant to accept sterner UN measures against Tshombe because of pressure exerted in Parliament and even in the Cabinet by commercial interests with major investments in the Union Minière and Northern Rhodesia. Even without these internal pressures, however, Britain's position would still be a difficult one. On numerous occasions Sir Roy has shown that he does not feel himself very greatly bound by London's decisions. If Britain were to go along with any of the really tough UN pressures, it would probably only be embarrassed by its inability to enforce them. It is hardly likely, for example, that Welensky would agree to closing the frontiers between Katanga and Northern Rhodesia, or that he would refuse to transport Katanga's exports.

It would be a major victory for British policy in the Rhodesias if the Federation could be brought to independence without bloodshed or anarchy. (Here the military training Kaunda's opponents are getting in Katanga is an ominous development.) Therefore Britain is willing to pay a heavy price to reduce further friction with Welensky while slowing down the increasing radicalization of Rhodesian politics. Both these ends are served by preaching moderation and negotiations in Katanga.

Furthermore, if the UN intervenes energetically and successfully to unify the Congo, the likelihood is that the majority of the General Assembly would press for similar action in other African trouble spots—*e.g.*, the Rhodesias. That, too, is a prospect the British would clearly prefer to avoid.

The last but perhaps most important force behind Tshombe is the Republic of South Africa. Although the Verwoerd Government has not yet been heavily involved in Katanga—to date the extent of its aid has been to supply Tshombe's army with mercenaries and equipment—it too has a vital stake in continued secession. For as long as Tshombe does not rejoin the Congo he will be dependent on the anti-nationalist forces which have given him such massive aid, and he can be counted upon not to back nationalist forces in the south. To South Africa this means that the advance of African nationalism and the movement for racial equality is kept that much farther from its own borders.

South Africa also has a vital interest in Portugal's continued presence in Angola. The collapse of the Portuguese position would give African nationalism its first boundary with a South African possession—the much-disputed mandate territory of South West Africa. Moreover, South Africa has a military pact with Portugal, and would probably intervene if the Portuguese forces prove unable to cope with the revolution in Angola.

But such involvement on the part of South Africa outside its own borders would open the way for claims that the Angolan conflict is a danger to world peace. Since the Verwoerd Government has no allies in the UN, the probable result would be the one thing that South Africa wants most to avoid—UN intervention.

Thus, a chain of interest exists between Katanga, Angola and the Republic of South Africa; and a somewhat similar chain can be traced in the Rhodesias and extended to Portuguese Mozambique. In any event, certainly much more is at stake in Katanga's secession than the mere exploitation of mineral resources: In supporting Tshombe, his backers see the opportunity to slow down—if not altogether stop—the entire timetable of national and racial emancipation in Africa.

It would be a mistake, though, to assume that Moise Tshombe is simply a tool of foreign interests. His own economic and political self-interests are also involved, and to understand this aspect of the Katanga secession it is necessary to examine Tshombe's career from the time the Congo first achieved independence.

As the leader of underpopulated but immensely rich Katanga, Tshombe could never hope to obtain political power commensurate to his Province's wealth within a unitary or even a federal Congo. In fact, his own party, the Conakat, gained only eight out of 137 seats in the Congolese Parliament. Even more important, Tshombe's position within Katanga itself was by no means secure.

Nothing shows Tshombe's political weakness better than the election results just prior to independence. Although the Conakat won a majority of two seats over the opposing Balubakat in the Provincial Assembly, it obtained a substantially lower number of popular votes. And the legality of the process by which Tshombe had been elected President of the Provincial government was widely disputed.

Since Tshombe had few allies at the national Congolese level, while his opponent, Jason Sendwe, had many, it was expected that the Central Government would intervene and either hold new elections or reshuffle the Provincial government in a manner unfavorable to Tshombe. It was this combination of economic and political factors, along with the traditional pressure from Belgian settlers, that was behind the Katanga leader's decision to secede.

When the Congo Army mutinied, the opportune moment for secession arrived. With the Central Government temporarily incapable of doing anything about it, Tshombe obtained the protection of the Belgian Army and proceeded both to expel the mutinous Congolese troops from Katanga and imprison the local opposition. Still, at this juncture his position was far from strong.

When the UN refused to reintegrate Katanga by force, Patrice Lumumba, then Prime Minister of the Congo, launched a two-pronged military attack against the Province from Leopoldville and Stanleyville. Despite the Army mutiny, it was said that the attack from Stanleyville had a good chance of succeeding. But at that moment President Joseph Kasavubu dismissed Lumumba, and in the ensuing political confusion the troops moving from Stanleyville, upon being paid their back salaries courtesy of the UN, agreed to return to their bases. It was after this that Tshombe built up his own army, aided by European and white South African mercenaries, and this soon became one of the most serious military forces in the Congo.

Having survived these threatening moments in the summer and early fall of 1960, Tshombe has failed in only two aspects of his effort to solidify his own power and Katanga's secession: (1) He has not been able to get recognition from a single power for his Province's independence. (2) He has been unable to control or conquer the northern portion of Katanga, which from the very first has consistently opposed his government.

In the attempt to subjugate the north, Katanganese army machine guns were pitted against the home made weapons of the northern Baluba in an encounter that has cost the lives of roughly 50,000 Baluba. Although sporadic fighting still occurs, the major battles appear to be over. But the loss of the north, though a serious setback, does not basically alter Tshombe's strength, since Katanga's mineral wealth is centered in the south. . . .

What can the UN do if Tshombe is once again only stalling for time? According to present plans, if the Katanga President does not accept the UN timetable economic sanctions would be initiated. In the last resort, these would go "to the extent of barring all trade and financial relations."

Can the UN in fact successfully exert such pressures? It is argued in some quarters that this could be done most easily through Belgian Government pressure on Union Minière: If the mining company could be made to cooperate with the UN, to stop its tax payments to Tshombe, and to channel all other financial transactions through the Central Government, the Katanga problem would be resolved. But Belgium, and in a sense also the Union Minière, have become the whipping boys of the Katanga problem. Actually, they are no longer in a position to change the basic power balance.

As things now stand, the Union Minière, rather than controlling the Katanga President, is clearly his prisoner. If the company were to refuse to deal directly with Tshombe, it would be no problem at all for him to seize its Katanga installations. Most of the Belgian personnel are sympathetic to his goals and could be expected to continue operating the mines. Should the Union Minière personnel oppose Tshombe, they would only become his hostages and could be replaced by Rhodesians or South Africans. In any case, the minerals would be mined.

Similarly, transport would offer no problem. Neither Portugal nor the Rhodesias, as we have seen, have any reason to close their railroads to Katanga exports. As to whether the minerals could be marketed, it is argued that the distributing organization would balk at selling "confiscated" goods. Tshombe, however, is supported by substantial elements of the Western world and international mining interests. Indeed, Union Minière has close ties with Rhodesian copper interests which, in turn, are connected with South African and United States metal companies.

Why should the buyers of Katanga copper boycott it, even if "UN politics" forces the Belgian Government to prevent the Union Minière from dealing directly with Tshombe? Would even the United States maintain such a policy for any length of time when 90 per cent of its total cobalt imports come from Katanga?

By and large, then, it is very questionable whether Katanga's financial and commercial relations can be "barred" in this fashion. The UN could, of course, interfere with the mining and transportation of Katanga minerals: The mine sites could be occupied by UN troops acting in the name of the Central Government, and the railroads leading out of Katanga could be placed under UN control. There is little doubt that such measures would accomplish the desired result. But the problem with applying this type of pressure is that it would be likely to result in another military engagement between UN and Katanga forces. Since it is no longer a secret that several Western powers are absolutely opposed to military hostilities, Tshombe may well calculate that the UN is bluffing or, if hostilities should start, would lose its support in a repeat performance of December 1961.

While achieving unification in the Congo may be agonizingly complicated and costly, the alternative is worse. Without an end to the present crisis, the Adoula Government can be expected to fall. And unlike Adoula, who has cooperated closely with the UN and has been a good friend to the U. S., his successor may ask the UN to withdraw from the Congo. If that happens, the Leftists can be expected to re-emerge. Once again the Central Government would attempt to conquer Katanga, and be forced to seek help from "anyone" willing to supply it.

Such a conclusion to the largely Western dominated UN efforts in the Congo would be disastrous for the world organization, as well as for the U. S. Future UN intervention in Africa would become politically impossible. And even though the U. S. has been the most determined Western advocate of Congo unity, it would probably bear much of the blame for continued Katanga secession. For it was the United States, acting unilaterally, which stopped the fighting between Katanga and UN forces in December 1961, at a time when it was generally recognized that one to four more days of military operations would have ended Moise Tshombe's secession.

Unless the Katanga situation is resolved, Africans and Asians are likely to remember that, when the chips were down, one or another Western power blocked the final push to unity.

Selection 41

The UN and the Use of Force*

STANLEY HOFFMANN

Stanley Hoffmann is an Associate Professor of Government at Harvard, and has specialized in the study of the United Nations.

There is one aspect of recent UN decisions which should not remain unnoticed. The UN military action in Katanga and the attitude of the members toward India's absorption of Goa constitute a thorough reversal of what one may call past UN doctrine about the use of force—a doctrine developed over the last ten years, and particularly under Mr. Hammarskjold.

The Charter of San Francisco barred the use of force as an instrument of national policy, and envisaged a collective security system under which the UN, led by the five permanent members of the Security Council whose agreement was indispensable, could have used force to put an end to aggressions and breaches of the peace. But as a consequence of the Cold War, and despite the Uniting-for-Peace resolution of 1950 (theoretically designed to make possible collective security operations aimed at a major power or at its allies, notwithstanding the veto provision), it became clear that most of the members of the UN had tacitly buried collective security. Some put their faith in military pacts outside the UN; others sought refuge in neutralism. Thus the UN, in case of breaches of peace, came to rely on non-military measures in order to put an end to fighting. The UN Emergency Force in the Middle East, UN observers in Lebanon, the UN presence in Jordan and Laos, the UN operation in the Congo under its original mandate were all predicated on the assumption that UN efforts to restore peace would *not* be military tests of strength: fire would be

* Reprinted by permission from *The New Republic* (January 8, 1962), pp. 11–13.

fought with water, not with fire. Never, since the ill-fated resolution of October, 1950, authorizing the UN forces to cross the 38th parallel in order to achieve the unification of Korea, has the Organization decided to use force in order to coerce its members to accept UN-sponsored terms of settlement in disputes which had led to breaches of the peace (Kashmir, Palestine, Indonesia, etc.).

The UN had to recognize that it would do little to prevent one of the Big Two from using force to promote its policies. For example, the Russians could not be stopped from crushing Hungary without the very kind of war which mankind hopes to avoid. At the same time, the UN has refused to condone the use of force (as distinct from the resort to subversion) by other powers; indeed, it is in the area of disputes outside of the "Cold War blocs" that the UN has repeatedly played its most useful role.

In the past several weeks, however, the UN has departed from its past practices. In the first place, the Security Council, which had previously authorized UN forces in the Congo to resort to violence only in order to prevent civil war, and only if absolutely necessary, now allows the use of force for the apprehension of foreign military personnel and advisers in Katanga. In the second place, the Security Council failed to intervene in the Goa affair, and after a Soviet veto, no effort was made to bring the Indian breach of peace before the General Assembly.

THE TEMPTATION AND ITS CONSEQUENCES

The immediate circumstances of those two events are well known, and one can find many justifications for what the UN has done. In the Congo, UN forces were placed in an almost impossible situation. Only one course of action would have been logical: given the breakdown of law and order within, and the danger of intervention from without, the territory ought to have been put under a UN trusteeship, so that the Organization could have assumed full responsibility. Such a solution was impossible, however: the Congo's independence had been proclaimed, and no majority in either the Assembly or the Security Council would have agreed to so expensive and drastic a new policy. Mr. Hammarskjold then tried to apply to the Congo the formula which had succeeded in the Middle East; it consisted of limiting UN intervention to the avoidance of civil war and foreign interference.

That left the responsibility for political developments within the Congo to the Congolese themselves.

Such a course was adapted to the pitiful mediocrity of the UN's real power, as well as being consonant with the principle of Congolese independence. But it condemned the UN to the unrewarding role of Sisyphus; for the very lack of political agreement between Congolese factions perpetuated the danger of civil war and of foreign help at the request of every faction, and it made of the UN force a stake in the struggle rather than a power capable of ending the struggle. It became indispensable for the UN to take a hand in shaping the political future of the Congo; the necessity, or the temptation, of using force on behalf of the blueprint was bound to become irresistible. As for Goa, it can of course be argued that there was nothing the UN could do anyhow.

The double departure from past UN doctrine is full of dangers, and the new precedents are extremely perilous both for the UN and for the U. S.

As for the UN. Mr. Hammarskjold's efforts tried to make of the UN *an impartial force* whose mission it was to keep new conflicts outside of the sphere of great power disputes, and to protect in particular the weak against the strong. The events of past weeks tend to make of the UN an instrument of *anti-colonialism, pure and simple.* Katanga is assailed because it is a prize example of neo-colonialism, India is whitewashed because it chased the last defenders of colonialism from its soil. Now, whatever the merits of those two actions, I would point out, first, that there is, from the viewpoint of the Organization's own moral authority, a major difference between having to accept the Soviet aggression in Hungary, and actually justifying the use of force—by itself or by some of its members—on behalf of anti-colonialism. The former decision merely reflects the structure of power between the blocs; the latter creates a double standard which destroys the claim to impartiality.

Secondly, from the viewpoint of the UN's practical efficiency, I would argue that the recent moves are also highly questionable. The UN is simply not equipped to cope with a world in which too many hunting grounds are left open; another aggression justified by anti-colonialism might, this time, provoke extensive bloodshed, and the UN would have to face the unpleasant alternatives of dangerous passivity or another hasty emergency action to stop a war that might have been averted. On the other hand, it is highly unlikely that the UN will be able to "keep the Cold War out" if it decides to use force in order to reach objectives defined by its anti-colonial majority. The expenses of such operations are essentially carried by the other powers, and particularly by the U. S. Inevitably, the involvement of one superpower in a military (as distinct from a non-shooting) operation will provoke the involvement of the other, and the expedition, even though it might start (as in Katanga) as an effort to inoculate the area from the Cold War virus, will become a stake in the great power conflict. For only the great powers have the means to provide the UN with military assistance—and only the U. S. and the U.S.S.R. are likely to serve as the secular arms of the anticolonial doctrine. I think it is precisely because such dangers are real that the last Secretary-General, as late as on the day of his death, and against the wishes of many of his "constituents"—the majority in the Assembly—and his personal representatives in the Congo, tried to settle the differences between Katanga and the Central Government, and the issue of mercenaries, without the use of force. His reports contrast strikingly with U Thant's almost belligerent Security Council statement of November 24.

As for the U. S. True, our representatives have stressed the limited objective of the UN presence in the Congo. However, the reasons given for helping the UN use force for a political purpose could be adduced for bigger objectives or in future cases of anticolonial expeditions. The basic reason is that to resist the tide, to oppose the anticolonial majority, would be to play into Communist hands. But it is not at all demonstrated that to go along with the majority does not achieve the same result. The least one can say is that none of the superpowers can be sure that it can control the operations of the UN; this being the case, *there is a serious risk involved in entrusting the pursuit of important national interests to a mechanism the next twists and turns of which one cannot predict*. The U. S., which was unable to get the Security Council to express any reservations about Mr. Gizenga, may find that it has weakened Mr. Tshombe for the benefit of Mr. Gizenga, and that the latter simply would not be opposed by the UN. In the "name" and on the ground of anticolonialism it is difficult for the U.S. not to be outbid and outwitted by the Soviets. Lastly, let us not forget that the Soviet "troika" plan aimed not only to prevent the UN from acting against Soviet interests, but also to make it easier for the

UN to act whenever there was a convergence of Soviet and "neutral" interests, in the belief that such a coalition would force the Western elements to sway with the wind, rather than be accused of paralyzing the UN. This is exactly what happened in the Security Council on November 24, when the U. S., despite its failure to get some of its key amendments approved, decided to support the resolution on the Congo sponsored by a number of the neutrals and backed by the Soviet Union.

Thus I would argue that it is not good either for the UN or for the U. S. to replace Mr. Hammarskjold's subtle policies (which did indeed coincide largely with U. S. interests—hence the Soviet Union's hostility and the growing hostility of the more radical new states) with a policy which condones the use of force either by the UN or by its members in the new "just war" against colonialism. There are better ways of serving that cause—ways less dangerous for world order, for the UN's own future and for the U. S. position in the world. The UN cannot be a substitute for a common Western policy in areas of vital interest to all Western powers, and should not be an alibi for the absence of such a policy.

Selection 42

Power Vacuum in the Congo*

William R. Frye

William R. Frye is an American journalist at present specializing in United Nations matters.

A four-year experiment in United Nations peacemaking ended in the Congo last week. The UN went to the Congo in 1960 to fill a vacuum left by Belgium, thus keeping East and West from violent competition to fill that vacuum.

There were other, derivative objectives, but the UN's essential role

* From the *San Francisco Chronicle, This World* (July 5, 1964), p. 11, and *This World* (August 30, 1964), p. 26. Reprinted by permission of the author.

was to keep the Congo from touching off a world war. It succeeded in more than that. The UN erected a shield behind which Western influence, working with the UN for progress and stability has elbowed out Communist influence, which sought turmoil and chaos.

As a consequence, the United States has won and Belgium has regained in the Congo a sphere of economic and political influence, a base from which to operate in central Africa. There is no assurance that they can retain this influence. Withdrawal of the UN will once again create a vacuum, one less dangerous than in 1960 because the Congolese are less immature, but still dangerous enough.

The real question to be answered in coming weeks will be: By whom will the new power vacuum be filled?

Because of the head start the UN has helped them obtain, Washington and Brussels are in much the best position to fill it. The Soviet Union and Red China are in a far less advantageous position. But Moscow and Peiping will not lie down and play dead. Communist money and influence are already detectable in at least two, and perhaps all three, of the provincial revolts now under way. . . .

With the UN gone, wraps will be off. The Congo will be free to request direct American military aid, and Washington will be free to give it. There is little doubt about Washington's reaction. This could mean that the Congo will become the cockpit of a direct East-West power struggle. If so, Western diplomats are saying, so be it. The prospect no longer alarms them. They are today—thanks to their own efforts and to the UN—in a much better position to fight and win that struggle. . . .

Moscow and Peiping, therefore, are not in a position to intervene directly in the Congo, through the front door, as they were at the time of Patrice Lumumba. They do not have a climate of receptivity in Leopoldville. They must try to jimmy the lock of the back door. . . .

. . . What Moscow and Peiping can and certainly will do is to continue stirring up trouble by proxy. There are plenty of disaffected Congolese ready and eager to accept Communist aid in troublemaking. Some of them are already doing so.

This continuing struggle for hegemony in central Africa will not be comfortable or easy. The outcome is very much in doubt. But it will be fought under terms and in conditions more favorable for the West than those which prevailed four years ago.

This, from the West's point of view, is the net effect of the UN's peacemaking stint in the Congo. [July 5, 1964.]

TSHOMBE COULD BE LEADING THE WEST TO A NEW VIETNAM

Moise Tshombe is a risky horse for the West to be riding in the Congo. . . .

The danger has been portrayed in Congress as a risk of an "African Vietnam." This is not the real peril.

It is inevitable that the United States, Belgium and perhaps France will progressively become more deeply involved in a direct power struggle for Central Africa. This has been inevitable ever since the UN was forced to pull out. Central Africa cannot be abandoned to the Communists.

COSTLY VICTORY

Such a struggle need not be particularly dangerous from a military point of view. It will not be like Vietnam—the rebels will have no privileged sanctuary, their supply line to Moscow and/or Peiping will be much longer, that line will be more vulnerable to interdiction, surface transport will be formidably difficult, and so on. The military advantages will be all with the West.

What is really dangerous is the prospect, not that the West will become involved in an African Vietnam, but that it will become involved on the "wrong" side—that is, on what many Africans will regard as the wrong side. . . .

And there is danger of precisely that happening.

SWEAR WORDS

Whatever side Tshombe is on is regarded by much of Africa as the wrong side. He is still one of the most unpopular men on the continent.

He has improved his image in the past few months, but many Africans still identify him with Belgium and with the whites of South Africa and Southern Rhodesia. . . .

Tshombe reportedly is . . . recruiting South African and Southern Rhodesian mercenaries to pilot the American planes he has been receiving. This step, though legal for him now that he is the Prime

Minister of a central government, would be extremely damaging psychologically. . . .

Yet Tshombe sorely needs help. He has no army of his own worthy of the name. Lacking trained officers, the Congolese army evaporates when it meets resistance. The United States does not wish to commit fighting forces at this stage.

Tshombe therefore is being urged to "Africanize" the Congo conflict—that is, to identify other African states mentally, emotionally and physically with his struggle to preserve the Congo's independence and integrity.

BACK TO THE FOLD

In response to these suggestions, though apparently with great reluctance, Tshombe has appealed to several other African countries—among them Ethiopia, Liberia, the Malagasy Republic, Nigeria and Senegal—to send him troops.

Some may agree. But they are not eager, and even if they do, the conflict will not have been "Africanized" effectively.

Other things being unchanged, the net result will simply have been to split Africa, as it was split at the time of the Lumumba-Kasavubu struggle in 1960—some countries backing Tshombe, others the rebels.

The one thing Tshombe could do that would genuinely align Africa, or a large part of it, on his side would be to appeal to the Organization of African Unity, charging the Communists with interfering in African affairs and undermining African independence. . . .

Given OAU sanction and American financing, several moderate and right-wing African states undoubtedly would be prepared to send troops to the Congo. The rebels then could be crushed both physically and psychologically.

It is a long shot. Tshombe is by no means Africa's fair-haired boy.

But Africa is mercurial, emotional, forgiving. Tshombe and Antoine Gizenga have been reconciled; Tshombe has even laid a wreath on Lumumba's grave. The big reconciliation—Tshombe and the rest of Black Africa—must now be attempted. [August 30, 1964.]

Suggested Readings—
A Brief Bibliographic Essay

An inexpensive, stimulating introduction to African affairs is found in Roland Oliver and J. D. Fage, *A Short History of Africa* (Penguin Books, 1962). H. A. Gibbons, *The Map of Africa* (New York: The Century Company, 1917), W. L. Langer, *The Diplomacy of Imperialism* (New York: Alfred A. Knopf, Inc., 1935), and Ronald Robinson and John Gallagher, *Africa and the Victorians* (New York: St. Martin's Press, 1961) assist in understanding how the map of Africa came to be (approximately) what it is today. E. M. Winslow, *The Pattern of Imperialism* (New York: Columbia University Press, 1948) discusses theories of imperialism.

A general introduction to present-day Africa is offered by Immanuel Wallerstein in *Africa: The Politics of Independence* (New York: Vintage Books, 1961), while Colin Legum in *Pan-Africanism* (rev. ed.; New York: Praeger, 1965) admirably covers this important topic. His account is brought up to date by Boutros Boutros-Ghali in "The Addis Ababa Charter," *International Concilication*, No. 546 (January 1964).

Vernon McKay's *Africa in World Politics* (New York: Harper and Row, 1963) is a valuable, if uneven, study of contemporary Africa's relations with the outside world. *Africa and the Communist World* (Stanford: Stanford University Press, 1963) edited by Zbigniew Brzezinski is a good source on this topic. Note also several readings (especially Selections 19 and 22) in another book in the Chandler Studies in International and Intercultural Relations series: *Red World in Tumult* (San Francisco: Chandler Publishing Company, 1962) edited by DeVere E. Pentony.

Thomas Hovet in *Africa and the United Nations* (Evanston, Ill.: Northwestern University Press, 1963) offers detailed analysis of African political participation in the United Nations.

Of great relevance to Africa is the recent report by Raul Prebisch to the United States Conference on Trade and Development, *Toward a New Trade Policy for Development* (New York: United Nations, 1964), in which recommendations on economic relations between developed and less-developed nations are made. Ali Masrui in "African Attitudes to the European Economic Community," *International Affairs* (January 1963) contributes insights into the political milieu of such relations, as do L. H. Gann and Peter Duignan in *White Settlers in Tropical Africa* (Penguin Books, 1962).

Also of interest is the book edited by William Friedland and Carl Rosberg, Jr., *African Socialism* (Stanford: Stanford University Press, 1964).